TELL ME WHY I CAN'T

WINNING MY BATTLE WITH CHINA BY MAKING IT IN AMERICA

★ RON SIMON ★

ISBN: 978-1-952483-21-9 (Hardcover)
ISBN: 978-1-952483-22-6 (Trade Paperback)
ISBN: 978-1-952483-23-3 (eBook)

Library of Congress Control Number: 2020925463

PRINTED IN THE USA

10 9 8 7 6 5 4 3 2 1

To my family, friends, and business associates
who have had a great and positive impact on my life.

TABLE OF CONTENTS

★ PREFACE

When I began writing this book, my initial thought was to use the title "At War with The Home Depot: A War Where Both Sides Won."

My reasoning then was that throughout my professional career, like most businessmen, I had fought many battles with many customers, but none of them matched the intensity of the ones I fought with The Home Depot, which began around 1984, after it emerged as the behemoth of American home centers. With its unprecedented purchasing power among home improvement stores, the company created what I felt was a David-and-Goliath war with its suppliers.

By then, I owned Perma-Bilt Industries, a bathroom cabinet manufacturer my dad, Sidney Simon, had started in 1949. He and I always had somewhat of a rocky relationship, so when my dad asked me to come on board in 1959, I reluctantly agreed, telling my wife at the time, "I will give it two weeks."

My prediction proved to be wrong. Two weeks turned into two years, and after overcoming a very rough start, I took over management of that company in 1961. The wars we fought with The Home Depot were always tough, and with the rise of Asian manufacturers, the battles became even more punishing with only bigger ones to come.

By 1987, I was totally burnt out and looking for an exit, which led me to sell controlling interest in Perma-Bilt, and this coincided with me being thrown out by Perma-Bilt's new owners, an Australian private equity firm run by extremely egotistical executives. Being cut out of the company I had built felt terrible at first but soon became a blessing in disguise. I used my retirement to recover and regroup from my exhaustion.

During that time off, I was developing a new company that would be successful doing business with the likes of The Home Depot. I was rejuvenated and more motivated than ever to do that, and so, in 1989, I started RSI Home Products.

While I've always been ambitious, little did I know that RSI would become the world's largest and most profitable kitchen cabinet, bathroom vanity, cultured marble countertop, and medicine cabinet manufacturer.

What I was certain about at the time was that, in a clear case of sweet revenge, RSI would put Perma-Bilt and its domestic competitors out of business. RSI did exactly that, but more important, RSI blew the Asian manufacturers out of the water. We proved that, done right, US companies could outcompete foreign rivals—just as RSI did with China, our first foreign competitor. RSI's ascent is one of my proudest life achievements and one that demonstrates the power of the American Dream.

But as I was writing my book, I began to see the limitations of the name, "At War with The Home Depot." While I was proud of my accomplishments, my life was much more than the successes I had manufacturing and selling products to the giant retailer. So I scrapped the title.

Many of the qualities I needed to make Perma-Bilt and then RSI successful were ones I already had as a kid growing up in Los Angeles. Specifically, I have questioned the status quo from as early as I can remember. Whenever I heard, "Ronnie, you can't . . . ," my mind went rushing to figure out why I couldn't. And sometimes, I wound up doing things that got me in big trouble.

Times were different in the 1930s, when I was born. If my own children would have done some of the Dennis-the-Menace-like pranks I did growing up, I would have really punished them. My parents certainly did let me have it when they found out about my sneaky antics, but that did not stop me. My unrelenting curiosity and questioning everything developed decades later into a creative force beyond anything I could have ever imagined back when I was a kid driving my parents nuts.

One of my main goals of writing this book was to leave a legacy for my children, grandchildren, and future generations. I also wanted to pay tribute to those whom I worked with throughout my career. And I wanted to inspire the hard-working men and women who are part of the Simon Scholars program. From 2003 to 2020, that program has provided over sixty million dollars in scholarships to more than 1,400 underserved students. And based upon past performance, over 90 percent of Simon Scholars will graduate from a four-year college or university. Our students have earned degrees from our nation's most elite institutions of higher education.

During these times of rapid changes in an unstoppable global economy, I also wanted this to be a testament to the power of free trade and a clear argument against protectionist measures that reward corporate laziness, slow innovation, and worst of all, hurt consumers.

I felt the best way to do this was to tell the story of my life on my terms, rather than have an account based on someone else's perspective on what I did and why I did it. Maybe a biography will show up in the future. If there should be one, I hope it's from someone I trust and who knows me well.

Also, as one ages, one's memory begins to fail, so I decided to write this book now while I still can.

In the following chapters, you'll read about my journey. We'll start with my childhood because those formative years prepared and led me to take the entrepreneurial path I would eventually travel throughout my adult life.

Given the current global trade debate and doubts about America's competitiveness and status in the world that make headline news every day, the story of RSI's rise is one as relevant today as it was three decades ago.

★ CHAPTER ONE

Our Neighborhood's Own Dennis the Menace

When I was in my forties, I enjoyed vacationing in Acapulco. If you've ever been there, you've seen the big gap between rich and poor. Either the locals have money to lead a comfortable life, or they're living in abject poverty. There's not much in the middle.

As a tourist, you're often approached by poor people peddling you stuff. Sometimes kids that couldn't be older than seven or eight are chasing after you with scarves, handbags, wallets, and more.

"How much?" I asked a little boy about the scarf he was waving around.

"Twenty dollars!" he said.

"Five dollars," I replied.

And so here I found myself as a grown-up businessman negotiating with a little kid.

As the saying goes, "Desperate times call for desperate measures." These children have little, and they may not even be able to read, but boy, do they have incredible street smarts, persistence, mental toughness, and all-around chutzpah.

Imagine these kids getting what they need: food, a roof over their heads, and an education. By the time they'd be teenagers, these same boys and girls would be ready to go into business and succeed.

*Ron at age eighteen months with his parents on the
driveway of their home on Harrison Street.*

I base my conclusion on the early lessons I had growing up. While my upbringing in Los Angeles came nowhere near the tough environments these kids have to endure, as early as I can remember, I had a similar tenacity as they did. And this usually meant questioning the status quo and refusing to take "no" for an answer. From as far back as I can remember, if something didn't make sense to me, I couldn't help but challenge it.

Even at four years old, an age when most little kids only dreamt of doing something that grown-ups were allowed to, I dared demand it.

"Daddy, I want to drive the car!"

"No," was his firm answer.

"Why?" I asked.

"Because you can't," he said.

His short reply didn't make sense to me. So in 1938, I was determined to sit behind the wheel of the family car and speed down Harrison Street. The busy road was in front of our East LA house, and all day, cars zoomed by it.

One afternoon while my mom was napping downstairs in my grandmother's bedroom, I found my chance.

Ron at age four.

Back in the thirties, kids regularly roamed their neighborhoods without any adults around. Even at just four years old, with my mom asleep, I was on my own.

Our detached garage was set about thirty feet behind the house, and the long driveway from where the car was parked spilled straight onto Harrison Street.

I hopped in the driver's seat and released the emergency brake. Because I was too young and little to see out the windshield, the car ended up crashing into the house. The jolt woke my mother from her nap. I can only imagine her shock as she wondered what the hell had just happened.

Unfortunately, for my mom, Belle, this wasn't the first time she'd seen my mischievous side. Actually, I prefer to call it fearless risk taking. And I blame it on my parents and their parents. In fact, I come from a long line of bold risk takers—immigrant pioneers who put everything on the line in order to escape adversity in their homelands and seek opportunity across the Atlantic.

The SS Polonia, *a Polish ocean liner, approximately 450 feet long by 56 feet wide, was constructed by Barclay, Curle & Company in Glasgow, Scotland, in 1910.*

My grandparents on my mother's side, Anna and Meyer Langer, were Russian Jewish immigrants who arrived from different parts of Europe. We grandkids called them Bubbie and Zayde, which are Yiddish for Grandma and Grandpa. They came from Czudnowo, which is a little town in present-day Ukraine. If you've ever seen *Fiddler on the Roof*, you have a taste of what life was like for them in what was a very poor part of the world with a harsh climate.

The Bolshevik Revolution was steamrolling over their country leaving behind death and destruction. Meanwhile, the Langer family grew in Czudnowo, where my mother, Belle Langer, was born in 1913, her brother Eddie in 1917, and her sister Lillian in 1918.

In 1921, Meyer and a pregnant Anna took their three children, escaped Ukraine, and fled to Poland, where their son David was born that same year. Because they left, my mom and her siblings were spared the violence, including kidnapping, rape, and murder, that destroyed the lives of so many innocent Jews.

The following year, the family of six Langers made the biggest move of their lives. Meyer had cousins who had already taken the cross-Atlantic trip to America and eventually settled out West in East Los Angeles,

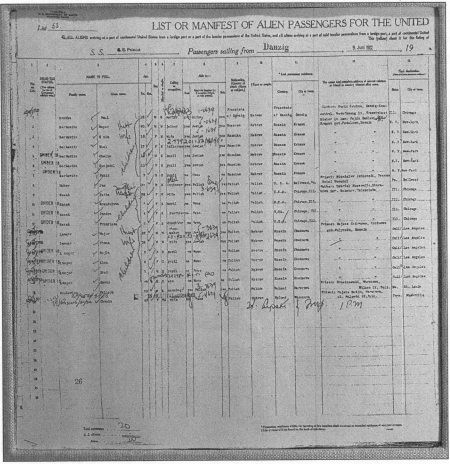

Manifest of passengers on the SS Polonia *arriving in the United States from Danzig on June 9, 1922. The Langers, numbers 13 through 18, listed Czudnowo as their last permanent city of residence.*

the city's Jewish epicenter. LA, at the time, was far from the sprawling metropolis it is today. With the help of Meyer's cousins, the Langers would start a new life in the United States.

Without speaking a word of English, they boarded the SS *Polonia* and set sail for Ellis Island. They arrived in the United States with what little belongings they had brought with them and twenty dollars—at least that's the amount of cash Meyer declared. But most likely the couple had other resources they didn't disclose that would allow them to establish their lives in their new country. At the immigration station, they registered their names.

Ron's father, Sidney Simon, 1934.

Once in New York, my grandparents wasted little time there. They bought train fare for their family of six and headed to the Golden State to reunite with their cousins.

Meanwhile, my dad's family, the Simons, had lived in England, Leeds to be exact. Toward the end of the nineteenth century, the northern English city had become home to Russian and Polish Jews, many of whom found work in the clothing industry. My dad, Sidney, was born in 1909. His mother was Sarah and his father was Morris, whose Hebrew name was Moishe, which is the name my parents gave to me.

Two years later, Sarah Simon gave birth to her second child, David.

Ron's mother, Belle Simon, 1934.

Like the Langers, the Simons left Europe to settle in the New World. In the Simons' case, however, pogroms didn't force them to flee England. But like the Langers, they had family who already had established themselves in North America.

Sarah had cousins, the Eisenbergs, who were living in Winnipeg, Canada. So, in 1912, she and my grandfather took their family of four and sailed to Canada, which is where my uncle Joseph was born in 1914, followed by my aunt Bonnie in 1916. That year, as they welcomed Bonnie, tragedy struck the growing Simon family when Morris died.

With the passing of his father, at only seven years old, my dad, Sidney, suddenly found himself the man of the house. His new role was made even more difficult by his devoted but tough-as-nails mother. Sarah was extremely philanthropic, was a strict observer of her orthodox faith, and ruled the household with an iron fist. My dad had to leave his childhood behind and grow up fast.

For the next decade, Sidney attended school in Canada while working to help support the family. In 1926, when he turned seventeen years old and after graduating from high school, he decided to move to Los Angeles. Prior to his big move, some of the Eisenbergs had already left Winnipeg and settled in LA and San Bernardino. Once in Southern California, they told Sidney of the job opportunities available there, which led him to leave Canada. A few months later, his mother and three siblings joined him in Los Angeles.

My father found an entry-level janitor job at Durasteel, a sheet metal company located near downtown LA. His superiors took quick notice of Sidney's innate intelligence and disciplined work ethic, and through a series of promotions, he eventually became superintendent.

At Durasteel, another Russian Jewish immigrant was hired. Belle Langer worked as a secretary, and after Sidney became superintendent, the two met and began dating.

In 1932, the young couple married. As newlyweds, they moved into a duplex that Belle's parents owned on Harrison Street. The Simons lived in the upstairs unit, and the Langers below them. I was born a couple of years later on July 26, 1934. My parents named me Ronald Maurice Simon—"Ronald" after Ronald Colman, an English actor, and "Maurice" for Maurice Chevalier, the French actor and singer. To keep ties to my Jewish faith, they also gave me the Hebrew names Moishe Yitzhak.

For the next ten years, I was an only child. Although I've never proved it, I'm sure my mischievousness may have made my parents think twice before having more kids. In fact, my mom claims I caused her to have a nervous breakdown. But she was probably highly exaggerating, as my Jewish mother often did. After all, out of the many stories in our family, none included any about my mom being admitted to a psychiatric ward. At the same time, I'll be the first to admit what a handful I was.

Decades later, fatherhood would teach me how tough parenting is, and I thank God my kids weren't like me. While I was overall pretty good, I wouldn't have wanted to rein in a boy like me. Being little Ronnie Simon's mom or dad wasn't easy.

My mom also liked to say that whenever the doorbell rang, she would have a checkbook in hand because the visitor was seeking compensation for some kind of damage I'd done—based on how much of a trouble-maker I was, that's a story I could believe!

For whatever reason, my fourth birthday marked a year of antics. All the calculated risk I'd take as a business owner later on had an early start.

That year I had a best friend, Dickey. His family lived next to mine, and we would play outside for hours together. One day, rather than running inside to go to the bathroom, we decided to take an outdoor leak. Between our homes, there was an empty lot with bushes.

We stood side by side in front of a shrub. My inner mischief-maker thought it would be hilarious to piss on him. So I turned around and sprayed him.

Dickey didn't find my prank funny one bit.

"I'm going to tell your mom!" he said.

And that's exactly what he did. When I saw my mom, she let me have it.

"Ronnie, you better never pee on Dickey again!" she told me.

I gave her my word, but inside I was really steaming at Dickey for snitching. So I decided to teach my friend a lesson while keeping my promise to my mom. The next day, I grabbed an empty milk bottle and peed in it.

When I saw Dickey, I poured its warm contents on his head. Dickey ran and told my mom, and once again, she let me have it.

"Ronnie, you promised!" she said.

"But I did not *pee* on him. I *poured* pee on him," I said.

My defense fell on deaf ears. I don't remember the punishment I got that day because it was just one among many I'd constantly receive. I later told Dickey I was sorry. He forgave me, and we continued to play together.

Then there was the time I saw the wringer on the washing machine. Back before washing machines automatically drained and then spun the water out of wet clothes, a set of electric rollers on top of the tub did the job of wringing out the wash. I wondered what would happen if I slid my arm between the rollers. So I turned the motor on.

When my bubbie saw my entire arm sandwiched between the two rollers, her look of horror was far worse than the pain of my arm being squeezed dry. She rushed over to me and stopped the washing machine's wringer as fast as she could. While I didn't break any bones, I certainly didn't try it again.

At times, I could have a grown-up temper trapped in a little-boy body. Again at four, I came down with tonsillitis. My mom made a doctor's appointment, and the doc asked me to open wide. He was poking around my throat. It hurt, and I didn't like it one bit.

"You son of a bitch!" I called him.

My mom was mortified. She washed my mouth out with soap on the spot, right there in his office. Afterwards, my condition worsened to the point my tonsils were removed, and she felt guilty because she thought the dirty bar of soap she used to punish me made things worse.

Since I could remember, I also closely observed my surroundings and people's behavior. This too served me well in business later on. We had a neighbor, Esther. She and my mom were good friends. When we'd visit Esther, she was often feeding her toddler who sat in a highchair in the kitchen.

Between our two houses was an empty lot, and I found a dead rat there. I picked it up and walked to Esther's kitchen with the rat hidden behind my back. Her son was sitting in the highchair waiting to eat. While Esther was turned away from her child, I dropped the rat on the tray in front of him. I then innocently waited.

The scream she let out nearly raised the rat from the dead. I knew my prank put me in hot water, so I ran out the kitchen as fast as I could.

I performed a similar stunt in school a few years later. I was in third grade, in Mrs. Seitz's class. Every morning, my teacher had the same habit. After we entered the classroom, she would take a seat, and without looking down, she would reach into the desk drawer and pull out a pen. I decided to shake up her routine.

Tony the Fishman would park his delivery truck on the street, and nearby housewives would buy seafood from him. One day, I asked Tony if he had any fish heads. He handed me one for free.

The next morning, I arrived at school early. Back then, teachers didn't bother to lock their doors, and I entered the classroom when no one was around. I slid the fish head in Mrs. Seitz's drawer and slipped out as fast as I could.

The bell rang, and we all took a seat in the classroom. I had told my friends what I had done, so we all sat with our eyes glued to Mrs. Seitz as she went through her morning ritual.

Like clockwork, she took a seat, opened her desk drawer, and reached in to get her pen. But she grabbed the fish head instead and then let out a scream. Right after, the entire class burst out laughing hysterically.

Ms. Seitz, by then all too familiar with my tricks, immediately knew who the prankster was. She dragged me to the principal's office, where I would receive a wooden paddle to the butt. . . . I experienced a few of those punishments during my time at Crescent Heights Elementary School. And I can honestly say I deserved every single one.

From time to time, I would have a double or even triple punishment to look forward to. For instance, once my mom found out what I'd done in Ms. Seitz's class, she took out a wooden coat hanger and swatted me on the rear with it. But sometimes, as she tried to spank me, I'd manage to escape. In that case, she'd let me know my reprieve was only temporary. Once my dad arrived home, he'd pick up where my mom stopped. But in his case, he preferred his razor strap.

"Go lie down on your bed!" he would say to me.

As bad as a razor strap sounds, though, and as painful as it could actually be, in my dad's defense, the lashes were pretty lightweight. In all honesty, lying face down on the bed silently waiting was a punishment way worse than the strap itself.

Sometimes, it seems as if people were waiting for me to cause mayhem. After all, I had a reputation in the neighborhood. In fact, my aunt, who lived about two miles away from us, once called my mom.

"Belle, you won't believe what I just heard," she said.

"What?" my mom asked.

"I was in the store's produce department, and I overheard some ladies talking about a little boy who lives on Harrison Street doing all this bad stuff. Can you believe they were talking about Ronnie?" she said.

While she wasn't proud of it, my reputation covered over two square miles. In other words, my mom knew they were talking about Harrison Street's own Dennis the Menace.

So all the neighbors should have known better than to feed my mischief-making.

"See that over there?" my grown-up neighbor asked me one day as he pointed to his carport. "It needs repairs because it's ready to collapse."

He explained that out of the two posts supporting his carport's roof, one of the front ones was on its last leg, . . . What the hell was he thinking when he told me this?

For Christmas that year, I had received a kid's carpenter set, an open invitation to all sorts of mischief, now to be put to good use. When the coast was clear, I took my tiny saw and began cutting away at the four-by-four post.

If I was a lumberjack, this is the moment where I would have yelled, "Timber!" as the carport's roof completely collapsed.

After my neighbor arrived home and saw what had happened, he marched up to our house and rang the doorbell. I ran for cover knowing the punishment that would come next.

Although risk taking and curiosity played a part in my mischief, I'm sure there were other reasons at play. My parents were very critical. They were the type of people that, if you showed them one hundred things you'd done and ninety-nine of them were amazing, they'd zero in on the one thing that wasn't.

So my stunts were probably a combination of getting any kind of attention I could, acting out, and being rebellious. And I didn't discriminate; young, old, male, female, Black, white, everyone was game, including my grandmother.

We were a tight-knit family, and since my grandparents lived in the duplex downstairs from us, I'd see them often. Bubbie was babysitting me one day in her home, and I went into their tiny bathroom. I locked the door behind me, shoved the rubber stopper at the bottom of the sink, and turned the hot and cold water on. The basin quickly filled, and water began overflowing onto the floor.

My grandmother eventually saw water seeping out from underneath the bathroom door. She knocked.

"Ronnie, let me in," she said.

I ignored her, and the flood continued.

In her panic to stop the flow of water into the house, she put towels along the bathroom door's threshold. Meanwhile, I enjoyed the water show from inside the bathroom.

"Ronnie, if you open the door, I'll give you chocolate," she said.

I loved chocolate. Sadly, I was allergic to it at the time. So her offer instantly caught my attention. I thought it over for a moment and then decided to unlock the door.

She rushed in and turned the faucet off and began the cleanup operation. I never received the chocolate, but I did get a spanking that day.

In addition to being a risk taker, I was also a religious skeptic. Both were about questioning the status quo, which would carry over to my adulthood. I was very close to my grandparents on my mother's side.

Zayde, my grandpa, would read me Bible stories such as Noah's ark. Like any good skeptic, I had trouble accepting the facts.

"Zayde, I do not believe it. Noah could not get all the animals on the ark because they would fight," I said.

"Well, God didn't allow them to fight," Zayde said.

That explanation didn't cut it, and I kept questioning the events Zayde read aloud to me. Eventually my nonstop doubts caused him to throw in the towel reading me Bible tales. My critical mind was also one of the reasons I never could be very religious. In fact, while I respect and appreciate the Jewish tradition I grew up in, from as early as I can remember, faith has not come easy for me; I was never afraid to question anything that didn't make sense. Thus I've not been a huge fan of any organized religion.

I recall traveling to Israel with friends a few years ago. During the trip, Joyce, one of my friends, told me, "Ron, you can't be Jewish because you don't go to temple every week."

That was the stupidest thing I'd ever heard.

"Joyce, I am Jewish, okay? . . . Go tell the Black guy he is not Black and then tell the Japanese guy he is not Japanese. Christ, I am Ashkenazi on both sides of my family. Meanwhile, you are Catholic and converted to Judaism, and you are telling me *I* am not Jewish?"

It was a harmless conversation between old friends. But it points to the complexity of the Jewish identity. Even my grandfather, who was Jewish through and through, reflected the nuances of what it means to be Jewish. Is it a religion or part of your DNA or both?

In his case, he wasn't very religious; in fact, he was more agnostic. But he was a total defender of being Jewish. If he witnessed anti-Semitism, watch out! He would not put up with it for a second. And, boy, was he a supporter of the Israeli state. He would help efforts here to raise money to send to Israel. My grandfather had a particular anger toward the British colonizers in Israel who blocked the flow of Jews into the region, which has been under a perpetual pressure cooker for thousands of years.

I visited the Wailing Wall once (also called the Western Wall), located in a holy site in Jerusalem for Christians, Jews, and Muslims.

An old Jewish man was praying, as many do, close up against the sacred wall. He dropped a pamphlet, and I picked it up and handed it to him.

"Thank you. Thank you very much," he said.

I recognized his accent.

"Are you Israeli?" I asked.

"Why yes!" he said.

"How often do you come here?" I asked.

"Oy . . . I come here every single day for the last forty years!" he said.

"Really? What do you pray for?"

"That there should be no more wars. That there should be peace between Jews and Palestinians and Arabs. That this senseless killing stops," he said.

He looked toward the ground, saddened when he thought about all the violence in his homeland.

"So you have been doing that prayer for forty years, and obviously nothing has really changed. How does that make you feel?" I asked.

He looked up at me.

"It feels like I'm talking to a fucking wall!" he said.

*Ron (*right*) with his friend Tom Tucker at the Western Wall in Israel, 2000.*

I actually never had that conversation. But I like to tell that story because it expresses my belief that maintaining humor is very important. If everyone would treat joking as just that and not be so quick to label humor as racist, bigoted, anti-Semitic, offensive, or otherwise politically incorrect, the world would be a better place.

In 1938, our family moved out of East LA and to the West Side into a rental duplex. Leaving LA's Jewish neighborhood meant encountering anti-Semitism, which was an unwelcome reminder of the poison the whole family had escaped from in Europe.

The signs on some rental units that said "No Jews" meant discrimination was nothing to hide and was, in fact, to be proudly displayed for all to see. After living in the duplex for one year, my parents bought a house at 2007 South Crescent Heights Boulevard where I lived until I got married at the age of twenty.

Nowadays, you hear lots of stories of families that cannot wait to live *away* from each other—good riddance, the farther the better! But my family was the opposite. The same ties that brought my parents and their families all the way from Europe kept them together in the United States, despite the many options they had to live apart from each other.

Shortly after we moved to Crescent Heights, my grandparents sold their duplex in East LA and rented a small apartment two blocks away from us. And then my mom's sister, my aunt Lillian, and her family, the Glucofts, moved in across the street from us.

Our move from Fairfax was positive overall—for one thing there was less bigotry. Because of their first-hand experience with anti-Semitism, early on, my parents taught me to respect others and never discriminate based on someone's religion or race. And these lessons included words I was told to not use because they were offensive.

One item on their list was the N-word. "Don't *ever* use it. It's terrible," they said to me. As a kid who questioned everything adults told me,

I asked why.

"If they hear you say it, they are going to get mad and beat you up."

I'm sure they were trying to spell it out to me in a way that would keep me from ever saying it. But it wasn't much of an explanation, so I needed to find out for myself.

One afternoon, when I was seven years old, I was walking in my neighborhood and saw a Black man across the street.

I yelled out the N-word.

He was furious and began chasing me, and I ran away from him as fast as I could. I entered the house through the back entrance, which opened to the kitchen. My mom was inside cooking.

"What's wrong?" she asked, seeing me out of breath after running as if my life depended on it.

"Oh, nothing," I said in my most innocent voice possible.

Then the door knock came. I'm sure my mom already knew I was up to no good and expected the worst. She opened the door.

The man I had just insulted stood in front of her. He was a real gentleman and politely explained what I had done. My mom profusely apologized for her son's appalling behavior and made it clear to him that such language was not tolerated in our house.

After he left, I received the two-part punishment: coat hanger from my mom and razor strap from my dad once he arrived home from work. They did their best to ensure that I'd never make the same mistake again. But that just meant I'd find other ways to cause mischief. Fortunately, sometimes my parents never found out—once, thanks to my best friend.

She was a gift for my seventh birthday from my uncle Dave. And it was love at first sight. Uncle Dave got the beautiful mixed German shepherd from the local Society for the Prevention of Cruelty to Animals, or SPCA.

Jippy was my first dog, and we created an instant bond. Sadly, a couple of days after we welcomed her into our home, she became very sick. We took her to the vet, and he diagnosed her with distemper, an often-deadly virus that affects dogs.

Nowadays, the illness is still serious but frequently treatable. Back then, however, it was basically a death sentence. The vet recommended we put her to sleep. But I begged and begged my parents not to, and they relented.

So we took her home and nursed her. Miraculously, Jippy fought off the disease and fully recovered. And that's where her name came from. We told Uncle Dave that he'd been gypped by the SPCA because they had given him a sick dog. The bond Jippy and I built from the start was the first of many I would have with my beloved dogs.

Although Jippy was officially the Simon family pet, she followed me everywhere, and no one questioned who her favorite was—maybe deep down she knew I had saved her life.

Ron with his companion, Jippy, and Daisy the Duck.

One day she got her chance to pay me back, the time I decided to test my pea-shooting skills on strangers. Through practice, I had become a pretty good marksman.

About a hundred feet away from our house, next to an empty lot, was La Cienega Boulevard. Just like today, it's one of LA's busiest and best-known streets. And along the boulevard was a billboard perfectly positioned about twenty feet above ground that advertised to heavy LA traffic. The billboard's wood frame basically invited a fearless nine-year-old like me to climb it.

"Jippy, stay put," I told my intelligent dog.

She sat and watched as I climbed the wooden frame.

Once I made it to the top, my targets were in clear view. I pulled the pea shooter from my pocket and scanned the road. Soon I spotted my perfect victim—a man driving a convertible with the top down.

As he zoomed below me, I took a deep breath and shot a few peas. Bullseye! He looked up, confused by what had just hit him. I couldn't have been more accurate—and I struck a moving target no less! I was ready to find someone else to shoot when I saw his car come to a screeching stop.

The man had clearly spotted me atop the billboard. Now I was in big trouble. I scrambled down as quickly as I could. But I barely had two feet on the ground when he caught me.

"Kid, where do you live?" he asked.

I pointed to the garage nearby.

"I'm going to take you there and tell your parents what you did," he said.

"I do not think that is a good idea," I said.

"Why not?" he asked, surprised by my boldness.

"Because I think my dog will kill you if you try," I said.

I looked at Jippy, who was behind the man. She was on all fours, her ears upright and stiff, raised hackles, and those teeth . . . fully showing and made to attack prey and rip their flesh apart.

The man turned around and heard the growl from my loyal German shepherd mix. By this point, Jippy's attack-dog stance made it obvious to both of us that she was ready to pounce at any moment. The man changed his mind.

"Don't do it again," he said.

He slowly, nervously returned to his car, careful not to trigger my protector.

While I did learn my lesson that day, how long I'd be able to stay out of trouble was anyone's guess. It would be a short break if the past were any sign—and I might not have my best friend at my side the next time.

Jippy was my constant companion at home and around the neighborhood. Back then, leashes were not mandatory, and my best friend didn't need one anyway. She was as smart as a whip and followed my every command.

While she did not come with me to school, by using her amazing internal GPS, she maintained her loyalty to me. Monday through Friday, after the dismissal bell rang, Jippy would be waiting for me halfway between Crescent Heights Elementary and our home. I always looked forward to seeing her furry face . . . and then, one day, she wasn't there to greet me.

I rushed home after school full of worry.

"Where is Jippy?!" I asked my mom.

She broke the bad news: My parents had sent her off to serve our country. It was 1944, and young men, as well as dogs, were enlisted to defend the free world.

At the time, deep patriotism pulsed in my veins; I would have gladly volunteered to fight for my country and against those evil Nazis had I been old enough. So, as awful as what my mom had just told me was, I could not have been prouder of Jippy.

I imagined her on the frontlines, dodging bombs, grenades, and bullets, constantly putting herself at risk in order to save our soldiers' lives. She was the ultimate dog hero! I thought of her treating American freedom fighters with the same amazing loyalty she had for me.

But years later I learned that, just like Santa Claus and the Tooth Fairy, the tale of Jippy's departure was totally make-believe.

Robert Simon, my baby brother, was born in 1944, the same year Jippy was supposedly sent to combat. My parents worried about having a big and sometimes aggressive German shepherd around their infant son, so they decided to get rid of her. And rather than tell me the truth, which could have potentially sparked a World War III in our house— who knows how I would have reacted had I found out what they had *really* done!—they made up a story that would appease their son who loved his dog and his country. Their tactic worked.

Although I missed my best buddy, my pride for Jippy's service offset my sadness . . . that is, until I found out what actually happened. But by the time the truth came out, I was old enough to understand their concern and why they decided to do what they did.

While the loss of my four-legged friend was tough when my parents told me Jippy was gone, that sadness paled in comparison to losing the closest people in my life.

Once I reached the age where I was allowed to play without grown-ups watching my every move, LA's streets were my playground. From Mid-City to coastal Santa Monica, as long as I had any say in it, I would spend as much time outside as possible.

I was an active kid, and my dark blue Roadmaster that my dad bought for me when I was about eight was my way around the neighborhood—my wheels were my life.

From hanging around with friends to making money through my paper route, it seems like I rode my bike nonstop and over anything that got in my way. And by the looks of the tires, there was some truth to that. The inner tubes had been punctured so many times they were practically held together by the patches I had to constantly put on them to keep them inflated.

When I was eleven, my front inner tube had nothing more left to give, and it needed to be replaced. I wheeled my bike to my grandparents' house. As usual, Bubbie was home, and I asked her for help.

"Can I have a dollar to buy a new inner tube?" I asked.

"I have to check with your zayde first. When he comes home from work, if he says it's okay, he'll give it to you," she said.

Back then, spending even a dollar required my grandma to ask her husband for permission. My, how times have changed.

I went home and waited. That evening, the phone rang. My mom picked up. It was my zayde. The color drained from her face as she spoke to him. She got off the phone and broke the news. My grandmother had died of a heart attack.

The news hit me hard because I loved Bubbie very much. I know I was a handful, but that did not matter to her. In fact, the only thing that mattered to her was family. So she was always a big presence in my life. But her death was not a complete surprise. Besides her advanced age, she also suffered from diabetes and was probably eighty pounds overweight.

The next morning my zayde came by the house.

"Ronnie, here's a dollar for the inner tube," he said as he handed it to me.

He told me that one of the last things my grandma told him before she passed was that I needed money to buy a new inner tube—I cried after hearing that.

Bubbie took care of me from the time I was born to her very last day on Earth. In fact, she took care of all the males in her life.

Her death meant my zayde had no one to keep him fed and organized. So he moved in with his daughter, my aunt Lillian, right after his wife died. And my uncle Dave, who was living with my grandparents at the time before he joined the US Navy, also moved in with my aunt.

As for Zayde, he lived well into his eighties. He eventually remarried a woman named Frieda. While we were happy for him moving on with his life, to be honest, none of us really liked her. Then again, the poor woman had really big shoes to fill! She was in many ways the opposite of Bubbie. In the end, my grandmother could never be replaced, so any comparison would be totally unfair.

Zayde was establishing his life with his new wife. Meanwhile, I was an adult building my business and raising my family, so we spent less and less time together. As time progressed, we mainly saw each other only at family celebrations.

My last visit to him was on his deathbed where we had a conversation about him and his beliefs. Never really religious, he was agnostic until the end; I probably took after him in this regard.

Zayde's influence in my life was one among many from close and caring relatives I had growing up. As a kid, I thought that kind of family presence was ordinary. But I see now what a gift that was. Besides all the love they showed me at the time, the lessons my family members taught me would support me throughout my life.

★ CHAPTER TWO
Lessons Learned

At thirteen years old, I had my bar mitzvah. In the Jewish faith, it's the rite of passage that marks a boy's transition into manhood. Bar mitzvahs are often associated with a big party. Mine was at the Congregation Talmud Torah, nicknamed Breed Street Shul.

The synagogue was in Boyle Heights. With around seventy-five thousand Yiddish-speaking Eastern European immigrants, the area had the largest Jewish community west of Chicago.

While most of my friends studied in Hebrew school for years and diligently prepared for their bar mitzvahs, I refused to do either. They learned Hebrew so they could read the haftarah, which are selections from the Bible you recite during your bar mitzvah. But rather than study ancient Hebrew texts, I preferred playing sports and working my odd jobs.

For me, some of the religious customs dating back thousands of years ago didn't seem relevant. And if there was a God, why did I have to go to a special place to pray? From a house of worship to a football field, couldn't I just do it anywhere?

To this day, I respect religions, but I'm not a religious person. For my bar mitzvah, however, I had to memorize the haftarah, so my parents had the rabbi come by our house and give their reluctant son a crash course. During my bar mitzvah, I successfully pulled off reciting my haftarah, which I'm sure made my orthodox grandma proud.

While I was able to stand in front of a group and recite at my bar mitz-vah, shortly afterwards, I developed huge anxiety when it came to talking in front of groups or strangers. I feared I would start stammering as my dad did.

For years, I had seen him struggle to speak under certain circum-stances. If he was in a comfortable setting, such as with family or friends, his speech was normal. But if he was put into a new situation, such as meeting strangers, he would have trouble.

Like a toddler trying to rise to his feet but landing on his rear end instead, my dad would make the effort, but the words would awkwardly stumble out. And by then it was obvious to everyone that Sidney Simon had some kind of speech problem. Even though my dad didn't show any sense of self-consciousness about it, I felt bad for him, and I definitely didn't want the same for me.

Now here I was, as a junior high student, afraid I might be going through something similar. The teenage years are a tough time—you're wanting to fit in, and you're definitely not wanting to stand out or be made fun of.

I had my share of insecurities going into junior high, partly because my parents were so critical and didn't instill self-confidence in me. And this new problem only made me feel worse about myself.

At the same time, my fear of stammering didn't come up all the time. Similar to my dad, if I was around anyone I was comfortable with, such as friends and family, I spoke without any worry or problem. But hav-ing one of my classmates discover my secret struggle terrified me, which made me scared of speaking in front of the class. So presentations and speeches were out of the question.

Fortunately, during my day, public speaking wasn't emphasized in school, so I didn't have to do it often. But when I did, a few times I went as far as staying home to avoid my peers seeing me choke up with ner-vousness. Although it was completely psychological, knowing that didn't make my problem, which was a biggie, go away.

Stubbornly, I refused to give anyone a clue about my struggle and developed tricks to avoid drawing attention to it. I fought hard to never let this inner demon out, and for the most part I succeeded. In fact, I had learned to hide it so well that I was the only person who knew about it. But my fear of it made me extremely self-conscious.

As good as I was at keeping it under wraps, my efforts took their toll. I felt a deep sense of shame and inadequacy about myself. Looking back, it's really unfortunate that a decent (albeit sometimes naughty) kid that was pretty smart, athletic, and hard-working thought so little of himself. Since putting that setback behind me, I can relate well with any young person who struggles with low self-esteem.

It wasn't till five years later that I would begin to overcome the major mental block. It was 1952. I was eighteen years old, just out of high school, and attending Los Angeles City College. I was sitting in my first psychology class, and the professor introduced himself. He shared about his background, and he told us he also had a private therapy practice.

By this point, my anxiety meant I sometimes had trouble even talking on the phone. If I needed to make an important call, I'd become very nervous, and I would sometimes hang up right after someone answered; my stress was too high.

I stayed after class that day and told the professor what I was going through. He listened carefully. I asked if he could help me but said I couldn't pay very much for therapy sessions. He offered to see me a few times and gave me a huge discount so I could afford it.

We met over the next few weeks. During our fourth session, he told me what he thought.

"Ron, I can't help you," he said.

"What lousy news!" I thought to myself.

"I can't help you because only you can help yourself," he added.

He described that my self-esteem was about as low as you could go. It was as if I had a little guy on my shoulder, constantly telling me I wasn't any good. Unless I dealt directly with this guy, he'd be sitting there for the rest of my life. But if I learned to quiet him down, he would no longer be able to influence me.

"I'll see you in class," he said. "But I won't see you here anymore. Now that you know what your problem is, it's up to you to overcome it. It's going to take a lot: You've got to be tough and keep fighting. This guy on your shoulder will keep showing his ugly face many times in the future. The only way to get rid of him is to force yourself to engage in exactly the situations that scare you."

His explanation made 100 percent sense. For the first time in my life, I felt I could handle this demon. It was all about choice. I could decide to ignore the guy on my shoulder. So I chose not to listen to him anymore.

Overcoming my insecurities sparked an intense drive and ambition that would emerge in my twenties, and it inspired me later on to establish the Simon Scholars program. Students who earn a spot in the program receive academic, financial, and most importantly, emotional support from high school through college. After facing my share of difficulties, I wanted to encourage and help young people through the Simon Scholars program to overcome the adversities they had in their lives.

My immigrant family members worked hard to build their own version of the American Dream. Meyer Langer, my maternal grandfather, worked at a luggage factory in Los Angeles, saved every penny he earned, and, in the late 1930s opened his own store on Third and Spring Streets in downtown LA. He called it Langer's Luggage. While the business didn't take over the world, it certainly provided his family a modest income and tapped into his entrepreneurial drive. I spent lots of time there and have fond memories of learning how he ran his store, working, and getting to know his employees.

Meyer hired two salesmen, Mr. Rubin, a Jewish man born in America but Germanic to the core, habits and all, and Mr. Steinman, an Eastern European Jew. Always serious, Mr. Rubin was the perfect foil for Mr. Steinman, who had an amazing sense of humor. Every morning, Mr. Rubin would enter the backroom. Before hanging his coat up for the day, he would spend whatever time he needed to smooth out any wrinkles he found on his jacket. Once in a while, Mr. Steinman would look on silently. Then, after Mr. Rubin had finished his daily coat routine, he would walk over to the jacket and ruffle it up, undoing all of Mr. Rubin's work.

"What the hell are you doing?" Mr. Rubin would yell.

The more irritated he became, the more Mr. Steinman wanted to rile him up again because he found Mr. Rubin's predictable reaction so entertaining. Mr. Steinman enjoyed making people laugh and always seemed to have a big smile on his face, which meant you'd never know how much suffering he had endured.

"Where were you during the war?" I asked him once, referring to World War II.

"Oh, I was in the consideration camp," he said, laughing at what he called it.

Far from anything considerate, I learned that Mr. Steinman had lost everyone he loved in a Nazi concentration camp. Yet here was this man, whose entire family was murdered in the most horrific way imaginable and had left his homeland, who got a kick out of playing practical jokes and spreading joy and laughter. I realized the funniest people are often those who have witnessed the greatest tragedy. He inspired me, and I respected his strength.

Starting when I was fourteen years old, I worked during times I wasn't in school. Zayde would sit in his chair most of the day and leave the selling to his employees, including me, even for some of the hard selling.

Once, on the Saturday before Mother's Day, business was slow. A man was window-shopping in front.

"Ronnie, go get him in the store," Zayde told me.

I walked outside and approached a man who was looking closely at a woman's bag set behind the glass.

"That is a beautiful bag you are looking at. We have one inside, and if you come in, I can show it to you," I said.

He saw the seventeen-dollar price tag next to the bag.

"Oh no, no, no. All that is too much money," he said.

"But isn't it nice? Is it for your wife for Mother's Day? Listen, my grandfather owns the store. Business is slow today. Maybe he can do better for you," I said.

Success! I convinced the man to enter Langer's Luggage. As I accompanied him, I let him know we had another bag just like the one he was looking at. We approached the glass counter, and I took it out.

"Is this the same one you were looking at?" I asked him.

He nodded yes.

Zayde bought the leather bags south of the border in Tijuana. He got a great deal on them there and then charged competitive prices that earned him a nice margin.

"But I don't have that much money," the customer said.

I asked him how much he did have. He told me fourteen dollars.

"Do you have any more?" I asked.

He dug in his pockets and pulled out all he had. He set his coins on the counter, and I counted them. Meanwhile, my grandfather was sitting close by, watching carefully.

"Zayde, this man, all he has is $14.85. But it is Mother's Day tomorrow, and he really wants it," I said.

"What!? Are you crazy? That's a seventeen-dollar purse!" Zayde said knowing that even at $14.85, he'd still earn a profit.

"Please, he really wants it," I said.

"When you grow up, I'll *never* bring you into this business! We'll lose money giving things away like that," he said.

I continued to make my case.

"Okay," Zayde said. "But don't do this ever again!"

I nearly closed the sale. But the man then remembered he needed a quarter for streetcar fare home. So I had to renegotiate with my grandfather, and he sold it to him for twenty-five cents less.

For years afterwards, Zayde loved telling that story. He was so proud of his grandson's sales skill. I once told what happened to my wife and friends, and she wasn't impressed.

"That's terrible!" she said. "Look how you cheated him."

"Cheated?" I argued. "In your case, you buy a bag on sale for 20 percent off, and it is still three thousand dollars. And what do you think that bag cost the manufacturer? One hundred dollars? So are you being cheated?"

In 1949, I started my first year at Alexander Hamilton High School in Culver City. Baseball was my passion, and I was excited to play at a higher level. Maybe I'd even join the big leagues someday! One of my close friends had a brother-in-law who played on a championship high school team and was now in the minor leagues. He was batting .240 and going nowhere in his career.

"God, I would like to go pitch to him," I said to myself, thinking I was a hotshot and could easily blow away this C-league player.

So I asked my friend's brother-in-law if I could test my pitching on him. He agreed. We met at Roxbury Park in Beverly Hills. I turned on my best pitching game ready to prove I had what it took to go pro. But despite my efforts, he hit my pitches with ease. At that point, I realized I needed to give up my Major League aspirations and focus on other professions.

I'm glad I was humbled that day because I would have gone nowhere and wasted my time had I continued holding onto my baseball dreams. I did, however, continue to play and perform well in high school and American Legion Baseball, as well as the Industrial Baseball League.

The following summer, after my first year of high school, I worked for my dad. The year before, he had started Perma-Bilt, a business that manufactured residential steel medicine cabinets.

He hired me to work in his factory, and his foreman, Floyd, quickly trained me to be a spot welder. Most of my co-workers were first-generation Mexicans. We all worked really well together and gained a great deal of respect for one another. They taught me lots of Spanish slang, including the curse words.

I think it's a universal rule that the bad and dirty foreign words are the ones that stick. At least that's what happened in my case. To this day, when joking around with Spanish-speaking people that I know won't be offended by my sense of humor, I'll throw in some of the curse words, and they always get a kick out of it.

After spending long days at my dad's factory for the entire summer, he came into my room one evening. He handed me twenty dollars for all the work I'd done.

"This is all I can afford to pay you," he said.

"Dad, you know what? I think I did a pretty good job," I said.

"You did."

"That is all I wanted to hear," I said.

And I meant it. For so long, I wanted my parents' approval. With a mom and dad who were often eager to criticize and scold but rarely complimented, I felt good finally receiving the recognition from him of my accomplishment and that I had contributed to his new business.

Earlier that same year, I spent an entire semester building something for them. From making a playhouse from scrap lumber taken from a construction project near my home to talking with my friend Arnie about starting a redwood furniture business, I had always enjoyed and been good at building things. So my wood shop class at Hamilton was one of the highlights of my school day.

We all had to complete a major project, and I decided to craft a piece of furniture for my parents. It was a magazine cabinet, and it folded and opened up. As it came together over the course of the semester, I grew more and more excited to show it off to my dad.

Lugging my completed project home was a major feat. I didn't have a car yet, so I had to carry it for about the longest mile ever. I set it down in the living room and couldn't wait for my dad to see the surprise gift.

He arrived home after work.

"Oh, that's pretty good," he said in about the most uninterested way possible.

His half-hearted response was a big disappointment, but I shouldn't have expected anything different, considering how he treated me most of the time.

Once I became an adult, my parents' tendency to focus on the negative continued, even though I was running a successful business.

I had moved to Newport Beach and was telling my mom about the wonderful friends I had made in my new community, which had many immensely creative, highly accomplished, and talented entrepreneurs and business leaders whom I respected. One of my closest friends was Byron Allumbaugh, CEO of Ralphs Grocery Company. When I told my mom about this, she became upset.

"Oh, he's a crook! They started scanning with barcodes at the checkout there, and they overcharged me many times," she said.

"Mom, Byron is not a crook. In fact, he is one of the most honest guys I have ever met. They were using new technology, and so of course it is bound to have lots of problems at first that need to be ironed out," I said.

She didn't stop with him. She found fault with all the highly accomplished and down-to-earth people I had become friends with.

"All you're associating with are rich people. How about the poor?" she asked.

As if being friends with people who had achieved a whole lot in their lives meant I didn't care about anyone else.

"Well, what do you want me to do? This is where I live," I said.

That short exchange is one example among countless others that sums up my mom's ability to find the negative in nearly any situation.

But back when, as a sixteen-year-old, I spent the entire summer of 1950 spot welding like crazy for almost no pay in my father's new medicine cabinet factory, the value of his words far exceeded the money he offered. For him to say he was proud of me was so rare that I've never forgotten our short conversation in my bedroom that summer evening. It was a high point in a year that would soon end in tragedy for our family.

The Glucofts, my aunt Lillian and uncle Julius, lived three houses north and across the street from us with their two kids, Linda and Richard, who were six and eight years old, respectively. As sisters, Aunt Lillian and my mother had a tight bond made even stronger through survival and fleeing Russia with their parents. Being close physically and emotionally, my family and I would visit Aunt Lillian's house often.

Ruben and Silvia Hausman lived next door to our home, across the street from my aunt and uncle. They also had two children, who were around the same age as my cousins, and along with my younger brother, Robert, the five would all play together. At fifteen years old, I had my own circle of friends.

Silvia's father, Fred Stroble, lived with them. Originally from Austria and a baker, now at sixty-eight years old, he was no longer working. From the little interaction I had with him, Mr. Stroble was very grandfatherly. He was a sweet and caring man that seemed to really love children, and we all enjoyed being around him. He would often play games with the five little kids. In his youth, he had learned judo, and once in a while, he would teach me some moves.

As my cousin Linda had done regularly, one afternoon she told her mom, "I'm going to play with Rochelle." She was Linda's best friend and the Hausmans' daughter.

Back then, six-year-olds like Linda could roam around their safe suburban neighborhoods on their own. My aunt gave her permission, and off Linda went to spend time with her closest friend across the street.

Hours later, my aunt called our house in a panic. She had checked the Hausmans', and no one was there.

"Linda hasn't come home yet. Is she with you?" she asked my mom.

We were alarmed at Linda's sudden disappearance, so we called the police, joined my aunt's family, and began scouring the neighborhood.

Meanwhile, the Hausmans had been out for the day and, in fact, had already left by the time Linda came knocking on their door earlier. They returned that evening to find that Fred Stroble was not home. Now, two people were missing, and the Hausmans joined us in the search.

We all kept going well after dark. Despite our frantic efforts, no sign of Stroble or Linda. Aunt Lillian's family and my family returned to our homes, clueless about what had happened and filled with worry.

But Ruben, Stroble's son-in-law, had his suspicions. He disclosed Stroble's criminal past to the police during their search for my young cousin. A few days before, the elderly man had failed to appear for his court hearing.

Six months prior, Stroble had been arrested for exposing himself to a ten-year-old girl whom he had also been accused of molesting. Ruben posted bail and let Stroble stay with his family.

But in a case of clear negligence, no arrest warrant was issued after he ditched his court date. Although Stroble had gotten away from his legal responsibilities, Ruben demanded that his father-in-law turn himself in or pack up and get out. Tragically, Stroble was still at home when Linda arrived.

Early the next day, the phone rang in our house, and my mom picked up. She broke down in tears during the call and then told me what had happened. As I heard the gory details, I felt like someone had put a knife in my heart.

Linda's body was found wrapped in a blanket, hidden under trash, and lodged behind an incinerator in the Hausmans' backyard, less than fifty feet from where we were receiving this horrible news. She only had on the yellow socks and red shoes she wore that day. Next to Linda's body was a bloodstained ax, hammer, ice pick, and butcher knife. But Stroble was still nowhere in sight.

My cousin's gruesome murder cast a gigantic spotlight on her case that drew coast-to-coast attention. Newspapers and radio and TV stations across the country reported on her death, as well as the suspect who was at large. The far-reaching media coverage resulted in the perpetrator's capture.

Two days after the murder, a truck driver tipped off the LAPD, and the rookie cop, Arnold W. Carlson, entered a downtown LA bar and took Stroble into custody as he was sipping a beer. He did not resist arrest. Under questioning, he said, "I had to kill her to stop her screaming." Stroble later added, "I wanted to play with her. She refused. This wasn't the first time; I had played with her once before."

He confessed that he had molested several other children in Los Angeles over the years. Popular with local kids, he was known for his generosity by offering them ice cream and candy, which was exactly what he had done when Linda had come looking for her best friend that horrible day.

My aunt Lillian told reporters, "Every home in this neighborhood has at least one child. We should have been warned, just like for a mad dog."

It would take decades for criticisms like hers to result in statutes, such as Megan's Law, written to protect children.

The day after Stroble was arrested, I was at my aunt and uncle's house when the doorbell rang. Uncle Julius answered. At the door was Ruben. I became enraged at the sight of him. My uncle joined him on the porch where Ruben expressed his deep sorrow for the heinous act his family member committed.

It took a ton of guts for Ruben to come over, and for a moment, my anger was replaced with sorrow for the man who obviously felt horrible for what his father-in-law did. But I quickly became angry again when I thought about how Linda's murder could have been completely avoided.

Why did he and his wife allow that crazy son-of-a-bitch to play with my brother and cousins—let alone their own kids? I wanted to rip Ruben to pieces. But I kept my cool and didn't say a word until he left.

I'm glad I didn't react because it wasn't my place and acting out of rage when our families were mourning would have made a terrible situation even worse.

In January 1950, Stroble pleaded not guilty by reason of insanity; he claimed alcohol made him commit the crime.

"I've been drinking steadily these last couple of months. . . . I can't believe that I killed her. . . . My head is on fire. . . . A million bees are buzzing inside my head. . . . I must have been crazy," he said.

Despite his insanity plea, four psychiatrists and one psychologist all rejected it.

His high-profile trial lasted twelve days, and for each one, the courtroom was packed with onlookers, many of whom may not have been fully prepared to hear the graphic details. Stroble described how he murdered my cousin on November 14, 1949. He recalled how he had slaughtered pigs in the past and slit her throat the same way. He then used his hammer and axe to mangle her head and face. One juror passed out after seeing the crime-scene photos.

Stroble was found guilty of first-degree murder, and the judge sentenced him to death.

The defendant's attorneys appealed the decision, arguing that their client's fourth grade education meant he couldn't understand his trial.

The appeal made it all the way to the US Supreme Court. Once at the doorstep of the country's highest court, it was denied, and the original conviction was upheld.

He was executed in the gas chamber in San Quentin on July 25, 1952, one day before my eighteenth birthday.

While Linda's murder would be the last thing I'd ever wish on any family, the public outcry afterward resulted in a series of new laws and a public awareness campaign intended to protect boys and girls and prevent this from ever happening again.

Prior to Linda's death, child molestation was only a misdemeanor in California. The crime eventually became a felony. And the sentence for a convicted first-degree murder of the sex killing of a child under fourteen years old grew to death or life in prison without the chance of parole.

Children's books and a short film, initially funded by John Wayne, taught kids how to identify and protect themselves from predators. These were distributed in schools. While novel back then, actions taken after Linda's passing resulted in public safety measures that seem common-sense today and have spared countless children from going through what my cousin did.

Well before my family's wounds began to heal from this tragedy, my brother, Robert, was diagnosed with a brain tumor.

My little brother was the opposite of me. Where I was defiant and rebellious, Robert was sweet and easy to love, and my dad was particularly affectionate toward him.

The timing of the diagnosis was especially hard for my parents since my father had just started his company, Perma-Bilt. So while my parents were working hard to make sure the new venture was successful, they were also taking care of Robert, which included a trip to the Mayo Clinic in Rochester, Minnesota. It was one of the best hospitals in the country, providing breakthrough treatments unavailable in Los Angeles, and offered hope for my parents desperate to keep their son alive.

For my mom, who had a fear of flying, hopping on a plane all the way to the Midwest showed her commitment to saving her son.

Unfortunately, his time at the Mayo Clinic didn't improve his condition.

When the phone rang the night Robert passed in late 1951, I was home alone.

My parents had been at work. Afterwards, they visited the hospital to see Robert at Cedars of Lebanon in Los Angeles and were on their way back to the house—little did they know the tragedy that had taken place shortly after they had left Cedars.

The call was from my brother's doctor. He told me that Robert had died. After that brief announcement, I hung up. Now I had to break the news to my parents. Until then, my brother's condition had not improved, so we had all been preparing for the worst.

When they arrived home, I relayed the doctor's message and told them to call him. I went straight to my room right after. Like many teenage boys facing difficulty, I just wanted to be left alone.

The death was big, but my family was extremely strong. My parents had experienced many losses up to this point: leaving their homelands and knowing that family members and friends had suffered tremendous and senseless persecution and death just for being Jewish. We drew from our strength and moved forward with our lives, as did, I believe, my aunt and uncle.

Two years after Linda's death, my aunt gave birth to Sheri. While Linda could never be replaced or forgotten, Sheri's presence signaled a new and bright chapter in their family's life.

In the summer of 1952, I graduated from Hamilton High, and in the fall, I began studying engineering at Los Angeles City College (LACC). Math had been my strongest subject, I'd always been mechanically inclined, and my father thought engineering was a good idea too. The choice was a right fit because I did well in my classes and they matched my interests and natural abilities.

While at LACC, I found work at a used car lot, called Murnat Motors. It was down the street from my school on Vermont Avenue and owned by two guys, Murray and Nat.

At the time, the car industry was booming, especially in sprawling Southern California. While consumer demand for cars was growing, the industry

Ron at age eighteen.

providing vehicles, especially used ones, was grossly under-regulated—to say the least. Once hired, I quickly realized the terrible reputation of used car salesmen had some truth to it. In fact, they are probably right up there with lawyers for the number of jokes about their bad behavior.

Murray and Nat ran their store as many men did during their day. Business was different back then because often salesmen would resort to practices that would not be considered acceptable today. This was the Wild, Wild West of business, before the many lawsuits and legislation that resulted in the long list of consumer protection laws, regulations, and organizations we have now like lemon laws for cars and the Better Business Bureau—let alone online review sites like Yelp. And thank goodness for that because the consumer has really benefitted as a result. Seeing good and bad business practices from such an early age certainly helped me: I rejected the negative and committed to upholding the positive throughout my career.

Murray took a liking to me right away. After a couple of months seeing me on the job, the co-owner realized I was hard-working, smart, and a quick study in selling well.

"Ron, you have a great future here. I want to teach you the business," Murray told me.

He told me to go with him to a car auction, so I could see firsthand how he bought his inventory. I was eager to learn the ropes.

We went to the city of Alhambra, and the auction was a warehouse full of cars in all different conditions. Some had notes written right on their bodies describing what was wrong with them.

I followed Murray as he inspected the inventory.

"Okay, we're going to bid on that," he told me.

"But why, Murray? It says, 'Cracked block,'" I said, knowing this meant the car was junk.

"Because no one will know that except us. So I'll get the same price for it as if it were fine," he said.

In other words, once he brought it back to his lot, he would figure out a way to cover up the defect. At Murnat, I witnessed the worst of the worst, including all the horror-story tricks that have earned the industry its horrible image: car odometers being dialed way back and major engine problems being bandaged with some kind of mystery goo poured straight into the engine block and even sawdust sometimes, just to create a temporary fix that would convince a clueless consumer to buy the car and drive the lemon off the lot.

The deception made me uncomfortable. The final straw took place when an elderly woman showed up at the dealership. I knew the car she was interested in was screwed up, but I sold it to her anyway. That night, I tossed and turned in bed filled with guilt over what I had done. I returned to Murnat the next day.

"I cannot stay here. I just cannot do business like this," I said.

"But you've got a great future here," Murray said.

"I do not want a great future with this. I quit," I said.

And that was the end of my car sales career. My short time at Murnat Motors provided me a lesson in ethics that would always stay with me. I realized that part of being proud of my work meant I also had to be fair, which meant I could also never run a business as Murray and Nat did. Thankfully, the car industry has become a much tighter and closely regulated industry since.

While I continued to take my work seriously once I started college, I still occasionally had moments of mischief. I was enrolled in a chemistry class, and we were learning about the periodic table and chemical reactions.

Magnesium is a highly flammable metal and produces a bright white light when ignited. It was used as one of the first flashes in photography and in weapons of mass destruction during World War II. My classmates and I were learning about magnesium's properties from our long-term substitute professor.

On lab day, we were instructed on the dos and don'ts with our magnesium experiment. Unlike so many objects on fire that are extinguished by water, magnesium loves H_2O. In fact, it's like pouring gasoline on a fire. So we were told to stay away from this combination.

In my mind, the professor was basically saying, "You can't mix the two!" As always, being told not to do something meant I needed to see for myself. Which is exactly what I did.

Holding strips of magnesium with tongs, I lit the metal. As I was warned, it caught fire immediately. I then dropped the flaming magnesium into a beaker of boiling water.

Poof! White steam shot from the beaker. The class's attention turned toward the small explosion that took place at my lab station. At that moment, my substitute professor's anger, if dropped in the same beaker, would have probably produced just as much steam.

"I warned you not to do this, but you did it anyway!" he told me.

My teacher was right, but once again, my curiosity had overruled my better judgment. Thankfully, apart from the anger he expressed, he didn't subject me to any additional disciplinary action. But he did, eventually, show me who was boss.

Shortly after getting in trouble at school, my close buddy, Arnie Naches, fixed me up on a blind date. Actually, the girl he was going out with at the time did the matchmaking. Arnie let me know that the young woman I was being introduced to was very sweet and pretty. He and his date arranged for all of us to go to a drive-in theater.

Date night, I picked up Arnie and his date, and we then headed to the house of the young lady they had set me up with.

I parked in front of the house and stepped out of my car.

"Aren't you coming with me?" I asked them.

"No, we'll wait here," Arnie said.

I didn't suspect a thing, but I later realized why they chose to stay behind.

Standing at the front of her home, dressed up and ready to impress her and her parents, I knocked and then nervously waited. The door opened, and I couldn't believe who was in front of me. It was the substitute teacher of the chemistry class I was taking.

"Simon, what are you doing here?" he asked. He was just as surprised to see me as I was to see him.

"I think I am here to pick up your daughter," I said.

He allowed me in, and to his credit, he let her go out with me. She and I chatted on the way to the movie, and the young woman was exactly as Arnie had described.

Although my teenage hormones may have tempted me to think or do otherwise, or maybe *because* they were tempting me, throughout the entire movie, I kept my hands securely fastened to the steering wheel. I had already landed on her dad's shit list once. There was no way I was going to risk making my professor angry a second time.

After I took her home and walked her to the door, I returned to my car and let Arnie have it. Meanwhile, he and his date were laughing their asses off. He really got me good that night after all the pranks I had pulled on him.

★ CHAPTER THREE
Zero Tolerance for Bigotry

"God, look at the pretty girl," Arnie told me.

We had just parked at a pizza place, and Arnie had spotted someone around our age who was standing with what seemed like a group of her friends outside the local joint.

"I don't know her, but I know the three guys she is with. Do you want to meet her?" I asked.

"Yeah!" he said.

We walked up to the group of guys I knew, and they introduced Arnie and me to their friend, Shirley. We all chatted, and at the end of the conversation, he got the prized phone number from her.

Arnie called Shirley Gorelnik afterwards, and they set up a date. It would actually be a double because Shirley had a friend that she offered to introduce me to.

The evening of the date, the four of us met. While I'd been set up with Shirley's friend, Millie, my attention was drawn to Shirley herself. She had a great personality that matched her looks. But she was also off limits because Shirley was Arnie's date, not mine.

The next week, Arnie called to see if she wanted to go out again. Shirley said she couldn't. He tried again later. She politely declined a second time.

Arnie told me how he couldn't convince Shirley to see him again.

At that point, I confessed to my buddy that I was interested in Shirley. Given his failed attempts, I asked if it was okay to reach out to her.

"She isn't going out with me. So, yeah, go ahead and call her," he said.

With his okay, I phoned her. During our talk, we hit it off and set up a date. We continued getting together, and I found myself falling in love.

Shirley told me she too took a liking to me when we first met. She wasn't crazy about Arnie the night of our double date, and when I reached out to her the first time, she was glad I called. I eventually proposed to her, and we married in 1955, a year after our engagement.

In 1954, when I told Shirley's parents about my plans to marry their daughter, I received an early insight into the family that would become my in-laws.

At the time, I was a college student and full-time employee. Shirley's mom, Minnie, had her doubts about me.

"What's Shirley going to do when you get married?" she asked. She was referring to her daughter's work situation.

"She is probably going to have to get a job after she graduates because I am still going to be in school," I said.

"What kind of man does that? To marry someone you can't even provide for?" she asked.

It was as if Shirley had picked some lowlife, not a hard-working young man with ambition and discipline.

"Well, Mrs. Gorelnik, would you rather I quit school and become a garbage collector? Or would you rather I invest another year in my education so that we can amount to something? And, yes, she would have to work for that year," I said.

That put an end to her nonsense . . . for now. Our conversation was just a taste of what I'd learn Shirley's mom to be—difficult.

When Shirley and I met in 1952, she was sixteen years old, and I was eighteen. I had earned my high school diploma and was off to college. Meanwhile, Shirley had just begun eleventh grade. While we both attended Hamilton High School, we never met there because I was two years ahead of her.

After attending drafting classes for one semester at LACC, I found work as a draftsman at Far West Engineering by answering a want ad in the paper. Being a full-time student and employee and having a serious girlfriend meant I was busier than ever.

The first few days, I was working my ass off trying to complete as much drafting as fast as I could. My boss took notice.

"Ron, you're doing a great job!" he said.

The praise was welcomed, but what he said after was the opposite of what I expected to hear.

"You don't need to work so hard," he said.

"What?" I asked.

"As a matter of fact, since you're a student, do you have any homework you need to do?" he asked.

"Definitely," I said, still a little bit in shock about this conversation.

"Well, go for it. I'll tell you when Hughes Aircraft visits the office. When they're here watching us, that's when I'll need you to put the homework away and work hard," he said.

At the time, Hughes Aircraft, which was designing the Falcon Missile, subcontracted Far West Engineering on a cost-plus basis, which can be summed up by saying it was nearly a blank-check arrangement. The company would charge Hughes Aircraft for the hours its employees logged. So the government, through the invoices Far West was sending Hughes Aircraft, was actually paying me to do my schoolwork . . . what a sweet deal!

At this job, I saw how much Uncle Sam wastes money through practices such as cost-plus pricing that essentially invites cheating. Although I didn't complain as a young student who needed to get his coursework done, it definitely made me critical of how Uncle Sam spent its revenue and my tax dollars. I was sure this was just one example of many representing government fiscal incompetence. It was an early lesson, among lots to come, that showed me how *not* to run a business.

I stayed at Far West Engineering for about a year until I found a higher-paying draftsman job. After I earned my degree from LACC, I was offered a position at Layne and Bowler Pump Company, located in Commerce in Los Angeles County. It was a profitable business with about two hundred employees, including its factory workers who were part of its foundry. At twenty years old, I was hired as a junior engineer and started in the fall of 1954. My salary was four hundred dollars a month.

Working in a five-person engineering department, I was the low man on the totem pole, eager to climb his way up. The benefit of a small team within a small company was I could learn a lot about many aspects of running a business, as well as be a big fish in a little pond. And I did both—I really grew within Layne and Bowler during my five years there, and my skills and drive were recognized by my superiors and colleagues.

My job marked the beginning of my ambition, which would only increase over time. While I entered the company still fighting against my low self-image, I left there confident I had what it took to succeed.

Because I was fresh out of school, I had lots of theoretical knowledge. Soon I became the smartest engineer in my department, and my boss leaned on me. The engineer that the company had previously depended on to design custom pumps had passed away, and I had replaced him. Layne and Bowler was expanding its product line, and I became the only one that could design the custom impellers for the company's pumps.

I had an insatiable appetite to learn and grow. In order to master the trade, I took a deep dive into my predecessor's work. And to continue building upon my expertise, I enrolled in evening hydraulics classes at UCLA.

Motivated by my ambition and the accolades my employer gave me, I knew I'd grow within the company. But my future within my current department was uninspiring. Seeing my boss, the chief engineer, sitting at his desk managing his team while they sat at their drafting tables all day was not my idea of an exciting career.

I wanted to take what I had learned in school and within the company and become more of a salesman and businessman than an engineer, which is not the typical path because generally engineers aren't interested in sales or running a company.

At the same time, basic engineering is great business training. As I realized within my department, you have to identify problems and then solve them. There's no gray area. If you don't do your job right, the pump won't work, the customer won't be happy, and you'll lose business.

You also gain tremendous focus. As I'd later learn, from engineering to personnel issues, so many people in business are solving problems all day. But they've missed one big step: They haven't identified the real problem, which means their supposed solution is useless!

I was ready to combine all the street smarts I'd gained through working the various odd jobs I'd had up to this moment and my competitive side I'd developed through sports and then apply them to my career. Luckily, I found the example I wanted to follow early on at the company. Clark Bower was the vice president of sales and marketing. He was smart, successful, and charismatic.

With his help, I was able to seize upon an opportunity to grow on the job and show everyone what I was made of. A customer came to Layne and Bowler needing a barge pump that we had never made. Now it was up to me to design it from scratch. Among the near endless list of important engineering questions to answer on the road to designing a pump that works was "Once you shut off the motor, how long will the pump run purely off its momentum?"

The question had stumped my fellow engineers, even my boss, Claude Wykes. I was the only one to figure out the answer to this question. But rather than tell Claude right away, I realized I needed to use this information to my benefit while making sure I stayed on good terms with everyone in the company. If I simply presented it to him, Claude would show it to his boss and then receive all the credit. But if I went to the higher-ups and his colleagues without letting Claude know, I would be undermining him.

Soon after, Clark Bower and I bumped into each other in the restroom. The VP had originally worked for a much larger company and was savvy about the interpersonal workings of businesses. During my time at Layne and Bowler, we had become friendly and respected one another.

We chatted in the restroom, and lucky for me, the conversation led Clark to ask me how the new barge pump was coming. This was my chance to let an important person know I'd solved a problem that none of my fellow engineers could and to get the recognition for what I'd done. But I had to act wisely. If I told Clark outright what I had discovered and my boss found out through Clark, I ran the risk of Claude thinking I was going around him. So rather than tell Clark my calculations directly, which I knew were correct, I framed what I would say into a question—one that was soliciting Clark's advice.

"Once the pump is shut off, I think it will run for three minutes. Does that make sense? I do not want to sound foolish when I tell Claude," I said.

"Based on my experience with similar sized pumps, that sounds reasonable. Ron, I'm really impressed you figured that out," he said.

I thanked him and then submitted my designs and calculations to Claude. My boss eventually presented the information to Clark. Had I not filled Clark in on my discovery that day in the restroom, he would have assumed Claude was behind it. While I'd never played office politics before, my first attempt worked.

I was rewarded for what I'd figured out. Clark invited me to his biweekly brainstorming sessions that included company executives. During those meetings, Clark encouraged participants to bring up any ideas. He explained that even a crazy suggestion could spark a great one. The experience taught me invaluable lessons that I carry with me to this day.

For example, during the brainstorming sessions within RSI, the company I would go on to found, I encouraged all participants to present any ideas they came up with related to our topic of conversation. Whether they thought it was legit, crazy, or even downright embarrassing, I invited their input because you never know what idea could inspire something brilliant in someone else.

As my time at Layne and Bowler progressed, I gained confidence in my professional skills and earned the respect of my peers. But when it came to the respect part, at first I was worried that could change in an instant.

Within the entire company, I was the only Jew. It was a mostly WASPy business, and back in the 1950s, being openly anti-Semitic was more acceptable and allowed than it is today.

Bob was second in command in the engineering department, and he and I had become pretty good friends. One day, he was telling me about his dad's furniture business and his father's sales strategy. Having been in conversations like these before, I had a gut feeling he was headed down the path of making a derogatory reference, one that uses "Jew" to mean to cheat someone, as in "I'm going to Jew these people down" or "Don't Jew me."

I wasn't sure if anyone in the company knew I was Jewish, so I could have easily let Bob say whatever anti-Semitic insult he wanted and not let on that it offended me. But considering how much persecution Jews had faced in the war that had just ended a few years ago, I would not allow it, even if it might not be in my best interest as Bob's subordinate.

"I think I know what you are going to say," I told Bob. "I am not sure, but if it is what I think it is, I like you too much, and I do not want to hear it."

"What's the matter?" he asked.

"I am Jewish, and I think you are going to say something about Jews," I said.

"You are?!" he replied.

Based on the look of surprise on his face, you'd think I'd told him I was a Martian. He had no idea about my background. But rather than backfire, speaking out worked in my favor. Bob was respectful, and I no longer had to be on the lookout for anti-Semitic language.

I don't tolerate bigoted comments about my Jewish background, but I'm not a particularly religious person. I respect my heritage and will never forget the twentieth century Jewish persecution that took place at the hands of, first, the Russian empire and, then, the Nazis. My emotions were running particularly high after World War II.

While during the war I knew the Holocaust was horrific, it wasn't till after the Nazis were defeated that the world saw the full horror of the Final Solution. Thinking about my family members murdered under the banner of anti-Semitism infuriated me to the point that anything or anyone associated with the Third Reich instantly triggered me.

While I was at Layne and Bowler, the company had a technology sharing partnership with a German business, which sent one of its engineers to work with us in Los Angeles. Hans was probably around twenty years older and much taller and bigger than me.

Friday nights, the engineering office team met at a bar to have a few beers and unwind after a week of hard work. Hans joined us. Given his age, he was an adult during World War II, so I had my suspicions about his background.

"Were you in the army?" I asked.

"Yes," he said.

"What was your rank?" I asked.

"I was an SS officer," he said.

Although I knew about the persecution of Jews at the hands of the SS, or Schutzstaffel, Hitler's elite paramilitary unit, Europe was a distant place. Throughout the war, I had been far removed from the land where Jews were rounded up and murdered. Still, SS had been burned into my mind as the title of those who had committed nightmarish atrocities against innocent people.

Growing up, I had heard many stories about how anti-Semitism before the rise of Nazism had directly harmed my family in Europe, and I saw it with my own eyes in LA as well. So from a young age, the inherent importance I've always placed on fairness combined with my outrage of bigotry meant I had no problem scrapping with other kids if I didn't see a better option.

Never a bully growing up—in fact, I couldn't stand anyone picking on the underdog—I was always willing to defend myself if I needed to. As Hitler's example showed, you give a tyrant an inch, and he'll send your people to concentration camps! So as far back as I can remember, I refused to back down—even if I knew I'd get the shit beat out of me.

One day when I was eleven years old, I was riding my bike in my neighborhood. Three kids standing on a lawn yelled out to me: "Dirty Jew!"

I steered my bike right into these three numbskulls. We all tumbled down like dominoes. I was outnumbered, so I would probably lose this battle, but that didn't matter to me. In the end, I was right. I did get my ass kicked. But I won over the long term: They knew I wouldn't go down without a fight, so they never picked on me again.

And now, years later as an adult in the job that I liked so much, in front of me was one of these Schutzstaffel demons I had heard about growing up. I couldn't believe I was face-to-face for the first time with a Nazi war criminal. Even worse, one who had gone unpunished for the atrocities he had committed against innocent people and was now leading a life as an upstanding civilian as if nothing had happened.

"What does SS mean? Did you kill women and children?" I asked.

"I was a soldier. I had to follow orders," he said.

Hans was no longer a friendly German engineer to me. He transformed into an SS officer of the Third Reich. I imagined him in his army uniform executing Hitler's Final Solution. I couldn't contain my rage.

"So you are telling me that is what you did . . . killed women and children?" I asked.

"I'm telling you I was a soldier. I had to do what I was told," he said.

I recalled the Holocaust footage, bodies stacked one on top of the other while survivors were skin and bones, many suffering from painful diseases brought about by inhumane living conditions and starvation. I thought of my innocent family members who were victims of the Nazi killing machine. I remembered the Nuremberg Trials, which showed the world the extent of Hitler's insane ambition and those charged to bring it about.

The next thing I knew, my co-workers were restraining me, dragging me from the bar, and throwing me into my car. I had clearly just lost it and gone into attack mode lunging toward Hans, the SS officer. By holding me back from trying to beat Hans up, my friends were actually protecting me. He was way bigger than me and would have easily won a brawl between us. With his military training, he could have killed me.

The entire weekend, I was filled with worry, convinced my outburst against my colleague meant I would be fired. By Monday morning, had my wife not said, "Ron, you've got to go," I would have skipped work altogether.

Sheepishly, I arrived at the office. I looked around and asked my co-worker where Hans was.

"He ain't coming back," he told me.

I found out that Layne and Bowler had sent Hans back to Germany. I couldn't believe the vote of confidence my company had given me. Here I was afraid I was about to be fired. Instead, Layne and Bowler accepted me for who I was and sent Hans away. I had always appreciated working for this company, but now I had even more loyalty and respect for it.

Since my run-in with Hans, my anti-German bias that was common among many Americans of my generation has vanished. Back then, if you had asked me if I'd ever buy a German product, my answer would have been, "Hell no! Not in a million years!" But time and peace have a way of putting past hostilities behind.

Where Germany and the United States were archrivals bent on destroying one another just decades ago—the Axis versus the Allies— today, we are two nations that have immense respect for one another. I'm happy to drive my BMW. More importantly, my second wife was of German descent. Her lovely mother, in fact, was born and grew up during World War II in Germany.

But despite all the reflection and remorse over how Jews were inno- cently killed during the war just because they were Jewish, you still see anti-Semitism all over the place. I remember confronting it even among those who were part of my close social circle.

On my calendar on September 12, 2001, was a monthly golfing event to play with the Long Whackers. This was a group of prominent Orange County businessmen.

In 1995, shortly after I moved to Orange County, I joined Big Can- yon Country Club and began to play golf. A couple of years later, Byron Allumbaugh, my friend and chairman of Ralphs Grocery Company, invited me to join the Long Whackers. We played in country clubs all over, including ones that would require plane travel, usually in one of the members' jets. Little did we know when we scheduled the golf date that the tragic events of 9/11 would take place the day before.

An unprecedented freeze on air travel across the country pointed to the gravity of the terrorist attack. But because the country club where we planned to meet that day was located in Los Angeles, this didn't affect us.

A highlight of each round of golf was the discussion after. We would meet for dinner where we would talk about political, economic, and business topics usually around a theme.

Herb Kalmbach, a fine gentleman and President Nixon's personal attorney, was also part of the group. I got to know him well. He always did a fantastic job as moderator, using his lawyer background to facilitate the discussion without ever taking sides and knowing how to motivate us to share our opinions.

"So I have *no idea* what in the world we'll talk about tonight," Herb said jokingly to me as we played golf. Despite being surrounded by the pristine Lakeside Country Club in Burbank, we felt our nation's stability shaken to the core—as did the rest of the country.

The Twin Towers' collapse the day before was fresh in our minds. We were all filled with both outrage over what had happened and uncertainty about the future. On the news, commentators talked about the possibility of World War III. I was sure the roundtable discussion would be one of the most interesting we would ever have.

After playing golf, as always, we started our discussion during dinner. The typical pattern was Herb would introduce a topic, often through a question, and then he would go around the room and give each person time to provide his insight.

"Why do you think we were attacked by these terrorists?" Herb asked to start the discussion.

The first member to speak was a Lakeside member that hosted the event.

"Because we support Israel. And the terrorists were fed up with everything we provide the Jewish state," he said.

"If that's the case, then is it in our best interest to support Israel?" Herb asked.

He directed his question to Bill Davis, who was an Orange County developer.

Bill was very supportive of the US friendship with Israel. He expressed his feelings on why we should continue to back the Jewish state. Don Beall, ex-CEO of Rockwell, was the next respondent.

"We should absolutely support Israel," Don said. "I've traveled in the Middle East. If Israel was not our ally, it would be necessary to have our military presence there. But Israel has its own military resources. So it's in the best interest of the security of the United States."

Don shared more of his opinion, which lined up with my thoughts.

A fellow I'll call Mark was next to speak. He was a local entrepreneurial legend who had built his business empire from nothing. I admired and respected him immensely.

"If supporting the Jews is going to bring us to war, then why should we support them? Hell, what have the Jews ever done for us?" Mark asked.

I couldn't believe what I was hearing. I thought I knew the man who was launching into an anti-Semitic tirade. It had been a while since I had heard such poison come out of someone's mouth—let alone a friend's. And it just got worse.

"Every time I did business with the Jews, I got fucked," he said.

By this point, the veins in my neck were ready to burst.

"Did he forget I was Jewish, or does he just not give a damn?" I asked myself.

I wanted to set him straight, but I needed to wait my turn. The next two men to speak were John O'Donnell, who was a prominent commercial Orange County developer, and Byron. They both disagreed with Mark's position.

When my turn came, I had already had enough time to cool off, so I no longer had the urge to verbally attack Mark for his offensive comments.

"Ron, what's your opinion?" Herb asked.

"Are you sure you want to hear it? After all, I am the only Jew in the room," I said.

I started speaking while seated. I then stood up and began walking toward Mark. As I put my hand on his shoulder, not in anger or a threatening way but in a friendly, respectful manner, I continued:

"Mark, go ask one hundred people what I think about you. And they will all tell you how much I respect you. So the last thing I want is to change how positively I feel about you. But when I heard what you said, I have to question it. If you knew all the facts, I believe you would change your opinion," I said.

I asked Mark to do more research about the history of Israel and its many accomplishments that have benefitted the world before he formed his opinion. Then I suggested after he did that, that he and I meet to discuss the topic further in a respectful manner.

Afterwards, a few members told me how proud they were of me for controlling myself the way I did.

When the dinner was over, all of us took a bus back from the country club to Orange County. Mark and I sat next to each other on the ride, during which we had a civil conversation. He had thought about what had happened during the roundtable.

"I'm sorry, Ron. I really don't know what's going on in Israel. And I don't know much about the history of the Jews and Israel after the war," he said.

I appreciated his words. At the same time, I had my reservations. Was he just blowing smoke, or was he really sorry for his anti-Semitic remarks?

About three weeks later, Mark and I attended an event where I was introduced to his sister.

"Just last week, Mark told me about you. He said so many nice things and has so much respect for you," she said.

With her kind words, I knew Mark had been sincere in his apology to me that day at Lakeside. And I was very glad and proud that I had expressed myself the way I had during our dinner.

In yet another instance of using my background to help others discriminate less, I played a role in removing racial roadblocks at my gym. Well, sort of . . .

Founded in 1880, the Los Angeles Athletic Club (LAAC) has a long history that spans the growth of Downtown LA. I was a member of the club and so was Perma-Bilt's CFO, Paul Vert. We would train there and unwind regularly after a long day at the office. Our workouts would often consist of a one-and-a-half-mile run on the track, some squash, and then another mile run.

We were there one night in the early 1970s, and I had really pushed myself hard at the gym that day.

"You know what, Paul? I think I want a mai tai," I said to him as we dressed in the locker room.

"Where are you going to get that?" he asked.

"The bartender can probably make one," I said.

We went upstairs to the LAAC's bar and ordered our drinks. By the time we finished our fourth mai tai, we were the only ones in the bar, and the entire club itself was empty.

Paul and I made the big mistake of drinking on empty stomachs. The result was some belligerent behavior. Paul typically was more a Dr. Jekyll. But after a few drinks, you'd see his Mr. Hyde side come out.

As we stumbled downstairs from the bar, we began getting rowdy. Acting like drunk sailors, we overturned ashtrays and pulled some paintings off the walls. While we didn't do any permanent damage, we definitely left our mark.

The next morning, I made my way to the office just in time for a meeting. At my desk I saw that the manager of the LAAC had left me a message.

"Oh shit!" I said.

I had been the one to sign the check at the bar the night before to cover our drinks. No one else was there by the time we had left, so it would be easy for anyone to figure out who had caused the damage. I knew I was in trouble with LAAC's management.

I ran over to Paul's office and told him about the message.

"You know what? I am just going to admit what we did—that we had too much to drink—and then ask how much the damage was and say I will cover it. Okay? And then I hope I am not kicked out of the club for good," I said.

Paul started laughing. And with his response, I knew exactly what had happened.

"You son-of-a-bitch. You really got me!" I said.

I was relieved Paul had pulled the prank on me. At the same time, I knew my reasoning about management finding out still made sense. Sooner or later, I would receive a legitimate call from the club.

Fortunately, I figured out a way to avoid getting caught. It involved addressing a black eye in LAAC's otherwise impressive history.

I called my friend Neil Bornstein. He was funny as hell, could impersonate practically anyone, and loved joking around as much as I did. I told him about my idea. He would call the club and take responsibility for the damage.

"Get the top people on the phone—the owner, the manager . . . anyone running the club," I said.

I gave him ideas of what to say; he came up with the script:

"You don't have any Black guys in the club. So the damage you saw last night is just a sample of what will happen if you continue to discriminate by not allowing my brothers in. I'll give you a month. If I don't see changes by accepting applications you've so far rejected, you're really in big trouble."

The civil rights movement and the Watts Riots put racism front and center on everyone's minds, so the LAAC's discriminatory policy was definitely a huge target for criticism.

Neil then called the LAAC. He let me know afterwards that he had successfully contacted the top guys.

"How did they respond?" I asked.

"'Oh no, no, don't worry! We're not prejudiced. We're not racists. We're considering these things,'" he said.

Neil's call worked, which meant I was off the hook.

Three weeks later, I was in the locker room sitting on the bench getting dressed. To my surprise, as I was looking down tying my shoes, I saw the legs of an African American man. It marked the first time I had seen a Black person in the club. I glanced up and recognized his face right away.

"Are you Mike Garrett?"

"Why, yes," he said.

I was awestruck seeing the winner of the 1965 Heisman Trophy during his time as a halfback for USC. He went on to have a successful professional football career with the Kansas City Chiefs and the San Diego Chargers.

I introduced myself.

"When did you get into the club?" I asked.

"Oh, about three days ago. But I've had my application in here for a while," he said.

"Oh really? That is interesting," I said.

Then about a week later, I saw another Black guy in the LAAC. And pretty soon, there were a few more Black members. So thanks to my drunken antics and my cover-up plan, the LAAC dropped its backwards policy.

★ CHAPTER FOUR
Family Secrets

Sarah Simon, my dad's mother and my grandmother, was a good woman. She was also extremely charitable. Four days a week, she volunteered at the local hospital and provided emotional comfort to patients. As adults, her children provided her financial support. She lived simply, and if she had money left over, she would use it to buy clothes, food, or whatever items that would help those in need around her. Sarah knew the suffering and mistreatment her family members and other Jews had experienced in Russia and throughout Europe during her time. Thus she was compassionate and quick to help the poorest among us.

My grandmother was equal parts giving and tough. She was a strict follower of her Orthodox Jewish roots. She kept kosher, which meant she followed Jewish dietary laws that included not eating certain foods such as pork and shellfish. Her observance sent waves of fear through her children into adulthood. If my parents knew that Sarah was coming to stay with us, my mom would stop cooking bacon five days prior. They had learned the hard way that Sarah could detect bacon had been eaten in the house even after four days of a pork-free kitchen. My grandmother would raise holy hell after smelling it. "How could you do that?" she would tell my dad, criticizing him for not following the same rules she had enforced when he was a kid. Five days of no bacon, however, and my grandmother wouldn't suspect a thing.

While not keeping a kosher kitchen would upset her, she would tolerate it—as long as the scent of pork products around her didn't remind her of breaking the rules. As adults, her other children, my uncles and aunt, kept kosher to different degrees of strictness. Whereas my grandmother was by the book, my aunt was kosher at home but ordered pork spareribs when eating out. Clearly, violating Jewish dietary laws would upset my grandmother. But there were other acts of religious defiance that were far worse . . . even unforgivable perhaps in her eyes.

Uncle Dave, my dad's younger brother, owned a laundry business. As head of his small company, he worked around the clock Monday through Friday. Uncle Dave would spend nearly every weekend in Phoenix to get away from his business and relax and then return to LA first thing on Monday to resume the business-owner grind. After my grandmother died, Uncle Dave felt it was safe to reveal the secret he had tightly held for years.

Rather than seek rest and relaxation in Arizona every weekend, my uncle announced to the family around 1970 that his visits had actually been to see his wife and kids. By that time, his wife and kids had moved to Kansas City. He had kept the news of his family secret because he wanted to avoid, at all costs, his mother finding out he had married a non-Jew. Had Sarah Simon discovered this, it would have broken her heart and she would have most likely disowned him.

Before receiving this jaw-dropping news of my uncle's secret family and the cousins I never knew I had, I'd always enjoyed our close relationship. Thus his announcement was a shock to me. But after hearing it, I felt terrible for him because I couldn't imagine what it must have felt like to keep this secret bottled up inside for so many years—as if he had committed some kind of crime. At the same time, I also knew I was a different type of man. No matter how anyone felt—my mother, grandmother, or otherwise—I would never hide my wife's and kids' existence for fear of rejection. But for Uncle Dave, the power his mom had over him meant he would rather lead a double life than cross a line she had drawn.

In fact, when my kids, Steve and Kathy, were younger, we were at my Uncle Joe's house celebrating Passover, which commemorates the Jew's liberation under Moses's guidance from slavery in ancient Egypt.

I was closer to my mom's side of the family overall because our chemistry and values aligned more with them than with my dad's side. The Langers were mostly secular Jews, so they were less observant of religious traditions. When it came to Jewish holidays, my family would spend them with my dad's side, who celebrated them all, attended temple regularly, and taught me about the high holidays.

During the Seder, which is the ritual meal on Passover, my grandmother and Uncle Joe started grilling me about my religious observance. Out of all his siblings, my dad was the renegade. He dropped most of the Jewish traditions he was taught to follow growing up, so I wasn't raised to live under orthodox rules. Uncle Joe, however, was a strict follower.

"Ron, do you observe Shabbat every Friday? Do you light the candles?" they asked.

Shabbat is the twenty-five-hour Jewish period of rest each week that begins on sundown on Friday. What a time to bring something like this up, I thought. Did they want to start an argument in front of everyone during what was otherwise a family celebration? Regardless, I wasn't one to lie or mince words.

"No, I do not," I said.

"Why not?" they asked.

Then they started criticizing me for what they viewed as my lack of upholding the Jewish faith. And because I had two small children, they probably thought they needed to remind me of the importance of passing traditions down to them. But I needed to put a stop to their badgering me, especially in front of my children, which really bothered me.

"Look," I said, "do you want to keep this up? I am here with my wife and kids because I love you. I respect the way you live. I am not a bad person, so respect the way I live. If not, I am taking my family, and we are leaving, and we will never come back," I said.

Those words put an end to my grandmother and uncle's attempts to bully me into following their way of religious observance. The two should have known better.

Then again, none of my grandmother's kids challenged her domineering personality, even as grown-ups. While that was an unpleasant argument, scuffles like that within both sides of my extended family, particularly during holidays, were rare. Overall, I was lucky to be surrounded by two loving sides of family. For instance, I would characterize my grandma on my mom's side as an old-fashioned Jewish mother. Her mission in life was to express her love by caring for her family. She enjoyed cooking for us and took pride in being the matriarch.

Compared to the relative harmony within my family on both the Langer and Simon sides, my first wife had it rough growing up. Fortunately, Shirley had some bright spots in her family to offset some of the negativity. She had aunts and uncles who were very nice people. Her maternal grandmother, Ida, was a sweet Russian Jewish lady who lived with Shirley's family. She always treated me well. Unlike Minnie, Shirley's mom, who criticized me because her daughter would have to continue working after we married, Ida saw that I had all the qualities to make a deserving spouse for her granddaughter.

When Shirley and I were dating, her parents would sometimes go out for the evening, at which point I'd receive a call.

"Come on over," Shirley would tell me.

Shirley's grandmother would usually still be in the house and didn't mind her granddaughter sneaking me in. On one occasion, her parents unexpectedly came home early. At that point, we scrambled to not get in trouble for breaking the rules. Fortunately, Ida was in our plan and was eager to protect us. She hid me in her bedroom closet. Once her mom and dad were in their bedroom, Ida let me know the coast was clear, and I quietly escaped.

Shirley's paternal grandfather, Hyman Gorelnik, was a successful Southern California developer. In fact, during World War II, he had built a lot of housing on Camp Pendleton, which is a 125,000-acre coastal

Marine Corps training base in San Diego County. He was a tough businessman who didn't hide his opinions.

I remember once visiting Hyman at his bedside when he was sick.
His three sons, including Shirley's dad, George Gorelnik, were all there.
I had met Hyman a few times prior. While I had not spent a lot of time
with him, we did have several discussions about business, and he really
liked my entrepreneurial spirit.

"Why can't any of you be like Ron?" he asked his sons.

I thought putting them down this way was terrible. It really made me
feel uncomfortable, to say the least. But based on their silence, this wasn't
the first time he had harshly criticized them.

Hyman was a powerful businessman who probably ripped into his
kids for their lack of his ambition and made them feel inferior throughout their lives. They didn't have the will to stand up to him, and his
bullying only ensured they never would. At the same time, I couldn't
disagree with him. His sons, particularly George, didn't have anything
close to their father's drive.

After Hyman died, Betsy, his daughter, took care of her mom. Betsy
was very sharp and tough as steel. But she was ruthless as well. Her parents owned the apartment complex where they lived. After her dad died,
Betsy moved her mother into the upstairs apartment in order to leave the
more desirable bottom unit available to rent.

Here was this elderly lady, who had trouble walking, being forced
to climb to her second-story apartment every day, just so her ungrateful
daughter could earn fifty extra dollars per month. After I found out what
Betsy had done to her mom, I let her have it the next time we met. I
knew I would be the only person willing to speak up.

"How could you treat your mother that way?" I asked.

I described how what she did was so wrong.

Betsy was taken aback by my bluntness. But she showed no remorse
for her terrible actions toward her own mother.

Afterwards, Shirley had some words for me.

"How could you talk to my aunt like that?" she asked.

"Anyone who would do that to her own mother, just to make an extra fifty bucks. . . . She is old and can barely walk! So no, I do not really care how your aunt feels about what I said. I meant every word."

Shortly after World War II, Los Angeles's housing market exploded. People were flooding into LA, and demand far exceeded the housing supply. The vast shortage meant if you had the means to build a residential property, you were nearly guaranteed to be able to rent it out or sell it for a hefty profit. Many of LA's most successful entrepreneurs made their fortunes in residential real estate development during Southern California's property boom. And among these real estate magnates were Holocaust survivors.

Jona Goldrich, Sol B. Kest, and Nathan Shappell were three examples of men who arrived in the United States as European refugees after the war. Jona and Sol went on to form the formidable development company Goldrich Kest. They came to this country with little money and big dreams and created massive fortunes by focusing on Southern California's growing real estate market.

Shirley's dad, George, had the benefit of having a father with the means and willingness to provide his son the resources to build his own apartment fortune. While not extraordinarily rich, his father was a financial success. To Hyman's disappointment, however, George lacked his dad's drive and ambition.

With that said, to succeed in real estate, George didn't even need his dad's deep pockets. At that time, LA's housing shortage was so extreme and the demand so high that banks were providing 110 percent financing. So while it required little business skill and seed money to get rich in real estate back then, George never managed to do so.

It's not that George didn't turn a profit. Whereas some people live paycheck to paycheck, George lived apartment to apartment. His formula was he would build an apartment and the money he made would be his excuse to stop working. His savings would dwindle away through a combination of supporting his family, betting on horse races, and drinking.

George had the means and the opportunity of a lifetime to join the ranks of LA's real estate giants and become a very wealthy man in the process. Had I been in his shoes, I would have never passed that chance up—to be lucky enough to catch an investment wave at its very beginning knowing it would only become bigger and bigger over time: How many people are presented a chance like that?

Even at just twenty years old, I knew George had missed the opportunity to become one of Southern California's premier homebuilders. And because of the vast number of people and tremendous capital flooding into the Golden State, the potential to succeed was unrivaled by any another part of the country.

In fact, I even asked George once, "Why don't you take the money you have made from one apartment and then build two, four, and then ten more? Instead of gambling all your money away, you could build another apartment." But he leaned on the lazy side and didn't share my enthusiasm or drive to succeed in business.

As was often the case for couples at the time, my soon-to-be in-laws hosted the wedding. The ceremony itself would be modest. Although Jewish, Shirley's family was secular, so rather than have the wedding at a temple (they didn't attend one), they rented a banquet facility.

Their choice of a non-religious venue was fine with me. We did follow tradition when it came to setting the date. Jewish weddings usually cannot be held on Saturdays before the end of Sabbath. If they do fall on a Saturday, after nightfall is typically the accepted time.

We scheduled our wedding on Saturday evening. Unfortunately, Shirley and I couldn't find an Orthodox rabbi to marry us. But we did find a Reform one, which meant he represented a strand of Judaism that dropped many Orthodox ceremonial practices. Being a Reform rabbi, he initially didn't plan to wear a yarmulke during the wedding. But I insisted. Our wedding's non-temple setting already drew enough criticism from our more traditional family members. But a rabbi without a yarmulke . . . that would be the last straw.

Ron and Shirley at their wedding, 1955.

"You are going to have to wear it," I told the rabbi. "If not, my grandma will walk out. So at least do that."

While I insisted on the Jewish skull cap, I didn't mind the rabbi dropping other formalities. That move, plus the non-religious setting, put me in the black-sheep category with my dad's side of the family, who strictly followed their Orthodox traditions. But I was okay with playing that role. My wedding wasn't intended to win their approval. If they chose not to attend, it meant they didn't love me enough to look past their expectations, and they didn't need to be there. And then there was Shirley's mother.

Two days before the wedding, we had a rehearsal. The wedding planner described how I would walk down the aisle until I reached the altar. The following groups would then come after me: the bridesmaids, the groomsmen, my parents, and last Shirley's parents.

Once her parents made it to the front, George would leave Minnie at the altar with everyone else and trace his steps backwards to escort Shirley to the altar . . . all traditional stuff.

But Minnie was not having it with tradition that day.

"George is *not* leaving me standing alone here!" she said.

The wedding planner, clearly having experienced his share of rehearsal meltdowns gently replied, "Mrs. Gorelnik, in that case, who will walk the bride down the aisle?"

But his effort to calm her down did the opposite.

"I don't care! I'm not standing here by myself."

Shirley, horrified at her mother's tantrum in front of our wedding party, broke down crying. Her maid of honor whisked her out of the room. I was furious at Minnie's blowup and immediately came to the defense of my wife-to-be with my own blowup.

"Thank you, Mrs. Gorelnik. I didn't want this fucking wedding anyway! Besides that, you are being ridiculous. What we are doing is customary. And as far as I am concerned, this will be the last time you do anything even close like this to your daughter."

By this point, the planner must have been concerned that the wedding might be cancelled, so he doubled down on Shirley's mother.

"Mrs. Gorelnik, Ron is absolutely right. It is totally customary for the father to walk his daughter down the aisle. If you won't allow this basic tradition, I'm not interested in putting the wedding on anyway."

Minnie threw her car keys on the ground and stormed out of the room.

We all stood in silence, confused at how quickly the wedding rehearsal went downhill.

"What a piece of work," I said to my buddies, the groomsmen. I had seen Minnie's unreasonable side before, but today was a new low.

Meanwhile, the wedding planner left the room to speak with Minnie. The rest of us waited around a few minutes, not sure what to do. Once Minnie had cooled off, she and the wedding planner returned.

In the end, everyone did attend the ceremony, and Minnie tolerated George leaving her at the altar to walk their daughter down the aisle.

After the wedding, the two of us would be off for a modest three-day honeymoon in Las Vegas.

"Here's some money, Ronnie. Go gambling," George said as he handed me one thousand dollars in cash.

He probably thought I enjoyed gambling just as much as he did. But as young newlyweds (I hadn't even turned twenty-one yet, and Shirley was eighteen), we had little savings, so there was no way I was going to blow all that money in Vegas.

"George, I am not even old enough to gamble," I said.

"They won't know. They probably don't even care," he said.

He was right. When my wife and I arrived in Vegas, I was able to gamble without any problem. But I tested my luck only with about ten dollars on twenty-one.

I appreciated George's money, but given his drinking, gambling, and lack of professional drive, there was no way I was going to follow in his footsteps. Worse, at one point, this Jewish man was an anti-Semite.

At dinner during Passover week, George became drunk and began saying more then he should have. My kids were little at the time, and George went on a tirade criticizing Jewish people and culture. It was ridiculous to condemn an entire group, and I couldn't believe my Jewish kids' Jewish grandfather was doing this in front of them.

I stood up and told him what I thought of his degrading words, fully prepared to leave with my family. My mother-in-law, Minnie, yelled at him, "You're wrong, George! Ron, please stay," she said. While I decided not to storm out of their house, George certainly didn't earn any respect from me that night.

In regard to gambling, he and I had different definitions of it. Now that I'm a financially secure adult with plenty of savings in the bank, if I were to go to Las Vegas and win lots of money, it wouldn't change my life. But, on the other hand, if I lost lots of money, I'd feel pretty stupid. So why do it? With that said, I used to play a lot of card games with my friends.

In the decades to come, I'd develop my own version of gambling that became one of the greatest adventures of my life. Running a business and making it grow and grow required taking lots of risk—that's the kind of gambling I get a thrill out of!

The moment George handed me the cash, I planned to put his gift to good use. One thousand dollars was a ton of money for me at the time. As a married couple, the next step for Shirley and me was to establish our family, which meant buying a home. George's financial gift was the seed money we needed to move forward with our plan. So when we returned from our honeymoon, I deposited the cash in the bank.

For the next two years, Shirley and I saved as much as possible to make a down payment on a house. Hard work and frugal living was our winning combination. We did our weekly grocery shopping at Boy's Market on Crenshaw Boulevard and Rodeo Road in Los Angeles. Saturday mornings were the perfect time to go to the supermarket because it was our day off and the store offered samples that often provided enough to eat so we could skip making breakfast at home. We also regularly ate dinner at Thrifty Drug Store. For fifty-nine cents per person, Thrifty offered a complete four-course turkey meal.

I recall the first couple we invited to our apartment for dinner. The menu we planned would fit our small budget. We made spaghetti, and our beverage was wine.

Before diverse and exotic wines from all over the world were on supermarket shelves across the country, Lancers was considered fancy for most middle-class Americans. Shirley and I bought Lancers wine, but rarely. What we did, however, was keep the clay pot bottle that most wine drinkers recognized right away. We filled the empty bottles with wine we found that was one-third the price but tasted the same.

"Oh, you have Lancers wine," our guests would tell us, impressed with our fancy preferences.

I remember my friends, who were also marrying around the same time, would receive money from their parents to pay for long honeymoons—similar to how George handed me the thousand bucks.

"As far as I am concerned, forget the wedding and honeymoon. I'd save the cash instead," I thought to myself.

I preferred the money so I could add it to our nest egg and build our future. This also explains our modest honeymoon to Las Vegas, which was an inexpensive car drive away. We also kept our vacation short to save money and allow us to return back to work right after our long weekend.

At the end of 1956, our discipline paid off. We had put a down payment on a twelve-thousand-dollar, eleven-hundred-square-foot house located on 13207 South St. Andrews Place in Gardena. It took us nearly two years to save one thousand dollars, which doubled the cash George had given us. The timing was ideal because the next year, 1957, our son, Steve, was born at Cedars of Lebanon on January 24.

Ron's children, Steve (age four) and Kathy (age two), 1961.

After Shirley's water broke, the doctor told us to wait until she went into labor before traveling to the hospital. So we stayed at my parents' house, which was closer to Cedars, and when Shirley was ready to deliver, we took the short trip to the hospital located on Sunset Boulevard in Hollywood. Steve was born a healthy baby, and as proud first-time parents, we brought him to our new home. Although Shirley's dad had intended for us to spend the money he had given us on entertainment and gambling, we turned it into the most important financial investment we made for our family, which grew to include our daughter, Kathy, born May 11, 1959.

We loved our kids, and Shirley was devoted to Steve and Kathy. In 1968, when they were older and more independent and Shirley had long ago quit her dental assistant job to raise them, she began talking about working again and possibly opening a dress shop. I encouraged her, eventually funded her small business, and spent hours helping her set up, which included building the display racks. She opened her store on Ventura Boulevard in Tarzana. Although her shop was never profitable, she liked staying busy, and the work there filled her time for the couple of years she had it.

While Shirley and I had our share of clashes, we also shared many fond memories together. Our relationship, however, was not helped by Shirley's mom. As the outburst at the wedding rehearsal had demonstrated, Minnie struggled with insecurities, which came out in her envy. She could become downright jealous of her daughter. This drove Shirley nuts, and I didn't blame her one bit.

After we married and Shirley moved out of her parents' house and we moved in together, I recommended she spend less time with her mom in order to get a break from her often difficult personality. Shirley took my advice, and the distance helped her.

Unfortunately, some of Minnie's insecurities had already rubbed off on her daughter, and even early into our marriage, they often appeared as jealousy. As one example, at Layne and Bowler's holiday party my first year there, I danced with the purchasing agent's wife. Shirley accused me of being in love with her. I had no intention of having an affair, so Shirley's claim was ridiculous.

My male friends weren't off-limits to her suspicions either. Of one of my best friends she once said, "He's in love with me." So she wanted me to stay away from him. But I knew what she said wasn't true. It was just another one of her jealous ploys to drive a wedge between my friend and me.

Shirley's jealousy extended to our pets. Our two dogs, Penny and Sam, were closer to my children and me than to her. When I arrived home from work every day, they eagerly greeted me, and I enjoyed passing the time with them. Her way of dealing with the insecurities she had when she saw how the dogs playfully interacted with the kids and me would be to complain how she didn't like them in the house.

One day, we invited friends over for dinner. Before our guests arrived, Shirley told me, "I want the dogs to stay outside."

Her excuse was that they would misbehave. But, as she and I already knew, Penny and Sam were friendly and did not jump on visitors. In fact, they were as well-mannered as any dogs I've ever had. I knew she was just jealous, and that made me angry. During our argument over the dogs, I stormed down the hallway of our house in Tarzana, which we moved into in 1970. Full of anger at her unreasonable demand, I kicked a hole in the door leading to our extra bedroom. But despite Shirley's ridiculous order, I relented and put Penny and Sam in the spare room and closed the door with the hole in it.

In the evening, our guests arrived. Before sitting down for dinner, Shirley gave our friends a home tour. She walked them down the hallway, and as we approached the extra bedroom, Shirley realized her plan to keep the dogs out of sight had only been partially successful. The opening I had made in the door was so wide that it left enough room for the dogs to poke their furry heads out into the hallway and greet our guests despite being banished. Shirley wasn't happy about it. While our guests probably didn't notice, my kids immediately recognized the look on Shirley's face. It said, "Those goddamn dogs! What are they doing there?"

To this day, my kids and I still laugh about Penny and Sam panting and smiling to our guests from the bottom of the door.

★ CHAPTER FIVE

Butting Heads with Dad

In 1959, I was twenty-five years old, and I had been working at Layne and Bowler for five years. My engineering skills blossomed at the company. By coming up with innovative designs, I knew I had a creative side. In fact, I was convinced one of my designs would work and produce amazing results. Unfortunately, I was never given the opportunity to test it out. By my boss shooting down without reasonable explanations what I thought to be great ideas, I realized that some people struggled thinking outside the box. I took this lesson with me later when, as a business owner, I made sure to foster a work environment that encouraged creativity and the breakthroughs it produces.

After honing my engineering skills, I sought to develop my sales and business abilities. At Layne and Bowler, the engineers weren't interested in sales, and the salesmen didn't have the technical background engineers did. While I never held a sales position at the company, on occasion, I did accompany salesmen on their calls. They were happy to defer their prospects' technical questions to me because the information I provided would help close deals.

The confidence I gained as a result of what I'd accomplished at the company sparked an entrepreneurial drive within me. Since childhood, I had always wanted to start a company, and now that I had the engineering, sales, and business experience, I had the background necessary to do so.

I knew the pump market well and thought a pump distributorship would be a viable business. Layne and Bowler sold to other distributors, and my company could be one of them. The startup would require little capital, and I'd saved enough by that point to be able to pay for the new venture.

As my plans came into clearer focus, I asked one of Layne and Bowler's salesmen to join me as a minority partner. Meanwhile, as I was dreaming of starting my business, my dad, Sidney, was asking me to join his company, Perma-Bilt.

"I've been in business now awhile. It's going well. It's profitable. I'm getting older, and I'd like you to come in and join me and run it," he said.

By this time, Perma-Bilt had reached its tenth anniversary. In previous years, my dad had proposed I quit my job and join him. I never thought twice about turning him down. But now, his appeal was different. Given my father's age, I knew he wanted to retire soon. But it never occurred to me that I'd be the one to run his company.

Our relationship had never been easy, so the last thing on my mind was to work for him. Spending even more time with him at Perma-Bilt would certainly not improve our already strained connection.

But his persistence prevailed. By saying yes, I believed working with my dad would be over in short order, and if so, I would then defer to my fallback plan, which was starting my pump business.

The truth is that joining Perma-Bilt interested me. Sidney Simon was my main problem. If any other business owner had presented me the same offer (take over a profitable business), I would have jumped at it. Running my own company had been my dream job, after all.

"I was planning on going into the pump business. But before I do, I will come and work for you," I told him.

Then I added one big condition.

"I am not coming on board to keep this company small. I want it to grow, and that is what I plan to do. But I do not think that is what you want," I said.

After trying for so long to convince me and eager to shift responsibility to his trusted son, my dad would have probably gone along with anything I told him. For now, he allowed me to take the company where I saw fit.

"I will give it two weeks," I told Shirley at home after my dad and I agreed to move forward.

My wife supported my career move. She would continue her role as homemaker, raising our growing family. The year Steve was born, we also introduced a four-legged member into our family: Tammy, a German shepherd.

I loved my dog, and maybe more so because she had an occasional mischievous side, especially when she was a puppy. My wife, on the other hand, didn't share my love for Tammy. One day, Shirley had hung Steve's washed diapers outside to dry. She went inside the house, and when she returned to bring the laundry back in, she saw Steve's diapers scattered across the backyard lawn. This was one example of Tammy's puppy antics, and by this point, Shirley couldn't stand it anymore. When I returned from work, she gave me an ultimatum.

"That's it! Either this dog goes or I go," she said.

For the sake of the marriage, I found Tammy a new home. In hindsight, considering how our marriage was going downhill and ended in divorce, I sometimes wonder if I should have called Shirley's bluff and taken her up on her divorce offer when she made it. But then again, my daughter Kathy wouldn't have been born had we split up then. So choosing Shirley over Tammy turned out to be the right thing to do.

With my decision to join my dad's business, I moved forward. Sidney and Ron Simon's professional history together wound up far exceeding my initial two-week prediction. While I guessed wrong about that one, I did accurately anticipate the conflict between us; my dad and I butted heads from the start.

At Perma-Bilt, I quickly realized that sometimes it is more important to learn from the wrong ways of running a business—and then correct course—than have someone teach you the right ways from the start.

By this time, I had had a strong taste of both. Layne and Bowler had shown me what a solid business looked like, and I was proud to be part of such a tightly run ship. Perma-Bilt was the opposite. If Layne and Bowler was a Division 1 baseball team, then Perma-Bilt was the Bad News Bears. Central to Perma-Bilt's problem was a lack of discipline within the organization. The factory workers and even some of its customers would take advantage of the company owner—in other words, my dad.

The lack of control Sidney Simon had over his business drove me nuts. By the time I joined Perma-Bilt, I was well aware of my dad's strengths and weaknesses. But now that we were working together, everything I knew about him was put under a magnifying glass. And the differences between him and me were more evident than ever.

He had a need to impress people that I didn't. While in and of itself, impressing people seems fine to me, his version of it was downright odd. As an example, if we were at a restaurant and the waiter provided terrible service, he'd leave a big tip. His reasoning was that server would treat him better next time as a result. Meanwhile, if the server was excellent, he'd leave a small tip because that person already treated him well.

I am 180 degrees different. I believe in being as generous as possible to my friends and family. I place a high priority on rewarding people who take care of me and are helpful and respectful.

At Perma-Bilt, my dad's personality reflected in his management style. In a variation of the saying, "When the cat's away, the mice will play," at Perma-Bilt, his employees played not only when the cat was away but even when the cat was in plain sight! Sometimes factory workers would be standing around talking instead of doing their work. Sidney would show up, and they would make no effort to shape up.

At Layne and Bowler, I was a lowly junior engineer with little clout. But if I walked on the factory floor and the workers were messing around and saw me, they'd straighten up right away—not because I had the authority to discipline them but because there was always the possibility that I could let their boss know they weren't doing their jobs.

Then there were my dad's customers. Or, more specifically, his one customer because about 80 percent of his business came from Acme Hardware.

Perma-Bilt had thirty-day payment terms. Meanwhile, Acme wouldn't pay for four or five months.

"Dad, this is ridiculous. Tell Acme you will not ship them anymore if they do not pay on time," I said.

"Oh no, I can't. They'll stop buying from me," he said.

"No, they will not. Who else will ever let them get away with what you are allowing?" I asked.

My dad still refused to force Acme to comply with our rules.

In another instance, we had a customer who was a part-time rabbi, part-time business owner. He hadn't paid us for six months.

"Jesus Christ!" I said. "You cannot allow this."

"He isn't going to cheat me; he's a rabbi," my dad said.

"I do not give a shit if he is God. Your terms are thirty days!" I said.

Just as I thought would happen, my dad never was paid by the supposedly religious man.

But where my dad held back his frustrations he had with others, he freely unleashed them on me. Early on, I had made a suggestion he didn't agree with. He blew up at me, yelling in front of Betty and Joy, the company's office workers.

"Let us go back to your office," I said, maintaining calm outside while my blood was boiling inside.

We entered and I quickly closed the door behind me.

"If you want to scream at me, even beat the shit out of me, that is fine. But if you *ever* yell at me like that in front of other people again, it is over. I am gone! This is not how a business is run," I said.

He knew I meant it, which is why he never did it again. Meanwhile, I certainly threatened to leave the company more than once. And I was ready to walk out each time I said it—I'm not one to dish out empty threats.

As I was taking over the management of Perma-Bilt, I dug deep into its operations. And the deeper I went, the more I realized what a mess the company was. We constantly fell behind in fulfilling orders. And now that I was the one fielding calls from frustrated customers waiting for late deliveries, I had to learn fast how to buy time. I mastered the art of apologizing and making up excuses for why our products hadn't shipped out to them yet. In fact, I had a series of excuses. Like an actor reading from his script, my lines were ready to go when the angry call came in.

Back at Layne and Bowler, I had prided my professional life on punctuality and being a man of my word. Now that I was taking over my dad's role at Perma-Bilt, I was full of anxiety because the company ran counter to my values. I'd wake up at three in the morning knowing a fed-up customer was probably calling the office about an order that hadn't arrived yet.

One day, I walked into work and saw one of my office staff in tears. I asked Betty what had happened.

"Harold Kitay just screamed and yelled at me on the phone because we hadn't delivered yet," she said.

At the time, Harold was president of Sunset Builder's Supply.

"Let me call him. I will take care of it," I told her.

I phoned our customer. I introduced myself to Harold and asked if we could talk in person. He agreed, and we met in his LA headquarters on Sunset Boulevard.

We sat in his office, and I apologized for the poor service he had been receiving. I explained that one reason I was brought to Perma-Bilt was to address the company's customer service issues. I reassured him I would do everything possible to straighten out the problems he was facing.

"In the future, if you have any complaints, I would appreciate it if you would take your frustrations out on me and not the office staff because they are not responsible for delivery dates and production schedules," I said.

I described how Betty was crying after speaking with him and politely asked that he never do that again. He appreciated my honesty and was receptive to my request.

Our meeting ended around noon, so he invited me to join him for lunch. We stopped by a nearby hotdog stand. Despite its rocky start, our initial meeting was the beginning of a deep friendship that would last until his passing in 2014. In fact, after he took Sunset Builder's public in 1970, he asked me to sit on his board of directors. And in 1993, I asked Harold to sit on our company's board of directors.

In order to address the production delays that I knew were due to the terrible management of Perma-Bilt's factory, I wanted to hire a plant manager. Despite backing off from his day-to-day role in the company, my dad was still boss. Thus, I had to receive his approval for major decisions like these, and he flatly rejected what I'd proposed.

But I kept pressing him on it because I knew how important the hire was. My dad eventually relented, and I brought on a plant manager. Unfortunately, about three months into his stint, I knew I had made a poor hiring decision. While we no doubt needed a plant manager, Forest Tash wasn't the guy. He just didn't have what it took to run the factory.

"Dad, I need to replace him with a more competent plant manager," I said.

Outright firing ran counter to Sidney Simon's way of doing business. This didn't mean my dad objected to my idea. He just had his way of doing it. Rather than blatantly telling the person he was terminated, my dad chose an indirect approach.

"Just give him a bad time, make his life miserable, and he'll quit on his own," my dad told me.

"Dad, that is not right," I said.

I asked him why waste time beating around the bush when I could keep it simple for everyone and just fire him?

We argued over it, but my efforts to convince my dad were pointless. Sidney Simon was boss, and he didn't like being the bad guy. So if I wanted the employee gone, I needed to follow orders and drive the plant manager to want to leave.

Over the next few weeks, I found myself putting someone nearly twice my age on edge throughout his workday. Being on top of the mistakes he made and rightfully pointing them out to him became my workplace mission. After getting tired of hearing me tell him about his incompetence, he quit.

Yes, my dad's plan worked. But it was yet another lesson on how not to run a business. I promised myself I would never do anything like that again.

Terminating people is never fun or easy. As the saying goes, "Where there's smoke, there's fire." So you'd better act quickly and make a change. I have learned that once you know someone is not suited for a job, taking a different course is necessary and should be done sooner rather than later and in a respectful manner.

My dad's approach was not fast, and it was definitely not respectful; I still feel terrible about the way I handled getting rid of Forest. In the years to come, I learned to avoid repeating the same hiring mistake. While my track record isn't perfect, when I reflect on the many subsequent decisions I've made that have resulted in people who have committed their entire careers to our company, I think I've done a pretty good job.

Throughout my history as a business owner, I've focused on recruiting people who are better than I am in the positions I needed to fill. In general, I think if you're right around half the time with your hiring decisions, which means you both hire people smarter than you *and* put them in the right position, you're probably making good choices.

By being surrounded by great people, I've been less inclined to make unilateral decisions. As I grew and evolved as a business owner, when I ran into a problem I needed to solve, I passed my ideas by those I trusted, had them play devil's advocate, and made sure I heard multiple perspectives before drawing a conclusion.

I've avoided digging my heels in the ground—saying, "I am going to do this!" and then going off and doing whatever "this" is—without first consulting those who will implement the action to be taken or those who have "been there, done that."

In the years that followed taking over the family business, I met and hired smarter and smarter people. Working with amazing individuals has been one of the keys to the success I have experienced. But I had to make some rookie mistakes first, as the Forest Tash example points out. After he left, we replaced him with a plant manager who performed exactly as I needed him to.

In addition to being a pushover as a boss, my dad was a pushover with the union. When he founded his company, he signed a contract with the United Electrical, Radio and Machine Workers of America (UE). In my opinion, he should have never let the union in from the start. By the time I came on board, the UE was manipulating him. If a foreman handed a two- or three-day suspension to a factory employee who was not doing his job properly, the union would defend the lazy worker by filing a grievance. Despite its ridiculousness, my dad would cave. He did this over and over again, which empowered the union to take advantage of him.

In 1963, our contract with the UE had expired. Since I was running the company by then, I took Sidney Simon's place in the contract negotiations. This meant the union could no longer push Perma-Bilt around. By this point, I was tired of the UE's unreasonable demands, and I was fully ready to put up a fight if necessary to bring fairness to the contract.

The UE and Perma-Bilt hit a roadblock. I refused to budge in regard to the union's outlandish salary ultimatums and requirements that would control the way I ran the business. The UE declared a strike. In its newsletter, I was unfairly blasted as the big bad business owner, which couldn't have been further from the truth. This only made tensions worse between the union members and the company. Our employees joined the picket line outside our headquarters, and union members made all kinds of threats against Perma-Bilt.

I took the warnings seriously, and in order to protect my factory from vandals and violence, I hired armed guards and dogs and brought in scab workers to keep the factory operating.

After three weeks of picketing and negotiations, Perma-Bilt and the UE came to an agreement and signed a five-year contract. Despite the protests and pressure, I refused to give in, and the contract didn't include any of the UE's nonsense. Workers returned to the factory, and my facilities were unharmed.

In 1968, the UE contract had expired again. By that point, I had had it with the union and would have been happy to have gotten rid of it. We hit a negotiation roadblock again, and the UE decided to go on strike. And once again, the factory workers joined the picket lines, and I hired scab workers. But this time, the protests outside Perma-Bilt got ugly with fights breaking out.

Despite the tension between the union and me, I maintained my position. I saw an opportunity to finally throw out the UE for good. By bargaining with another union, the Teamsters, I could replace the UE. During contract negotiations with the Teamsters, we were able to come up with an agreement that was favorable for both sides. We signed a deal, and with the new union on board, the UE was out, and I hired back my factory workers who were now Teamster members.

As much as my dad and I had a volatile relationship, the fireworks grew less frequent as my dad pulled back from Perma-Bilt and I took on running the company. He would come into the office at eleven and leave by two. With me in charge, he gladly worked less. He felt comfortable doing this because he knew he had made the right decision by choosing me to take over. While my dad avoided directly telling me he had confidence in my abilities, others would tell me how proud he felt.

As time progressed and I gained experience running a business, Perma-Bilt began growing just as I had wanted from the start. I added new customers, and our sales territories were expanding. I was learning how to balance upholding Perma-Bilt's values and meeting customer demands and how to compromise when the two were in conflict. But some of my lessons were harder to learn than others. Dave Heerensperger dished out one of them.

Dave was leading a buying coalition that included Eagle Electric and Plumbing Supply (which he founded in 1959), Buzzard Electrical and Plumbing, and Grover Electric and Plumbing Supply. They were all based in Washington. The coalition was created to compete with Pay 'N Pak, which was the regional home improvement behemoth at the time. Former Pay 'N Pak store managers, including Dave, went on to found these companies that would directly compete with Pay 'N Pak. Bad blood between Pay 'N Pak and its new rivals boiled as a result.

Dave himself was a creative, business-savvy renegade who was tough as nails both in and outside the office. He was built like a linebacker and wasn't easily intimidated by anyone. Dave told me the story once of driving in his fancy car with his wife and waiting at a stop sign. A pedestrian passed by yelling, "You rich son of a bitch!"

Dave hopped out of his car and started to fight with the loudmouth. Lucky for the poor guy who was outmatched by a long shot, the cops intervened and broke up the brawl before the pedestrian was pulverized.

I reached out to Dave to see if Perma-Bilt could supply his buying group.

As a young man eager to grow the business, I was being handed a huge opportunity to expand in the Pacific Northwest. Unfortunately, Dave added a major catch.

"If we agree to work together, you can't sell to Pay 'N Pak because we're competing with them," he said.

As the saying goes, "A bird in the hand is worth two in the bush." In other words, even though Pay 'N Pak was the major industry player, I wasn't sure if I could sell to the company, so I agreed to accept an offer that would guarantee to grow my business.

Soon after, Ken, the son of Pay 'N Pak founder, Stan Thurman, reached out to my company expressing interest in buying from us.

I wrote him a carefully and politely worded letter describing that I wasn't in the position to be able to supply his company.

Stan was a brilliant businessman and just as tough as Dave. He wasn't afraid to duke it out, either, if he needed to stand up for himself. One time at a bar in Houston, Stan and Dave were talking over a drink. The two got into a yelling match. The argument escalated until someone pulled the first punch. And then, just like in the movies, a full-blown bar brawl broke out: fists flying, stools toppling, and a crowd cheering on the fight.

Five years later, enough time had passed to where Dave and the companies he represented were succeeding. He was no longer concerned about Perma-Bilt selling to Pay 'N Pak, so I made an appointment with Stan to pitch my products.

I met with Stan in Pay 'N Pak's Seattle headquarters and sat in front of him in his office.

"You want to sell to us?" he asked.

He then pointed to the letter that he had pinned on the wall next to his desk. My stomach sank in embarrassment. Despite the passing of time, I recognized it right away. It was the one I had written five years ago, explaining that I wasn't in the position to sell to his company. Stan had been looking at it every day for years as a reminder of what I had done.

I apologized over and over and blamed my mistake on my youth and inexperience when I first sent the letter. Despite the grand error I had committed five years ago—being bullied by Dave into an arrangement that put me on Pay 'N Pak's shit list—Stan eventually agreed to buy from us.

Years later, in an odd twist of events, Dave Heerensperger wound up returning as CEO to Pay 'N Pak, the company he had jumped ship from in order to launch his own business. By the time he took control, Pay 'N Pak was one of our biggest customers.

"It was déjà vu all over again." Except this time, as I sat in Dave's office, he insisted that I not sell to one of Pay 'N Pak's competitors. The memory and subsequent humiliation of sitting in Stan's office had forever been seared into my memory. I wouldn't cave this time.

"Dave, I made this mistake once before. I am sorry. I am not going to refuse to sell to anybody," I said.

He was a shrewd and tough businessman who was used to getting what he wanted.

"If you don't agree, we're throwing you out," he said.

"Dave, I have learned a lot of things about you. Mostly good. One thing I know is you are a man of your word. So, my friend, it has been very nice doing business with you," I said, fully aware that Dave was cutting ties with me.

Losing a major account was not my best moment, but I needed to stand by my convictions. Despite reaching this impasse, we both were men of impeccable integrity and held a high level of respect for one another. While I didn't know it then, this mutual respect would benefit me when I launched RSI and Dave would be my first customer. His trust in my company was the spark that ignited my startup. But that event would have to wait until several years later.

Back in 1964, I was thirty years old and in charge of a business I was proud to have turned around. In the next two years, I had set my sights on even more growth, and I knew that Perma-Bilt would achieve this. It was just a matter of time and hard work. So I approached my dad about giving me stock in the business.

The company wasn't worth a whole lot of money so it made sense for him to give me the stock now when he'd pay little gift tax versus later, when the company would be valued at much more. Plus, given Perma-Bilt's success under my leadership, I wanted some ownership. Last, my dad and I agreed that he would eventually pass the business to me anyway, and there was no advantage to delaying the transfer process.

At first, my suggestion was met with reluctance, which didn't come as a surprise to me considering how hard it often was to get him to agree to move forward with many ideas I proposed. The bottom line was he was afraid of losing control of his business, so he didn't want to give away any of it.

Over the course of a year, we had a series of intense discussions about my ownership in Perma-Bilt. My dad called me into his office one day. Jules Henig, his CPA and an all-around good guy, was there as well.

"So, I'm going to promote you to VP," my dad told me.

The title meant nothing to me. He and I, our customers, and Perma-Bilt's employees all knew I was running the show.

"And I'm going to give you stock," he added.

"Finally!" I thought.

Back then, the company had a total of four hundred shares. He handed me a stock certificate. I couldn't believe it when I saw the number: four shares. In other words, he was handing me 1 percent of the company.

I was beyond pissed. "Was that the value he placed on everything I had done?" I asked myself.

By this point, I loved my work. I spent long hours at Perma-Bilt because I could see my efforts paying off. But I was willing to walk away from it all. He would not have been able to run the business without me—nor was he interested in doing so. I'd given him exactly what he had wanted when he had asked me to join his company. Now this was how he showed his gratitude. I looked at him and said:

"With all due respect, you can take these shares and shove them up your ass. It is over."

"See, Jules," my dad told his CPA. "You give him a finger and he wants the whole hand!"

"Fuck you, Dad. I am out of here. You could not have paid me a bigger insult," I said.

I stormed out of his office, grabbed an empty cardboard box, and went directly to my desk. Betty saw me tossing my belongings into it.

"What happened?" she asked.

"Betty, it's over. I quit," I said.

By this point Joy had entered the conversation. Both she and Betty started crying.

"You can't leave!" Betty said.

"I am sorry. It is no reflection on you, but I have to go," I said.

That evening, I received a phone call from my mother. She couldn't believe what had happened in my dad's office and tried to bridge the impasse between him and me. I wanted no part of that. I doubled down.

"If you were involved with this, I would feel the same about you as I do of him. He could not have done anything more devastating. Nothing. You guys are not part of my life anymore. I never want to see you again," I said.

We ended our conversation.

A week later, I received a call from my dad's lawyer, Maury Castle.

"Ron, your dad and everyone is upset about this. I'd like for both of you to meet in my office," he said.

Despite my anger over the matter, I agreed. The day of the appointment, I, along with my mom and dad, sat in his office.

Maury asked me to tell my side of the story. I described how I had been working around the clock, the new customers I was bringing on, my sales projections, and what the company's profits and value would be. Maury was impressed and saw my point.

"Sid," Maury said, "if Perma-Bilt achieves its growth plans, the company will be worth substantially more, which means when you die, the government's going to basically own the business because you'll have to pay a ton of gift tax. And where will that money come from? So why not do it now when it won't cost you a thing?"

My dad reluctantly listened to his lawyer, who went on to say, "You have no idea how lucky you are, Sid, that you have a son this capable running the company. He has the respect of everyone, including the employees and customers, and he's growing the business."

To Maury, my dad's stubbornness about the matter made no sense, which led to his ultimatum.

"If you don't do this, I won't be your attorney anymore," he said.

By the meeting's end, I thanked Maury for understanding my perspective and trying to beat some reason into my dad.

"Just let me know what you decide, and I will let you know what I will do," I told my mom and dad. I then left the meeting.

Eventually, my dad came to his senses and proposed to give me 40 percent of the company. I agreed with the arrangement, and my parents and I reconciled.

"Dad, all I wanted was ownership in the company. I did not need a title or a salary increase. This job is my life. I am looking at the future opportunity and what I can build this into," I said.

The near-forever fallout I had with my dad taught me a hard lesson in shared success. If you talk to any of the executives I've worked with, they'll describe how they all benefitted from our company's accomplishments. They all had equity in the business, and some have become millionaires as a result.

A golf pro once told me, "When you hit a bad shot, you learn. You learn what *not to do*. You analyze what you did wrong. In the end, you try not to repeat the same mistake. When you hit a good shot, what did you learn? Nothing. You're just happy you hit a good shot."

Perma-Bilt's early days gave me more bad shots to learn from than I can even count. But I'm not complaining. As a result of seeing how my dad ran it, I committed to doing things differently. I learned to be tough but fair. Both qualities are vital to being a successful business leader.

★ CHAPTER SIX

The Pains of Growing the Family Business

When the firetruck pulled up in front of our South Los Angeles building on Graham Avenue, I knew we were in for yet another production delay. We literally ran out of the space necessary to support our growth.

We had no place to store the corrugated shipping boxes and various raw materials necessary for production. As a result, they would sit on the factory floor before and after the workday. Every morning, in order to begin production, we would move those items and place them on the sidewalk outside the building. This ordeal would take thirty minutes. And then we would need to spend another half-hour at the end of the day moving the materials back inside to store for the evening. That sixty minutes of lost productivity could stretch even longer on days the fire department showed up. The firemen would tell us the contents we placed outside posed a fire threat. At that point, we would have to halt some of our production and move the items inside.

With our expanding customer base, we couldn't afford delays like these. I insisted to my dad that we needed to grow our facilities, but he refused. He thought my plans were too ambitious, and he was quick to criticize.

"Who do you think you are . . . General Motors?" was one of his common comebacks.

I thought my dad was out of touch with the needs of the growing business. But looking back, decades later, I also think he struggled letting go of Perma-Bilt. On the one hand, he wanted to relinquish control, which is why he gladly let me run it. But on the other hand, I'm sure it wasn't easy for him to have his son constantly telling him what to do with the business he had started.

As a tough negotiator, I loved the challenge of growing the business, was willing to take risk, freely spoke my mind, was open to learning new ways to run the company, and refused to back down from my position if I knew I was right. All of this meant Sidney and Ron Simon were polar business opposites! The contrast between father and son probably posed a threat to my dad's ego. Then again, my tough negotiation side was nothing new to him.

When I was nine years old, I was at the annual family Seder, which is a ritual Jewish dinner on the first or second night of Passover. My grandparents, parents, uncles, aunts, and cousins would gather every year. The Seder is traditionally led by the man of the house, and it commemorates the Israelites' escape from Egyptian slavery thousands of years ago. My uncle Dave, my dad's brother, usually headed the ceremony.

Matzoh, which is a cracker-like piece of unleavened bread, plays a central role in the Passover celebration. In one part of the meal, some pieces of the matzoh are broken and passed to the participants to eat. What is left over is wrapped in a cloth napkin and eventually hidden. In most families, the man of the house hides the matzoh from the children in a game. The child that finds it wins a prize.

My family's version of this game was that the kids would hide it and hold it for ransom, and the man running the Seder would have to pay the children to get it back. This invariably called for negotiation—unless the matzoh was found, you couldn't finish the Seder.

When my cousin Jackie and I were nine years old, we were charged to hide the matzoh. If we did a good job, it would give us negotiating leverage to ask for a hefty ransom, which was a big motivator to make sure no one would find it. Jackie and I thought hard and found the perfect spot where no one would look.

Uncle Dave had reached the part of the Seder that required the matzoh.

"Did you hide it?" he asked.

"Yeah, Uncle Dave, we did," I answered. He offered us a ransom to get it back.

"I'll give you fifty cents," he said.

Fifty cents was nowhere near what Jackie and I had in mind.

"No, Uncle Dave, that is not enough," I said.

"How much do you want?" he asked.

I mulled it over for a second and thought of a *huge* amount.

"Ten dollars," I said, which was equivalent to nearly two hundred dollars today. I knew there was no way he'd give us that much, but I demanded more than the small sum he offered.

He balked. But he bumped up his original offer to two dollars, which would be one dollar for each of us. That was more like it! Puffed up by my ability to convince him to up his offer, I stood firm.

"I told you, I want ten dollars," I said.

He became impatient.

"Goddamnit, you're greedy," he said. "I'll go find it myself, and when I do, you're not getting anything! So I'm warning you to take two dollars."

"Go ahead," I said. "Try to find it."

I said this hoping he would up his offer to four dollars (which meant two dollars for each of us). This amount was my original target.

He began looking for the matzoh. Jackie and I knew he'd never find it. As the minutes passed, Uncle Dave looked all over the house. His patience had reached its limit.

"Sid, what kind of kid are you raising?" he asked my dad, angry that he couldn't find the matzoh and that I wouldn't accept his offer.

Left up to me, my dad knew I wouldn't have budged, no matter how angry my uncle became and how long everyone had to wait.

"Ronnie, go get the matzoh," my dad demanded.

I did as I was told. The Seder wrapped up, and just as Uncle Dave had said, I didn't get anything. Had I played my cards right, my cousin and I could have received one dollar apiece. That Passover, I learned an early lesson in the art of negotiation: The deal has to work for both sides. It's a strategy that would serve me well later in life.

Uncle Dave got angry because I was being a smart-ass kid who was not respecting his authority. But for me, the back-and-forth between us felt more like a game.

At the time, I didn't know my bargaining at the Seder was a sign of being motivated by negotiation, entrepreneurship, competition, and the thrill of victory. The potential to earn money and the independence that it offered through being tough and clever really got me excited. There was nothing like the freedom and satisfaction that came from having something I wanted in mind and then figuring out how I could buy it on my own.

My parents always provided me a comfortable place to live and food on the table. But from BB guns to baseball bats, I knew if I wanted anything outside my basic needs, I was the one responsible to make it happen—just as my parents had to do when they were growing up.

Unfortunately, too many kids today feel entitled and do not have a great work ethic. So while I had a side that challenged nearly everyone and everything and got a kick out of mischief-making, I was also extremely self-motivated, independent, and disciplined. I think this has to do with a combination of being fiercely competitive and having strict parents. For instance, I excelled in sports, and I loved to win. But I hated even more to lose.

I found whatever ways I could to make money. I used to ride my bicycle west to the beaches of Santa Monica and Venice and collect Coke bottles that people left on the sand. I took them to markets that would pay me two cents each for them. And after school, I had a paper route delivering the *Daily News*.

Billy Shapiro, who had four years on me, taught me another way to earn money: by raising pigeons. Based on what I saw him do with his birds and the coop he built for them, it also seemed like a cool hobby.

I bought the supplies, and he showed me how to make a coop. Once mine was ready, I started with two homing pigeons, and eventually my collection grew to a dozen. Their ability to find their way back home, no matter how far I took them away from it, provided hours of fun. I then expanded to squab, which were basically fat pigeons that I could sell to neighbors to eat.

Here, too, my friend was my guide. But unlike Billy, I found that raising squab for slaughter wasn't for me. Billy showed me how to kill a bird, and I'll never forget the first time I tried. There were two techniques: wringing its neck or chopping its head off. I chose the chopping block. With one hand, I pinned the bird down. In my other hand, I held the ax high. It took me a while to work up the guts to swing the ax down. And nerves probably kept me from using the force necessary to cut off its head. My first strike left the poor bird with only half its neck split open. Despite wanting to call it quits, I knew I needed to put the bird out of its misery. With one more swing of the ax, the job was done. Soon after that, I quit the squab business.

Harming animals was absolutely unthinkable for me . . . but I had no problem scrapping with humans if the need arose. While I didn't pick fights and didn't get into them often, when duty called, I was ready. During school one day, one of my friends, Jerry Katz, and I began arguing with each other. The tension reached the point where we were ready to brawl. Despite our rage, Jerry and I knew better. If we traded blows right there, we'd be caught and punished. So we postponed our fight to off-campus after school.

Word spread fast. After school, we, along with about fifty kids, met in the backyard of a vacant house near our school. The crowd of our classmates surrounded us, and we went at it.

Man, did we go at it!

We beat the bejesus out of each other. I arrived home that day, and there was no hiding the scrapes and bruises.

"What happened to you?" my dad asked.

"A bunch of lumber fell on me," I told him.

I'm sure he didn't believe me. But he probably didn't want to know what really happened, so he accepted my silly answer.

The big personality difference between my dad and me probably made him sometimes wonder if we were related at all. At the same time, my tough character served Perma-Bilt's interests well, especially when it came to working with our growing customer base that now was stretching across the country.

Simon's Hardware and Bath, New York City's oldest hardware store, was interested in Perma-Bilt's products. I had never done business with New Yorkers. Perma-Bilt at the time didn't have a manufacturer's representative in New York, so I hired Sam, who lived in Cherry Hills, New Jersey.

Sam knew I was a newbie working with businesses in the Big Apple, so he provided me tips when it came to negotiating with Willie, the store's buyer. My plan was to fly to New York City to meet Willie, and Sam prepped me for the meeting.

"Willie is very interested," Sam told me. "He's really hot to bring in your product line."

He added that, because he wanted me to come all the way from California, I was essentially guaranteed an order from the prospective customer. But knowing Willie, Sam believed the order would be for only about ten thousand dollars.

"Well, that is not very much," I said, "especially considering the time, money, and effort the trip would require."

"Exactly. That's why when he makes his offer, don't take it. Say something like, 'What are you talking about? I didn't come all the way from California for a measly ten-thousand-dollar order,'" he said.

The response he was suggesting was over the top and out of character for me.

"Sam, I do not do business that way. He will throw me out," I said.

"Ron, you're in New York. It's very different. He ain't going to throw you out. Trust me," he said.

I asked him what counter offer I should make, and he recommended an order totaling one hundred thousand dollars. Asking ten times the amount of what would be his original offer seemed risky, but I was open to following Sam's advice.

I flew to New York. Willie and I met. He showed me the order he had put together. Just as Sam had said, it was nowhere near what I wanted.

"I am looking at these quantities, and what you are buying are the right products for your business. But my God, your order is going to come to less than ten thousand dollars," I told Willie.

He looked at the paperwork again.

"You're right. But that's what I want to order," he said.

I played back my conversation with Sam in my head.

"Willie, you know I have a business to run. I did not hop on a plane all the way to New York just to get an order for ten thousand dollars. You think I am crazy? If that is all you want to put in stock, then I do not know if I want you as a customer," I said.

Now, he knew I meant business. The meeting's dynamic shifted in my favor.

"Oh . . . okay. But what do you recommend?"

I made my product suggestions. He listened. In the end, I walked out with a fifty-thousand-dollar order. I closed my first deal playing by East Coast rules. Had I taken the New York approach with a California customer, I might have been shown the front door.

As much as the experience was jarring at first, I actually began enjoying doing business with New Yorkers as time went on, and I was able to get many more East Coast customers.

With Perma-Bilt expanding into new markets, my frustration and insistence that we move to larger facilities grew to the point where I threatened to leave if my dad didn't authorize the expansion. He finally gave in, but not before the Watts Riots torched a large stretch of LA.

On the evening of August 11, 1965, a rebellion broke out in Watts, which is a neighborhood of southern Los Angeles. Tension between Black residents and LA's law enforcement had been escalating prior to the riot, which was triggered when, at around seven in the evening, police officers pulled over Marquette and Ronald Frye, two Black stepbrothers. Marquette was arrested after failing a sobriety test, and a fight broke out between him and the officers. Ronald, in an effort to protect his brother, joined the scuffle.

As the scene grew tenser, a crowd gathered, and more police showed up. A second fight between an officer and a bystander broke out. The stepbrothers' mother, Rena, arrived. Convinced the officers were harming one of her sons, she attempted to pull the officers off him, and the scene became more violent.

As the crowd swelled, so did the police presence. Hostilities reached fever pitch, and several other fights broke out. By 7:45 p.m., what had started out as a small traffic stop blew up into a riot that eventually engulfed South Los Angeles in flames. For the next six days, angry crowds threw rocks and bottles, shot passersby, looted stores, attacked motorists, and lit businesses on fire.

The warzone grew wider. Eventually, fourteen thousand National Guard troops were sent to the city to contain the rebellion. One way they did so was to erect barricades. Meanwhile, fires throughout the riot area came within a block of Perma-Bilt.

My friends called me while I was at work, concerned for my safety. They followed news reports and insisted I take an alternative route home because snipers were targeting drivers and crowds were blocking cars, pulling people out of their vehicles, and attacking them. So if I got caught in the mayhem, my life would be in danger.

I listened to my friends and took a different route. But I was so worried I made up my mind that if anyone were to try to stop me, I'd run him over. Fortunately, I arrived home safely without having to implement my emergency strategy. The riots started on a Wednesday and stretched into the weekend. By the following Monday, the violence had subsided, but it would take until Tuesday for order to be restored.

We closed the office on Monday, and I worked from home. I phoned customers and let them know that the riots had affected our operations.

Business resumed as normal that week after the riots had ended.

A year later, despite my dad accusing me of acting like the head of GM, he gave me the green light to construct a new and larger factory. We hired an architect and a general contractor and started looking for a site to build it on. We found one on 19106 South Normandie Avenue in the city of Torrance, located in Los Angeles's South Bay. Perma-Bilt's new home would wind up being 120,000 square feet, which marked a major step up from the 28,000 square feet of the prior factory.

With the bigger facilities, we could move full speed ahead with my growth strategy, which was to direct our focus to the expanding home improvement market. This was a change from when my dad had started Perma-Bilt; back then, his customers had all been builder's hardware suppliers.

The investment community saw the pace at which consumers were remodeling their homes, and economic forecasts signaled tremendous future growth many times larger than that of new home construction. Not only was the retail sector booming, but it offered the added benefit of being less cyclical than the homebuilding market.

Perma-Bilt still served our customers who were providing hardware, milling, and building materials to new residential construction. But I knew DIYers across the country were redoing their bathrooms, and that's where the opportunity would be.

Over the next few years, I pointed Perma-Bilt's marketing efforts toward the home improvement industry. I hired a sales manager, Frank Xavier. He had been a captain in the marines, and his military background showed in his hard work and honesty. A talented, effective, and personable sales manager, Frank headed a successful sales campaign and opened up important home center accounts for Perma-Bilt.

Through top-notch sales and marketing and developing revolutionary products, Perma-Bilt transformed from a regional player into a national one. Outside of California, I had sales representatives all over the country. We had accounts with home centers such as Angel's, Builders Emporium, Builders Square, Cashway Lumber, Channel Lumber, Handy Dan,

STYLES FOR EVERY DECOR

BEACON HILL

COVENTRY

CLASSIC

MILL VALLEY

CONTEMPO

BISCAYNE

*Perma-Bilt's product line of decorative medicine cabinets,
vanities, and cultured marble sink tops, 1985.*

Hechinger Company, Ole's Home Center, Payless Hardware, Rickle, and Sutherland Lumber Company.

We introduced decorative cabinets that didn't look anything like what our competitors sold. At the time, medicine cabinets were boring, practical pieces. We added beautiful frames that could match the surrounding bathroom décor and tri-view mirrors that swung out on the sides so people could see multiple angles of themselves. When Perma-Bilt showed our product line at the National Hardware Show, retailer interest made it clear that my company was onto something with great potential.

With the fast-paced growth that would continue for the foreseeable future in the retail industry, I set my sights on an initial public offering. In order to gain personal liquidity and provide the financing to support Perma-Bilt's growth, in 1968, I hired Paul Vert as our CFO. As a soon-to-be public company, we needed a capable chief financial officer. Paul had been a senior accountant with Arthur Young & Company, so he had the background necessary to support our ambitious plans.

The three of us, Frank, Paul, and I, formed a great team, and Frank and Paul represented some of the wisest hiring decisions I have ever made. All of us shared a common vision to make Perma-Bilt the best company possible. We worked hard, played hard, and created a wonderful professional environment full of fond memories I cherish to this day.

In order to complement our medicine cabinet line, I bought Del Mar Manufacturing, a company that made bathroom accessories such as towel bars and rings and toilet paper holders.

With business growth also came my personal and professional growth. To guide my future decisions, I asked myself, "What type of businessman do I want to be?" And my answer was clear: Integrity was the most important value for me to uphold. I would not tolerate dishonesty or cheating employees or customers. I was maturing and being tested constantly. One such test came from our customer, Ole's Home Center, which was a large account for Perma-Bilt.

Frank broke the news to me that he had spoken to Ike Danan, Ole's buyer. Ike told him that we had lost Ole's business.

"What was the reason Ike gave you?" I asked Frank.

"He said it was because of the horrible service record we had with them," Frank told me.

By this point in Perma-Bilt's history, I had resolved many of the customer service issues I'd inherited when I'd first joined the company.

"That is bullshit. And I have heard through the grapevine that Ike is on the take from other salespeople," I said.

In other words, Ike was accepting bribes by our competitor. I told Frank that I wasn't going to sit back and lose this battle without a fight.

"So what are you going to do?" he asked.

"I will make an appointment with Ike's boss and tell him his employee is a thief!"

"Are you sure about that? You'll be thrown out of the meeting," he said.

While Ole's Home Center had dropped us for now, in this competitive industry, nothing stayed the same. Thus, the company could change its mind later.

Frank feared that accusing Ike of accepting bribes in front of his boss would put Perma-Bilt on Ole's blacklist forever. While his point made sense, I didn't care. It was more important to do the right thing than to stay quiet out of fear of the consequences. If I was thrown out, I'd know it happened because of upholding my integrity, so I'd feel good about what I did.

Plus, if my buyer was awarding business to suppliers because they were paying him off, I'd want someone to tell me. And I'd have all the respect in the world for a person who had enough guts to be honest with me, despite the risks of telling the truth.

I arranged a meeting with Ike and his boss. Frank nervously came along, and I came fully prepared. Like a well-armed lawyer, I brought with me what I would use to make my case. My biggest piece of evidence was a sixteen-inch-high stack of purchase orders and invoices that proved our impeccable shipping record with Ole's. In other words, Ike's argument was bogus.

As we sat together at our customer's headquarters, I explained my position to Ike's boss, and then I dropped the news.

"I think Ike is being paid off by our competitor," I said.

The claim I had made was met by total silence. While Frank and I didn't get abruptly thrown out of the meeting, neither Ike nor his boss appreciated what I had said. I'm sure the last thing Ike's boss wanted to imagine was that his employee was cheating the company. At the end of the meeting, Perma-Bilt didn't get Ole's business back, but I had no regrets. I knew I had done the right thing. Several months later, Ike lost his job. While we didn't confirm why he was terminated, we assumed his boss had found truth in what I'd said.

My ethics were put to the test again when I received word that Handy Dan, a successful LA-based chain of home center stores, had dropped Perma-Bilt's bath accessory line and had given the business to our competitor.

Stan Cohen was the sales representative behind Handy Dan's decision. Two years prior, he had been Perma-Bilt's manufacturer's representative, and I had fired him for paying off buyers in order to land business. After I had let him go, he went on to represent a rival's bath accessory line, and Handy Dan had awarded its account to that competitor.

Based on Stan's track record, Perma-Bilt's competitive prices, and our impeccable service to Handy Dan, I suspected that Stan had been up to no good again by paying off buyers. In order to get to the bottom of what had happened and to confirm my suspicions, I arranged to meet with Bob McNulty, Handy Dan's vice president of merchandising.

During my appointment with Bob at Handy Dan's LA office, I asked him why Perma-Bilt had lost the business. None of his reasons was legitimate, so I left the meeting fully unsatisfied and even more convinced that Bob had accepted a bribe from Stan.

Now I needed to take action. After leaving Bob's office, I headed right to the receptionist's desk and asked to speak to the company's president, Bernie Marcus . . . yes, the same Bernie Marcus who went on to found The Home Depot.

While it wasn't a common move to go straight to the top, especially without a prior appointment, I was in Handy Dan's office and decided that since I was there anyway, I might as well try my luck.

The receptionist reached out to Bernie's secretary, telling her one of his suppliers wanted to see him. My gamble paid off. Bernie agreed to meet. I entered his office and introduced myself. He immediately proposed that Perma-Bilt participate in Handy Dan's advertising campaign that would roll out in a couple of months. His pitch provided the perfect opening for me.

"Bernie, I was informed that we had lost Handy Dan's bath accessory business. So I am not going to pay to participate in a promotion that would sell my competitor's products. I am also convinced the only reason we lost the business was because my ex-salesman was paying off McNulty," I said.

Similar to the response I had received from Ike's boss at Ole's Hardware, Bernie wasn't pleased to hear what I had told him. At the same time, he wasn't defensive and didn't question my integrity. In fact, I left thinking that he respected my honesty, or in the least that I had left a lasting impression, which would be confirmed when we met for the second time. That event would have to wait another three years.

★ CHAPTER SEVEN
Taking the Family Business Public

In 1973, at age thirty-nine, I divorced my wife. I moved out of the family home and into an apartment, and then shortly after, I bought a condominium right on the beach in Marina Del Rey. The divorce itself was relatively uncomplicated with the exception of how it broke up a friendship.

Shirley and I were close friends with another married couple. While friends taking sides during a couple's divorce can create tension, the husband went overboard when he decided to show up in court and back up Shirley's ridiculous claims against me. His wife wanted nothing to do with her husband's decision and stayed out of the divorce. Thankfully, his betrayal didn't affect the divorce settlement, but it did put a halt to our friendship.

In the end, Shirley and I decided the kids would continue to live with her, but I saw them often. During ski season, in particular, we'd regularly hit the slopes nearly every weekend.

As a newly minted bachelor, I began dating. Once, I had asked a woman out who let me know that she was already seeing someone else. But she had a single friend who might be interested. She gave me Donna's number. I phoned her and set up our first date. While our relationship never became serious, over the next few months, we enjoyed each other's company. She had a great personality and was fun to be around. And that wasn't just my opinion; my daughter thought so too.

Kathy was in high school at the time Donna and I were dating. I eventually invited Donna to join us on our ski trips to Mammoth where I'd rent a condo for the weekend.

Upon returning to Los Angeles, my ex-wife would grill my daughter about her time with me.

"What did you do with your dad?"

"We went to Mammoth with Donna," she said.

And with her honest and innocent answer, my ex-wife had ammunition to come after me. She called her divorce lawyer, and the next thing I knew, she dragged me to court.

Although I'm sure it would be unheard of today, back then my ex-wife was able to convince a judge that if I took my daughter skiing, my girlfriend couldn't be there.

So the next time Kathy and I went to Mammoth, I planned it for just the two of us.

"Is Donna coming?" Kathy asked me.

"No," I told her.

"Why not?"

"Because I have this court order. If Donna joins us, I would be in contempt of court. They could put me in jail," I said.

"But, Dad, we have way more fun when she's there," Kathy said.

"I know we do. But I cannot do it," I said.

"Well, I'm not going to tell anyone," Kathy said.

With my daughter's promise, I invited Donna to join us. And she was right. We did have more fun skiing with her. This was one example among many that showed the close father-daughter relationship that Kathy and I have to this day.

While my marriage to Shirley went south, business was soaring higher than I could have ever imagined when I first took over Perma-Bilt as a twenty-five-year-old. In 1972, I took the company public.

Prior to this big step, we first had to set the business up for a successful initial public offering. Critical to a solid launch would be to create interest from investors. Among the countless options in the stock market, Perma-Bilt, a relatively little company, had to stand out. The key to doing this was to tell investors a compelling story: Where was our company currently and what was our growth potential?

In order to ensure we had a great story to back up our strong financial standing, we enlisted a professional who would guide us through the process. We engaged Fred Taylor, who was previously an investment banker at Kidder, Peabody, & Co., which was a US-based securities firm. He helped us select our underwriter, Morgan, Olmstead, Kennedy & Gardner, Inc., a Los Angeles–based investment banking and securities brokerage firm. G. Tilton Gardner, the company's youngest partner, guided us through the complicated underwriting process.

Paul Vert had been our CFO since 1968, which is also when we brought on Arthur Young & Company as our accountant. Perma-Bilt began receiving audited statements from the firm in 1969. We hired Howard Sterling, from Rifkind, Sterling, Kennedy, and Gardner, as our lawyer who would ensure our offering complied with all Securities and Exchange Commission regulations.

The plan was to sell about 30 percent of the company. My dad and I would retain the rest with a 60-40 split: 42 percent of the company would be my dad's, and I would have 28 percent.

We described a company whose growth would not be dependent on the residential homebuilding cycles. Instead, we would sell through home center channels, which offered tremendous growth opportunities.

The financial community already saw what was on the horizon and was investing in do-it-yourself retailers. The size of that market was massive. Specifically for us, the number of already-built homes requiring new cabinets vastly exceeded new construction, and Perma-Bilt was perfectly equipped to meet ever-increasing DIY-consumer demand. In sum, we would offer investors an ability to tap into a booming retail sector.

But before all the heavy lifting required to take Perma-Bilt public,

I had one hurdle, which was bigger than any that even the experts and big firms we hired had to overcome—I had to convince my dad of my ambitious plans for his company.

He was immediately opposed. My dad was still Perma-Bilt's president, and he was reluctant to relinquish the title of the business he had started. This was despite the fact that his position in the company was in name only. I was the one running the show, and Sidney Simon and the underwriters knew this. They made it clear that my dad had to step down as president.

"Ron, he's not even involved in the company. When Perma-Bilt goes on its dog-and-pony show to sell itself, analysts will be asking the president tough questions and demanding clear answers from him. There's no way your dad can do that. Only you can, which is why you have to be president."

To which my reply was: "You go tell my dad that. And then watch him have a shit fit."

Rather than try to convince him one person at a time, which could backfire, we followed a strength-in-numbers strategy and met with him together.

The approach was a success. In the end, two arguments stuck out to him. First, rather than take away a coveted corporate title from him, we would be replacing it with another.

"Dad, you will be chairman. That is more important than president," I said.

"Oh, it is?" he said.

While dropping the president label was a big blow for him, becoming chairman lessened its impact. He also realized going public would eventually result in a big payout, which made the deal too sweet for him to pass up.

With my dad on board, we aggressively moved forward with our IPO. In the end, we had a one-million-dollar offering at three dollars per share.

Approximately a year later, in 1973, Perma-Bilt's stock price dropped from three dollars to one dollar per share. On the one hand, the company was growing, profitable, and financially strong. But on the other hand, its market value was going south. I believed the main reason for the decrease in stock value was lack of interest on the part of investors.

Whatever the cause of the two-thirds decline, the bottom line was, as Perma-Bilt's president, I felt immense responsibility to our shareholders to deliver on the investment opportunity that attracted them in the first place.

In order to create interest in the company, I came up with an unorthodox yet logical idea. It was based on the fact that stock splits usually attract the attention of investors. If a company splits its stock, it's almost always only when the stock has increased, and not decreased, in value.

But I rationalized there was no reason for the stock to be trading at one dollar per share versus three dollars per share based on the company's performance. Thus, if we split the stock three for one, there would be a strong possibility it would continue to sell for one dollar per share and, as a result, triple the company's market capitalization.

My plan immediately brought me relief because it made so much sense. At the same time, I had no clue if it was possible, or even legal.

I called Fred Taylor to receive his expert feedback.

"I have this crazy idea. What if we split the stock three for one, and now everyone has their investment back if the stock stays at a dollar per share?" I asked.

"Ron, you can't. Nobody does that."

His reply wasn't what I wanted to hear and reminded me that he was a conformist and not a risk taker. But more importantly, his explanation was far from convincing.

"I do not care what anyone does or does not do. Give me a good reason why I cannot," I said.

"You never split stocks when they're going down. Only when they're going up," he said.

"I know all that. Any other reason?"

"If you split it, what happens if you don't attract investors? Your plan will do the exact opposite of what you intend, and the stock may drop to nothing. And where does that leave the company?" he said.

But I was confident the move would create the interest in the company we needed. From there, the analysts would look into Perma-Bilt's financial situation, marketing approach, and growth potential and see what a good opportunity we offered. Unconvinced with Fred's reasons against my idea, I continued pressing him.

"But if I went ahead anyway, would I be doing anything wrong?" I asked.

"Well, you can't. That's all there is to it," he said.

He didn't answer my question, but I didn't push him on the subject more because I knew where he stood and wouldn't budge.

Fred's personal limitations came through during our conversation. He was what I call an "in-the-box" thinker. Fred opposed my idea based on the grounds that he didn't know of any other instances of a company splitting a stock when it was decreasing in value. "But so what?" I thought.

I wonder where the world would be today if everyone was an in-the-box thinker. The Wright Brothers would have never taken flight if they had listened to the naysayers who said their dream was impossible. And we'd still probably be reading by candlelight if Edison had refused to give up on his seemingly impossible idea.

When something out-of-the-box comes to mind, I'm open to receive feedback and criticism about it. If I run the concept by someone I trust, no matter how great I think it is, I'm willing to change course if I'm provided good reasons explaining why my idea is terrible. Fred's reason was far from convincing, so I reached out for second and third opinions.

John Marshall and I were initially introduced through our kids' friendships. Our families lived on the same block after his divorce. He was a mergers and acquisitions specialist for Merrill Lynch. From the moment we met, we hit it off and became close friends . . . or so I thought until he would betray our trust in a big way years later.

I described my plan to him.

"Shit, Ron, that's interesting!"

John, unlike Fred, was enthusiastic about my stock-split idea. And John, like me, was an out-of-the-box thinker who also had a strong financial background, so his opinion mattered to me.

"Do you see any reason why I should not or cannot do it?" I asked.

"To my knowledge, no one's done it before, but I don't see any reason why not. Maybe you'll create investor interest," he said.

Investor interest is exactly what I wanted!

I then called Howard Sterling, Perma-Bilt's SEC attorney. I asked him if there were legal reasons why I couldn't move forward.

"Absolutely not, of course you can do it," he said.

After receiving two votes of confidence, one from a financial expert and another from a lawyer, I reached out to Fred again, who also was on Perma-Bilt's board of directors.

"Fred, I have run my idea by Howard Sterling and John Marshall, an M&A guy at Merrill Lynch. They thought it was interesting and worth trying out. And I really want to do it," I said.

"I don't want any part of it," he said.

So I called a board of directors meeting at Howard's office.

I invited John Marshall, who, with Howard, would provide his opinion. At the meeting, I asked John what he thought about my plan.

"I think it's a great idea. In fact, I don't know what the downside is," he said.

I turned to Howard.

"Are there any legal issues?" I asked.

"None whatsoever," he replied.

Fred wasn't pleased.

"Ron, I don't want any part of this. If you do this, I'm out of here," he said.

"Goodbye, Fred," I said.

Fred walked out of the board meeting. Shortly after, we sent him a resignation letter, he signed it, and that was the end of his history with Perma-Bilt.

We moved forward with our plan. Truth be told, as much as Howard, John, and I believed it would work, nobody knew for sure what would happen.

We split the stock three for one and waited. Then my phone started ringing. Analysts wanted to speak to me: "What's going on with your company?" "What are your growth plans?" "What's your marketing focus?"

Clearly, we had created the buzz necessary for Perma-Bilt to stand out.

Within a few days after the split, Perma-Bilt's stock was back up to a dollar a share. The major difference between before and after the split was the original investors now had three times as many shares. I had fulfilled my commitment to provide our investors a good opportunity.

In business, calculated risk taking is key to growth. Today, when I'm confronted with a big problem and come up with a creative solution, I reflect on my track record of successful decision-making and then tell myself, "Go ahead and try it. What do you have to lose?"

Perma-Bilt was expanding as a publicly traded company, landing business from the country's biggest home center retailers.

After the honeymoon phase, I realized that being public was initially fun and exciting, but eventually it turned out to be a big pain in the ass. All the reporting, restrictions, such as how much salary I was going to draw, and the huge headache of working under so much oversight outweighed any advantages. And, beyond the initial public offering, Perma-Bilt didn't need additional cash to grow because we were generating enough of it from within.

While I saw the benefit of taking the company private, I knew it was a big decision and thought hard about it. I finally pulled the trigger in 1977. The lengthy process took a year to complete and, in 1978, Perma-Bilt bought all its stock back and was no longer chained to its previous restrictions.

After I first spoke with Bernie Marcus in 1976 during our impromptu meeting in his Handy Dan LA office, the next time we saw each other, his career had taken a dramatic turn that would forever change America's home center and retail landscape.

Between our two meetings, he had been fired from his position at Handy Dan. While the news was devastating at first, it ended up being one of the best things to happen in Bernie's career. He and Arthur Blank, who was Handy Dan's CFO and had also been fired, teamed up with Pat Farrah and Ken Langone. Together, the four of them founded The Home Depot with its first store's grand opening in 1979. No doubt, its early and subsequent success was due to the brilliant retail minds behind it.

Bernie, Arthur, and Pat moved to Atlanta, which became The Home Depot's headquarters. In 1979, thanks to the goodwill my company had built, we were awarded The Home Depot's bathroom accessories and medicine and vanity cabinet business. I flew to Georgia to have dinner with Bernie, Pat, and spouses. Our previous conversation in 1976 had left its mark on Bernie.

"Wow, Ron, you're one tough businessman," were the first words that came out of Bernie's mouth when we sat down for dinner.

Since we had met only once before, I knew he was referring to our first meeting, when I had told him I thought his VP of marketing was taking bribes.

"Bernie, I may be tough, but I am honest," I said.

We went on to have a memorable talk over our meal. In addition to working with Bernie's company during his Handy Dan days, Perma-Bilt also had done business with another founder of The Home Depot in his prior post. The year before teaming with his business partners, Pat launched Homeco, which was an ambitious big-box home improvement retailer that, while Pat didn't know it at the time, became a precursor to The Home Depot.

Pat was a brilliant visionary. Prior to Homeco, he had been vice president of merchandising of a small home center chain called National Lumber. Pat launched his Homeco store in Long Beach, California.

While Pat's retail model would change the face of home improvement through The Home Depot, his first business failed. Due to Pat's marketing savvy, Homeco sold tons of merchandise. Unfortunately, it couldn't turn a profit. After about ten months of operation, the company filed for bankruptcy, and Pat lost everything, including his home.

Perma-Bilt was one of his company's suppliers, which meant we would become a creditor and not get paid for outstanding invoices. But bankruptcy didn't mean Pat let himself off the hook. In the midst of his professional and personal crisis, he came to visit me at Perma-Bilt.

"Ron, I'm so sorry that I can't pay our invoices," he said.

As a business owner, I knew the risks required to be a successful entrepreneur. I thought of what it would be like if my business went under and how I'd feel letting so many people down.

"Pat, whatever loss my company has encountered, remember we did have a margin. Not to mention all the orders we shipped that you paid for and the profits we made as a result. The bottom line is our loss is nothing compared to yours. If you would ever want to start a new business, I would jump at the chance to be your supplier again," I said.

"Thanks, Ron. I really appreciate your understanding," he told me.

While Homeco's demise was unfortunate news for me at the time, any disappointment I had was short-lived. After that meeting, Pat would partner with Bernie, Arthur, and Ken to start a new company. Little did I know at the time the retail behemoth The Home Depot would become.

When I first learned about their ambitious plans, I thought, "How will anyone be capable of growing a business that quickly?" But, boy, was my question quickly put to rest! Bernie, Arthur, Pat, and Ken would go on to create one of the greatest retail businesses in the history of US entrepreneurship.

Before the online giants, such as Google and Facebook, became household names, here was this nuts-and-bolts business that went on to make business history. From The Home Depot's early years, Perma-Bilt was a very important supplier. Perma-Bilt and then my next company, RSI, would proudly be a part of The Home Depot's astonishing growth.

During the many years Perma-Bilt supplied The Home Depot, I was always comfortable discussing business issues with Pat and Bernie. The beauty of working with The Home Depot in the early days was the importance the company placed on integrity, which reflected Bernie's, Arthur's, and Pat's values, as well as mine.

If I had a business issue I needed to address, I always knew I could go straight to Bernie or Pat. Our conversations were often tough, but they would always be direct and honest because we respected one another. Our straightforward communication was based on mutual integrity and trust. As a result, we'd get to the heart of the problem and solve it quickly without the layers of nonsense driven by incompetence that, later on, would make business difficult for all of us.

As my business life was taking off, my personal life was too. Around this time, I fell in love with Eleanor Neumeier-Allerton. I had actually met Ellie in 1973 after Shirley and I had divorced and when I hired her as my secretary at Perma-Bilt. We began dating in earnest around 1975, after which point we agreed that we should no longer work together, and Ellie left the company.

Ron and Ellie's wedding, 1980. Left to right: *parents Sidney and Belle, Ron, Ellie, Kathy (Ron's daughter), Oma (Ellie's mother), and Colby (Ellie's son).*

By 1978, I had purchased a house in Encino, and I asked Ellie to move in with me. We then married in December 1980. We skipped a fancy wedding and instead opted to exchange vows in the judge's chambers in Beverly Hills, followed by a small reception of around one hundred guests a couple of weeks later at Jimmy's. The Beverly Hills restaurant, founded by Jimmy Murphy, a native of Ireland, was popular with Hollywood actors and powerbrokers in the 1980s and 1990s.

When it came to Ellie's mom, she couldn't have been any more different from my ex-mother-in-law, Minnie. While Shirley's mom was harsh and tough to be around, Ellie's mom was sweet and a joy to spend time with.

Her name was Elizabeth, but I called her Oma, which means grandma in her native language, German. Oma lived in New Jersey, and I always looked forward to her visits to California. And when I was on the East Coast for business, she let me know how she felt about me not visiting her:

"Why didn't you come to see me?"

Oma didn't have to ask me twice. On several occasions, I would have business associates with me during my trips to the East Coast. While it would have been more convenient to depart from JFK, we would fly out of Newark instead—just so we could visit her. I would drive my associates to her house in Weehaken, New Jersey, where she would have a warm meal waiting for us. Then we'd fly home. Everyone enjoyed her amazing cooking and her kind company.

Unfortunately, her son, George Neumeier, didn't inherit his mother's character. He was about as ungrateful of an asshole as you could imagine. George had become a successful dermatologist—thanks to his mom. Oma had worked two jobs, one requiring scrubbing floors, in order to put him through medical school.

George never ever expressed any gratitude for his mom's sacrifice. And he would have never accomplished what he had without her. His refusal to give back and to provide her comfort as she grew older and required help showed a deep selfishness and a complete lack of integrity.

Oma had contracted pancreatic cancer, and by the time Ellie and I found out, it had reached an advanced stage and she had to be hospitalized. I was in Mexico City when Ellie told me that her mom was admitted to a hospital in Edison, New Jersey. Ellie flew from California and was with her mother.

"She's not doing well; she's in a coma," Ellie told me.

We knew she would be passing soon, so I told Ellie that, rather than return to Los Angeles, I would fly from Mexico City to New Jersey.

When I arrived at the hospital, I saw George in the hallway outside her room. He told me she hadn't been responding to anyone and had been in a coma for the past two days. As George and I spoke, all of a sudden, we heard yelling from her hospital bed.

"Ron! Ron! Ron is here! Ron is here!"

George and I looked at each other shocked that she had come out of her coma. At the same time, George found himself both baffled and disappointed.

"Why is she calling out to you and not me?" he said. "I'm her son!"

"I could give you a million reasons why. But now is not the time to get into it with you," I said.

I left it at that and then entered her room. Even in her most difficult state, she maintained her wonderful, loving character.

"Ron, you didn't have to come here. It wasn't necessary, but I so appreciate it. I'm so happy to see you," she told me.

We had a brief conversation, and then the next day, Oma died. After her passing, I was ready to answer the question that George had asked me the day before.

"Remember when we were in the hospital and you were wondering why your mom was asking for me and not you?"

"Yes," he said.

"It is because of how you treated her. You did not deserve to have a mother like that," I said.

I really let him have it. The years I had put up with him mistreating his mother came out all at once, and I called him all kinds of names.

During her memorial service, George publicly apologized to his deceased mother for being an awful son, pretty much repeating the points I had made to him earlier.

Afterwards, I talked to him.

"It took quite a man to say what you did . . . to fess up like that.

While I do not have respect for the way you treated her, I do respect you for what you said."

But any redemptive quality I thought George had instantly went down the drain once we divided his mother's limited belongings after her death.

Around a year before her passing, Ellie and I were visiting her at home and noticed she had an old TV that hardly worked. Meanwhile, George lived nearby. He clearly didn't give a shit about whether his mom had a working TV because, based on his doctor's salary, he could have easily afforded to replace it.

During our visit, Ellie and I bought her a new TV. She appreciated the gift, and we were happy to add comfort to her daily life. After she died, Ellie and George inherited her estate—split fifty-fifty—which was not very large.

Ellie and I were back in California when I heard her talking to George on the phone.

She was telling her brother how their elderly aunt, who lived upstairs from their now-deceased mother, had a lousy television.

"Let's give her mom's TV," Ellie said.

George refused to do so.

"But Ron and I bought mom that TV. It was a gift from us!" she said.

Listening to the conversation, I realized George was arguing that because the inheritance was divided evenly between them that meant part of the TV was his, and he didn't want his half going to their aunt.

I couldn't believe what I was hearing. To think that, even after expressing regret at his mom's funeral for being a bad son, he hadn't learned a thing and had reverted to his old ways.

I yelled out to Ellie so that George would hear, "You tell that SOB the TV cost $700, so we will write him a check for $350, and then your aunt can have her TV!"

She repeated what I had said to her brother.

"That would be fine," was his cold reply.

I've met a lot of people over the course of my lifetime, and George ranks among the most selfish people I've known.

Ellie, unlike George, had inherited her mom's personality. She was a sweet woman who had a soft spot for her young son, Colby Allerton. Our marriage went smoothly, and I treated Colby as if he were my own kid. He was bright and athletic, and I saw lots of potential in him.

With Los Angeles Unified School District having a busing program that, depending on the luck of the draw, would take kids to schools clear across the city, I decided to enroll him in a private junior high located in Brentwood. It was a good choice because he excelled in a very academically rigorous environment. After he graduated, I thought the logical step would be to send him to an equally challenging private high school. But he insisted on attending a nearby public school in Van Nuys.

Although he had his strengths, he was still only fifteen years old and needed a lot of direction. Having two kids of my own who had already gone through the school system, I was convinced private school would be a perfect fit. It would be academically competitive, but I knew, rather than sink under pressure, Colby would rise to the challenge because he liked to push himself. The school would also give him the structure and smaller class sizes he needed to thrive.

"He has so much talent and intelligence and is so far ahead academically that he is going to coast through the first two years if you send him to public school. You are letting him take the lazy route," I told Ellie.

She disagreed. Colby was a great kid, and I really loved him. He never knew his dad, so he and I became close. We both were sports fans and had fun together. Despite my protests, Ellie went along with her son's wishes, and so off to public high school in Van Nuys he went. As I expected, he had no homework for the first two years because he had already studied those subjects in private school and now breezed through them.

When he reached his senior year and it was time to go to college, Colby planned to major in business. At the same time, he wanted to attend UCLA in order to be close to home. Unfortunately, UCLA didn't have a business program.

Together, Colby, Ellie, and I paid a visit to the high school counselor. I asked the counselor to tell him about different career paths to open him up to options beyond business. Afterwards, Ellie let me know she wasn't pleased with what I had said.

"You just want him to be an engineer like you!" she said.

"That could not be farther from the truth. I just want him to be able to maximize his potential. I am here for him, not for me!" I said.

We had one hell of an argument that day. It was one of many on how to raise Colby. I thought he was a kid trying to find his way and needed direction and discipline. Meanwhile, she thought he needed to be left alone and I was being overbearing.

Colby wound up going to UCLA, even though the university did not have an undergraduate business school.

In 1993, Ellie and I were planning to move from Encino to Newport Beach. Or so I thought. We had been talking about the move regularly, but that stopped the day she broke the news to me.

"I don't think I want to move to Newport," she said.

"Why?" I asked.

"Because I've been to a divorce lawyer. I told him about the move, and he talked me out of it. He has connections with Los Angeles judges but not ones in Orange County. So if I moved there, I'd have to file there, and he recommended against it," she said.

I knew we had problems in our marriage. But her announcement came as a surprise to me.

"You have already talked to a divorce lawyer?" I asked in disbelief. "It is over. Goodbye."

The betrayal was unforgivable. There was no way I would have thrown her off guard like that. And if there was anyone who would have benefitted from making the first divorce move, it would have been me, considering I had the successful business to protect. I moved out that day.

To make matters worse, I soon learned she had hired an attack-dog divorce firm. Trope & Trope was a notoriously vicious family law practice. As much as what she did was terrible, part of me doesn't hold her fully to blame. Before the divorce and after, Ellie was a sweet, kind person. But she made the mistake of seeking advice from one of her girlfriends about what she should do. This woman had gone through a nasty divorce and prepared Ellie to go to war when arming herself for battle was totally unnecessary.

In fact, like a cancer that goes into remission and then comes roaring back with a vengeance, a couple of years later, her lawyers came after me again. The first time around, the divorce was a stressful event that I'd never want to go through again. But the second time made that one seem like a picnic. I'm certain Ellie didn't initiate this move. She didn't have that kind of conniving side to her.

It was just another example of how her attorneys were ruthless sons of bitches. Eventually after the divorce, my business really took off, and its profits increased. As a result, the company was worth a lot more than when Ellie and I had agreed on the final settlement decree.

Two years after our divorce, Ellie's lawyers came up with a cockeyed claim that during our original settlement, I had intentionally devalued RSI by telling The Home Depot to slow down its purchases and buy less from us for six months. Then, after half a year, I allegedly began shipping The Home Depot more products. After the first negotiation between Ellie and me, her lawyers now saw a chance to strike again by essentially accusing me of fraud.

Could they have thought of anything stupider? As if The Home Depot would tell its customers they would have to wait six months to receive products and as if the customers would be willing to go along with that without taking their business elsewhere. And most importantly, as if any big business would hold back orders to help a supplier going through a divorce!

Thanks to hiring and paying for wise legal counsel and having a fair judge overseeing the case, Trope & Trope lost. I have no respect for her divorce attorneys who turned what could have otherwise been an amicable breakup into one that ruined our relationship, making us enemies for life. In fact, I'm sure that given our personalities, we would have maintained a connection after the divorce under less hostile circumstances. But because her attorneys were out for blood, there would be no reconciliation between us. I never saw Colby again, and with the exception of depositions, the same was true for his mother.

★ CHAPTER EIGHT

From Burnout to Success

After being in business for thirty years, Perma-Bilt was facing fierce competition from Taiwanese companies. They were manufacturing and selling the high-volume medicine and vanity cabinets at prices 50 percent less than ours and our more than thirty competitors'. And we weren't alone.

The entire furniture and building-products industry was taking a huge hit. US businesses were closing their stateside factories and setting up shop halfway around the globe. States with high concentrations of furniture factories, like North Carolina, were being hammered.

Perma-Bilt was being squeezed tighter and tighter in a vice grip. On one side were my Asian adversaries, and on the other were my customers such as The Home Depot, which was beginning to sell its Asian-made products in its stores as special promotions. With its massive purchasing power, The Home Depot was using its clout like a billy club to beat our prices down.

So there was Perma-Bilt, stuck between two giants, one across the Pacific and the other right next door, with our profit margins and tensions tightening.

An example of one of the battles among many that tired me out took place in 1985, just before the National Hardware Show in Chicago, where John Wickes, The Home Depot's buyer, stooped to new lows.

Frank Xavier, Perma-Bilt's very capable vice president of sales, broke the news to me.

"John told me that unless we drastically lower our prices, we'll lose The Home Depot's business."

I was outraged. Our prices were competitive with all other American manufacturers. The stakes were very high for Perma-Bilt because of the large volume of our business that The Home Depot represented. Despite the risk, I knew this was a case where I had to stand my ground and say no, even if it meant losing one of our most important customer's business.

But to see if we could salvage the deal, Frank suggested we all meet in Chicago because we would be there for the trade show.

"All right, Frank, but make sure Jim Ingliss is there too because I am not going to meet John without him," I said.

Jim Ingliss was The Home Depot's senior vice president of merchandising, as well as John's boss. A tough but fair man, he was one of the first senior executives that the founders had hired. I respected him for his intelligence and integrity. He had done a tremendous job by playing an important role in the company's remarkable growth. With our business on the line, I wanted to make sure our big customer's senior guy was there.

Frank, Jim, John, and I met in a hotel room that The Home Depot reserved for meetings during the trade show. The whole thing started amicably. In fact, Jim spent the first couple of minutes telling Frank and me what a valuable supplier we were to The Home Depot. The praise and gratitude were quite different from John's earlier threats to take his business elsewhere. But Jim had a reason to be so complimentary.

"We're launching a national advertising program, and we'd love for Perma-Bilt to participate. It'll be a win-win. With our combined advertising dollars, I'm confident your business will increase. So what do you think?" Jim asked me.

I thought the meeting was to see how we could keep The Home Depot's business, so I wasn't prepared for Jim's pitch.

"I have listened carefully to your presentation. And all I have to say is that I would be a stupid idiot to participate in the cost of the ads," I said.

His silence told me that he hadn't seen my response coming.

"What do you mean, Ron?" he asked.

"It is simple, Jim, because we are not going to be your supplier anymore," I said.

"Why not?"

"Ask him," I said. I pointed at John Wickes. "He told Frank that we were out because we would not lower our prices. And because of that, I guess it has been nice doing business with you."

"Is what Ron's saying true?" the senior VP asked Jim.

John stuttered his answer. "Well . . . I did tell them that. But I was just negotiating," he said.

"John," I shot back, "how the hell were we supposed to know that you were 'just negotiating'? And because there is no way we are going to cut our prices, I figured we had lost the business," I said.

I am not one to throw a buyer, like John, under the bus—especially in front of his boss. But the truth was that he was threatening to take The Home Depot away from us. So I had no other choice than to tell Jim the truth.

"You're not going to lose the business. That's ridiculous. You're too valuable of a supplier," Jim said.

"Well, Jim, I have to tell you something. We do not have the money to invest in an ad campaign. We just do not have those margins. So I am sorry. We cannot do this. I hope you understand that I cannot give you the advertising dollars," I said.

While I was willing to walk away from the deal, fortunately, I didn't have to. The result of all this was that we did end up keeping The Home Depot's business without contributing the advertising dollars.

Although this was a lesson of knowing when to say no—and an example that would stick with me when I started my next business only a few years later—it was just one more instance of getting beat up. So while it was a pretty big victory, it didn't bring me a whole lot of satisfaction.

By this time, I was tired of constantly being thrown in the ring with the likes of buyers like John; I just didn't have it in me anymore to keep fighting. Despite the challenges, my executives and I had been able to keep Perma-Bilt profitable. But winning was becoming harder and harder, and given the aggressive foreign competition, there would only be more battles to come. "To hell with this. I want to sell the company and get out" became a thought I regularly had.

I FELT TRAPPED, BEAT UP, AND BURNED OUT.

For months, I had been discussing selling Perma-Bilt with my friend John Marshall from Merrill Lynch.

In late 1986, John had found a buyer for my business. Austram was an Australian private equity firm. At the time, private equity money from Down Under was pouring into the United States.

John introduced me to Efrem Goldhammer, who was Austram's managing director. Efrem proposed a deal. Austram would buy a 48.5 percent stake in Perma-Bilt. I would retain 48.5 percent and a seat on the company's board of directors, and I would step down from being CEO. Meanwhile, Austram would bring in a new CEO. John, as part of his compensation for brokering the deal, would have the remaining 3 percent, which would be held in a voting trust.

I liked the arrangement because I would receive enough cash to sustain my lifestyle, and I would still have a voice in the direction of the company. I ran the offer by Allan Liebert, my attorney and close friend. He reviewed the terms and thought the deal was clean—except for one key part.

"Ron, this could work against you; you could lose control," he told me.

"Allan, I understand that, but if I never get another penny out of Perma-Bilt, that is fine; I just want out," I said.

While I wasn't sure about my next career move and even though my instincts warned me that I was about to get in bed with someone untrustworthy, I wanted out so badly that I went ahead with the sale. Unfortunately, shortly after signing a definitive agreement, my instincts proved right. I still might have had a chance to back out at this point, but the burnout made me decide otherwise.

In 1987, the National Hardware Show took place again in Chicago. Perma-Bilt's sales team appeared in full force. Efrem, who would soon become one of Perma-Bilt's owners, flew in to check out the event.

As we had done in years past, Perma-Bilt hosted a hospitality room where we served cocktails and hors d'oeuvres. Customers would stop by after show hours. I was talking to Frank Xavier when Efrem arrived. Back in Australia, Efrem had a wife and children. Frank and I were shocked to see him walk in with a young lady—that wasn't his wife—on his arm.

If a person decides to have an affair, that's his business. But Efrem showing up like that basically said, "Look who I'm sleeping with," to Frank, me, and everyone else at the Perma-Bilt–sponsored event.

I thought to myself, "Holy shit, is this who we sold the company to?" He demonstrated a lack of humility, an overinflated self-image, and a cavalier attitude.

In fact, Efrem's egotistic display that evening gave me sure signs of the arrogance both he and the entire Austram team would have in taking over Perma-Bilt. Armed with their all-knowing attitude, they wasted no time addressing Perma-Bilt's problems their way.

The day after the deal closed, there was a kickoff staff meeting I wasn't invited to, where Austram's new CEO made a sweeping announcement.

"We're starting from scratch. The days of Ron Simon are over," he said.

He then told them I'd no longer be involved in the business and, from that point forward, Perma-Bilt employees could not seek my advice.

After the tense meeting, my secretary at the time, Barbara, came into my office. I had been packing my belongings. She told me what had happened.

"My God, they can't talk about you that way," she said with tears running down her cheeks.

Although it did not represent the spirit of the deal I had made with Austram, based on what I had experienced so far, the news didn't surprise me. Working decades in the business world meant I had seen my share of backstabbing—it was never my leadership style, but being on the receiving end of it thickened my skin. It also taught me what goes around comes around and often results in sweet revenge. While I didn't know it at the time, I would soon discover that the CEO's words were mild compared to what would happen under his leadership.

A couple of days after the meeting, the CEO called Frank Xavier into his office. Frank and his sales team were accused of cheating and padding their expense accounts. Working with Frank for fifteen years, I knew he was an honest and trustworthy man of integrity. He was highly respected by his colleagues, customers, and subordinates. The groundless and unthinkable claim coming from his new boss caused Frank to nearly leap across the desk in outrage. Angry, Frank phoned me immediately after. My advice to him was to "cool it for right now; his time will come."

Within weeks, the CEO fired several Perma-Bilt executives. It was tough to watch fiercely loyal employees, some of whom had been with me for many, many years, forced out of their jobs. Then there were those who left on their own; these men and women found the new work environment and its incompetent CEO unbearable. After these waves of departures, both forced and voluntary, Perma-Bilt under Austram bore no resemblance to the company I had built.

In the meantime, after working hard for so many years, I welcomed the break to be out of the trenches being beaten up by The Home Depot and our other customers. But I didn't put my feet up completely either. Together with Barbara my secretary and her boyfriend Marty, who was a private detective, we started a small company that performed background checks for businesses seeking to hire high-level employees. Before the internet, companies had a tough time finding information about potential executives.

During this time away from Perma-Bilt, I had a chance to regroup, catch my breath, and objectively rationalize the company's predicament. I still wanted to figure out a way that Perma-Bilt could succeed in such a competitive environment. But maybe more importantly, if I was going to go all in, work had to be fun.

At Perma-Bilt, I had lost the excitement and motivation to go to the office every day. This was not acceptable for me. I wanted to look forward to showing up at work. A fulfilling, enjoyable job for me meant having the thrill of growing a business, a value proposition that would kill the competition, and fighting battles when necessary—ones that might beat me up but I could actually win . . . and win big.

About the time I sold Perma-Bilt Industries, the Taiwanese cabinet manufacturers began moving their production to China. By then, Chinese wages were far lower than in Taiwan. In addition, Taiwan had focused on manufacturing only high-volume products. The companies didn't have any credit issues because they obtained letters of credit. They did not have to deal with returns, provide in-store service, or offer advertising allowances.

I reasoned the only way to compete with Taiwan, and now with China, was to create a very focused product line, which would greatly enhance production efficiency resulting in much lower costs. Furthermore, in order to be profitable selling to giant companies like The Home Depot, we had to offer a program they could not get from any other US manufacturer. In other words, we had to be irreplaceable. This would allow us to stand up to customers. Rather than get the shit kicked out of us, we would have the ability to say no to any demands that would adversely affect our manufacturing efficiency. We would have prices that were around 40 percent less than our US competitors and provide the best service and quality for the high-volume products our customers purchased.

My plan would result in our ability to have selling prices within 5 to 10 percent of China's versus being almost twice as much. In addition, we would have no letter of credit requirement, have thirty-day payment terms, provide delivery in two weeks rather ninety days, which was the turnaround time from China, and offer products of higher quality. Last, when it came to delivery, the word "backorder" would be forever cut from our vocabulary.

In another instance of "sometimes it's more important to learn from the wrong ways of running a business than having someone teach you the right ways," Perma-Bilt had developed a bad backorder habit. This was a result of our very broad and complex product line we had developed to keep the competition out of the space allocated to us in our customers' retail operations.

For our largest customer, The Home Depot, we were regularly shipping orders 70 percent complete with the remaining 30 percent on backorder. Meanwhile, The Home Depot required a minimum of a 97 percent completion rate. So Perma-Bilt going way beyond The Home Depot's backorder threshold made us a pretty lousy supplier.

In fact, Bill Hamlin, the company's vice president of merchandising, was fed up with Perma-Bilt's delays. I had a long-standing relationship with Bill. We shared similar values; namely we were both outspoken and men of integrity. And when we weren't duking it out in the negotiations ring, we both appreciated a good laugh. Bill and I had a similar sense of humor. When it came to our most recent conversations, however, they were no laughing matter.

"You've got to clean up your act, or you're going to lose this business," he told me.

I actually appreciated the harsh words because had it not been for the goodwill Perma-Bilt had established with The Home Depot over the years, we would have most certainly already been thrown out. Bill gave us a way to salvage our relationship.

"Here's what we're going to do," he said. "I'm going to give you ninety days to correct things. You're going to have to ship 97 percent. Anything less than 97 percent and we're going to penalize you. After ninety days, we'll review your performance and see if you've shaped up."

My company had been thrown a life preserver. I agreed to what Bill proposed. Perma-Bilt had to quickly pull itself together, and I made sure we put all our effort into hitting our target.

After ninety days of hard work, we were ready for The Home Depot's evaluation. While we did not reach 97 percent, we were very close and, most importantly, enough so that we satisfied our customer. In fact, we were so close that the penalty for not reaching 97 percent was only about three thousand dollars—a small amount I was more than happy to pay.

Complying with The Home Depot's demand eased some of the tension between the two companies. Feeling good about what we had accomplished and knowing that Bill appreciated a joke as much as anyone, I thought of a memorable way to pay Bill what we owed his company.

Rather than mail The Home Depot a check or offer a three-thousand-dollar credit, I decided to hand Bill what we owed in person. To make the payment unforgettable, I wanted to load a wheelbarrow with three thousand dollars in pennies. I'd then roll the change into his office and dump the coins on the floor.

"Bill, here is your penalty paid in full!" I would tell him.

Then I'd leave him with a mountain of pennies to remind him that Perma-Bilt had met his ultimatum.

I talked my prank over with my Perma-Bilt team. We thought that if anyone would get a kick out of it, Bill would. *But*, if he wasn't in the mood or didn't find it funny, the joke could backfire and piss Bill off, so in the end, we decided against it. Instead, I arranged to meet Bill in person without the wheelbarrow.

During our appointment, I handed him a check and then told him how I had really wanted to present him the money.

"Damnit, Ron. You should have done it! It would have been funny as hell, and I would have remembered it forever," he said.

While I didn't leave a permanent impression on him with my wheelbarrow prank, I did build trust that would provide me a big break later on when I needed it most.

Although The Home Depot was satisfied with 3 percent backorders, my aggressive plan for competing with Asia called for 0 percent, meaning I would accept only 100 percent completed orders for my business. While I did not know it at the time, this daring and aggressive plan would be the genesis of RSI, a company I would eventually start.

But for now, I was focused on resuscitating Perma-Bilt. The plan to transform it into an irreplaceable supplier was what I presented to Austram. Our unrivaled quality, prices, and service would make us bulletproof. And by being bulletproof, we would have negotiation leverage. No company could ever put a gun to our heads and force us to say yes to demands that went against our values.

I concluded the only way to survive and be profitable selling to The

Home Depot and our other customers was to not be a "me too" supplier. Instead, we had to be unlike any other supplier in all our product categories. Perma-Bilt needed to offer our customers a value they could not find from our competitors, which would give us the ability to stand up and say no to any unfair demands our customers placed on us. Sticking to our principles meant we risked losing business from our biggest customers. But that was a worthwhile tradeoff for me; I would rather lose business than cave to demands that would compromise our profitability and make my life miserable.

But executing my plan that got me excited to jump back in the ring would have to wait because, again, I was told, "You can't."

A little over a year after Austram took over, I was attending a Perma-Bilt Board of Directors meeting and introduced my idea.

"Ron, you can't. You're crazy for even thinking this is possible! If we do any of this, we'll lose The Home Depot," Perma-Bilt's new CEO told me, which is exactly what I expected to hear.

At the time, Perma-Bilt offered its customers a product line comprising over sixty stock-keeping units (SKUs) of medicine cabinets. In addition to my 100 percent shipping requirement, my plan would reduce our line to only fourteen SKUs, which represented approximately 80 percent of total sales.

"Let our competitors sell The Home Depot the other low-volume items," I said.

I added that even if The Home Depot dropped us, we weren't making any money with the retailer anyway. But I knew we wouldn't lose The Home Depot because we would be competitive with Taiwanese companies.

My proposal was flatly rejected.

Then, in 1989, more of Austram's unethical business practices emerged. Upon reviewing the company's financial statements, I saw blatantly fraudulent activity. Austram was understating the reserves on Perma-Bilt's balance sheet. This was to cover up the amount of money Perma-Bilt was losing. At the next board meeting, I let the CEO and Efrem Goldhammer know what I had found.

"You are defrauding the bank. I am not going to be a party to this. I am resigning from the board. And you know what? Once I am out of here, I am going back in the business!" I said.

"You can't compete with us! We'll sue your ass," Efrem countered.

"Go right ahead. Your big egos got in the way of having me sign a non-compete agreement. So you guys can go fuck yourselves," I said and immediately left the meeting.

A few weeks later, I received a phone call from Efrem.

"Leucadia has offered to buy Perma-Bilt," he said.

Leucadia, a multi-billion-dollar holding company, owned General Marble, which was Perma-Bilt's competitor. If Perma-Bilt agreed to sell, Leucadia would perform its due diligence.

"They are not going to buy this company," I said. "They only want to get access to all our trade secrets, customer pricing, manufacturing processes, and everything else. I am warning you not to talk to them."

"No, they really want to buy. And we want you to vote your shares, so we can move forward with the deal," Efrem said.

In my mind, it made zero sense for Leucadia to purchase a company on its deathbed. And even if I was wrong, once Leucadia performed its due diligence, it would quickly realize buying a losing business was a stupid move. At the same time, after a botched turnaround plan and with an incompetent CEO at the helm, Efrem was desperate for a deal that would cut him loose from Perma-Bilt.

During our call, I didn't budge. Not only did I question Leucadia's motives, but also I was starting to create a company that would compete head-to-head with Perma-Bilt and General Marble. So there was no way I wanted to give my rivals an upper hand by providing them access to Perma-Bilt's corporate secrets. I did, however, make the conciliatory move to meet with Joe Steinberg, Leucadia's president. After my call with Efrem, I reached out to my lawyer. We decided to hold the meeting with Joe in Allan Liebert's office.

On the day of my appointment with Joe, he arrived at Allan's office accompanied by his attorney. The conversation between us started amicably but quickly went south.

"Joe, do you know I am going back into the business?" I asked.

"I don't care. We're not worried about that," he replied.

He then made his offer. I'd earn a hefty amount from Leucadia's buyout.

"Why do you want Perma-Bilt?" I asked.

Joe's reasons were weak, which convinced me more that my suspicions were spot on. I was furious.

"You know what? I am not approving this," I said.

"So that means you're going to vote against us?" he asked.

"Absolutely!" I said.

Joe dug in.

"Ron, I wanted to give you a chance. But the truth is, we don't need you anyway. Between Austram and John Marshall, we've got the votes we need," he said.

So John Marshall, my friend, was voting against me? This was the first I had heard about his flat-out betrayal. "He will get his," I thought to myself.

I knew my new company, RSI, would destroy Perma-Bilt. So neither Perma-Bilt, Austram, Leucadia, nor anyone who stabbed me in the back would get in my way. I then looked at Joe, wanting to throw the guy right through the window behind him.

"So you are telling me I have to agree to sell Perma-Bilt to Leucadia?" I asked.

"Yeah, I am," said Joe.

My attorney held his breath.

"Then let me tell you what *you* have to do," I said. "You have to leave right now. Because if you do not, you are going through that fucking window behind you."

With my reply, and after only ten minutes together, the meeting ended. From the very start, I knew my position, and I had no intention of budging; Joe wasn't going to bully me into changing my mind. Joe and his attorney left using the door and not the window, and I moved forward with my ambitious plan full force.

The first step was to create a team. I looked no further than trusted Perma-Bilt employees who were fired from the company. So a bunch of Perma-Bilt rejects, let go from their posts, would form an industry dream team that would lead to Perma-Bilt's eventual undoing. Perma-Bilt's new owners deemed us idiots, with me probably labeled the biggest among all of them. But we had fires in our guts and were ready to prove them wrong.

I brought on Ron Shewach, Perma-Bilt's materials manager and hired him as vice president of operations.

We came up with a company name. High on the list was LAMCO, which stood for Lean and Mean Company. In the end, however, I called it RSI Home Products, which stood for Ron Simon Industries, and incorporated it in April 1989.

Ron Shewach and I then went about securing component suppliers, equipment, and an assembly facility. In the city of Gardena, California, I found all three. Arkay, a small, family-run company had all the equipment required to make the components RSI would need for its medicine cabinets. During my talks with Arkay's owners, a widowed Armenian woman and her two adult sons, I described how I was also looking for space to house an assembly plant.

"We've got nine thousand square feet right here next to us we're not using," one of the sons told me.

We then negotiated how much the family business would charge RSI to supply the parts. I initially balked at what they quoted me. They then balked at my counteroffer.

"We'll lose money," the son told me.

"Listen, I have been doing this for years, so I have a thorough understanding of what the costs are," I said. "I am putting my whole reputation at stake here. And it is based on the fact that you will make a profit if you do what I tell you. If you do not, I will lose my supplier, and I will be out of business. Do you think I am going to take that kind of risk?"

They trusted my word. We moved full force with the deal, and I rented the nine thousand square feet to be used as my assembly facility. RSI could now begin taking customer orders.

Soon after, I hired Norton Krinsky, who had been Perma-Bilt's comptroller, as RSI's first CFO. He set up all our accounting systems. With our financial controls in place, including software, RSI was ready. Norton played an integral role in our management team and contributed to RSI's eventual success. After about four years of hard and productive work, Norton decided to retire. Steve Goldstein took his place, and Norton stayed on to make sure the CFO transition was seamless.

I also brought on another former Perma-Bilt employee, Joe Varela, who had been the company's plant manager. Austram had previously terminated Ron, Norton, and Joe. And at the end of 1989, when RSI was growing and performing very well, I convinced Frank Xavier to quit his position at another job. After leaving Perma-Bilt, he was working at Donner, a manufacturer of bathroom accessories. He resigned from Donner and joined RSI as vice president of sales. This amazing team built from Perma-Bilt rejects went on to become industry superstars. Meanwhile, I still had a stake in my old company, which Leucadia supposedly wanted to buy.

In April 1989, I called a former Perma-Bilt customer, Dave Heerensperger, now at Pay 'N Pak as CEO. Over the years, the company gave Perma-Bilt tons of business. Although he and I had clashed many times negotiating business deals, we had an immense amount of respect for each other's honesty and business skill.

We arranged to meet in Seattle. I flew in, and Dave picked me up at the airport and drove me to his office. I showed him my product samples, which he loved, and then quoted my prices, which he loved even more. We spent the rest of the day catching up, and he gave me a tour of the boat he was building. He then dropped me off at the airport where we sealed the deal.

"Ron, how big of an order do you need to start your company? What if I gave you an order of thirty thousand cabinets?" he said.

"Dave, that would be unbelievable! If you did that, I would kiss your ass on both cheeks," I said.

I agreed to begin delivering by September. With his commitment, RSI had its first customer.

I then contacted Bill Hamlin, still The Home Depot's VP of merchandising. Once again, he came through for me. The integrity at the core of our relationship from the start certainly played a major role in his decision to take a risk with RSI. He committed to buying RSI's products for his western stores, and I agreed to begin delivering by July.

With huge orders only months away to fulfill, Ron Shewach and I forged ahead with RSI's operations. The pressure was on to never repeat what had happened at Perma-Bilt. I let my team know that as long as I was running this business, I would not tolerate hearing, "We can never ship 100 percent complete." Instead, I would accept no backorders, not even one . . . ever! The reality was I didn't have to beat anyone into submission about it. The all-star team I had put together was equally as committed as I was. They were self-disciplined and pushed themselves harder than anyone could do from the outside. We all knew that this would be one of the keys to our company's success.

RSI would ship 100 percent complete 100 percent of the time. If that meant working twenty-four hours a day, that's what we would do. Remembering the embarrassment and pain of backorders at Perma-Bilt, I vowed to a 180-degree turnaround—even though I knew that a small percentage of backorders was normal, that would never be normal for us.

Many aspects of Perma-Bilt were examples of how *not* to run a business. Now, RSI would demonstrate how *to* run a business—one with the ability to say no and mean it because of what we offered our customers. My new company's success would eventually lead to Perma-Bilt's demise.

★ CHAPTER NINE

Battling Our Customers' Changing Cultures

With RSI, I hit the reset button. I had the opportunity to use all my previous lessons, accomplishments, and mistakes in order to start fresh.

And I was ready for it.

In a short period, the burden and burnout from running a business that had made me miserable disappeared. Instead, I was filled with excitement about the journey ahead of me. I was leading a startup I was passionate about and knew that, done right, RSI was destined to succeed.

As promised, we began delivering our first cabinets to The Home Depot in July and Pay 'N Pak in September. And thanks to the trust the Armenian family put in me, they wound up earning even more money than I initially had told them they would.

Although Dave Heerensperger and I had butted heads several times during my years at Perma-Bilt, he took the leap of faith and ordered from RSI because we fundamentally trusted one another. Pay 'N Pak and The Home Depot lit a spark that ignited RSI and would allow my company in the coming years to change the course of the kitchen and bath cabinet industry.

Perma-Bilt's innovative product, Marlan.

By 1990, we decided to expand our medicine cabinet product line to include bathroom vanity cabinets and cultured marble sink tops. But because of environmental issues in California, rather than manufacturing the sink tops in-house, I would outsource production in Mexico. And, thanks to a relationship I had made during my Perma-Bilt years, I had the perfect person in mind to take care of our needs.

For three years, Ramón Soto had been producing cultured marble sink tops and other products for Perma-Bilt in his fiberglass manufacturing company in Tijuana. We had introduced Marlan, which we designed to compete with DuPont's Corian countertop surface, and Ramón produced it for us in his factory. While Corian offered many benefits, such as being stain resistant, easy to clean, and seamless, it was expensive. Our product cost less than half.

Mr. and Mrs. Joe Varela (left) and Mr. and Mrs. Ramón Soto, 1993.

By the time I started RSI, Ramón and I had already known each other for over four years; I respected him for his work ethic and integrity. Unfortunately for Ramón, Perma-Bilt's demise hit his business hard. In fact, when Perma-Bilt sank, it dragged his business right down with it. With his business gone, he was scrambling to support his family.

When I reached out to him, the timing couldn't have been better for both of us: Ramón was in terrible financial shape, and I needed someone trustworthy to meet RSI's rapid expansion.

Ramón was confident he could set up a new production line. While he had the skill to manufacture cultured marble sink tops, he lacked the capital to start up a business. I offered him a life preserver, which would also benefit my business.

"Give me a budget on the startup expense," I said.

Ramón came back with an estimate of one hundred thousand dollars, which in today's currency is more than double that.

I knew and trusted Ramón, and the amount sounded right to me, so I told him I would send him the money he needed for purchasing equipment to get started. We agreed that he would pay the loan back from the profits he generated selling sink tops to RSI. Our deal was sealed with a handshake—goodwill and honor.

I told some of my friends about our arrangement.

"Ron, you're crazy. He's in another country. He can just take your money and run, and you'd have no recourse whatsoever!" one of them told me.

"We will see. That is always a possibility. But I just do not think that is going to happen," I said.

In the end, trusting my gut turned out to be a good move. Our arrangement was a win-win: Ramón not only dug himself out of his debt; he also wound up making far more than he had anticipated. Meanwhile, thanks to Ramón's efforts, RSI was able to sell at prices that continued to beat the competition. Had Ramón not demonstrated his character over the years we had known each other, I would have never taken the risk, which was one that paid off for both of us over the long term.

★

Preparing to serve Christmas lunch to all RSI's employees, 2015,
left to right: *Frank Xavier, Ron Shewach, Ron Simon, and Norton Krinsky.*

In 1991, I made the best hiring decision of my career. Alex Calabrese was only twenty-five years old when the recruiter sent him to us. He was interviewing for RSI's materials manager position, which dealt with production control and purchasing. During our meeting, I immediately picked up on his intelligence and the passion he had for our business. When it was Alex's turn to ask questions, his quick and insightful thinking stood out. Rather than focusing only on the materials manager position he was applying for, he took a global perspective that demonstrated the type of vision and leadership RSI needed. . . . I was impressed.

Succession planning is a must for any successful business, and I was looking for someone who could fill my shoes when it came time for me to step aside. While I had a great executive team, a CEO requires a certain skillset that I hadn't found yet. Hiring Alex was a no brainer. I called the recruiter right after.

"You made my day. Given my age, I have been thinking about a successor, and I have a good feeling that I may have just met him," I said.

Once Alex started at RSI, his performance impressed us all. As time went on, I gave him more and more responsibility until eventually he became president in 1996 after less than six years of being hired.

After I made Alex president and as a result of his remarkable performance, my confidence in him kept growing, and the bond between us kept getting stronger. So in 2009 when a competitor phoned me to ask if RSI would be interested in acquiring it, Alex and I flew to Dallas and negotiated the purchase of Continental Cabinets.

By then I believed that Alex was very capable of managing the acquisition process and putting him in charge would be a great experience for him. So that's exactly what I did, and the deal was completed to both sides' satisfaction.

After it closed, I received this very heartwarming letter from Alex, which I have cherished for all these years.

Dear Ron,

Thank you so much for giving me the opportunity to take the lead on making the Continental acquisition. The significant level of confidence that you had in me on this deal meant the world to me. I can't begin to thank you enough for all of the lessons you have taught me over the years, and so many of them resonated throughout this process. I am ever thankful for that training and remain very eager to continue to learn from your wisdom and invaluable business insight. I thank God every day that our paths crossed some twenty years ago and look forward to the next twenty.

Alex and the many outstanding people from Perma-Bilt who joined me at RSI ensured our success. But when I started RSI in 1989, I had no idea that we would become the country's most successful manufacturer within the kitchen and bath industry. RSI's business plan that allowed me to be a tough but fair CEO resulted in us selling and manufacturing more cabinets than our rivals and with operating margins more than twice that of our most profitable competitor.

As the nation's biggest home centers grew, new leaders were hired, and the rapid expansion brought about shifts within their organizations' cultures—often for the worse.

In 2000, Robert Nardelli, one of three top General Electric executives vying to replace Jack Welch as GE's CEO, lost the battle but was then hired as The Home Depot's CEO. The Home Depot was bullish about what the gifted and disciplined executive would bring to the company. Unfortunately, his time at The Home Depot was marked by a series of controversial decisions with mixed results and ended in his termination.

One of the moves Nardelli made to signal the new leadership at The Home Depot was to erase the company's phenomenal past.

I always enjoyed visiting The Home Depot's Atlanta headquarters. The huge lobby told the story through photos of the company's rise. From its scrappy roots to becoming one of the greatest success stories in the history of US entrepreneurship, the images couldn't help but make you feel proud of being one of its suppliers. As someone who knew its founders, Bernie, Arthur, Pat, and Ken, I had a particular appreciation for and understood the blood, sweat, and tears represented on the company's walls.

The founders of The Home Depot, as well as most of the first group of executives they brought on to run the day-to-day operations, were extremely smart and tough businessmen with high integrity. They and RSI had the same goals: to provide the best products and services to our customers. And because we were all very passionate about achieving success by focusing on this shared goal, we had many heated but productive discussions. These were direct and honest where people said what was on their minds without any politics involved—exactly how business should be.

The Home Depot's demanding policies helped make RSI a great company. Its founders were like the best boxers. RSI would enter the ring, and to avoid getting the shit beat out of us, we had to train harder, get stronger, and never let our guard down. And we became better from it. While the founders were tough, they were always fair—no low blows. And they were hands-on. If RSI had an issue, I could reach out to them directly and they would work hard to resolve the problem. I never had to deal with layers of bureaucracy.

Too many people resort to playing games in order to meet their self-serving interests. This is corporate and office politics as usual. It's anything but normal for me, though. In fact, I have zero patience for it.

I am fully willing to duke it out in the negotiations ring, as long as the rules are fair. But mix business with someone playing underhanded tricks, and you have a formula that I want no part of. I'd rather someone tell me, "Ron, you're full of shit!" than smile to my face and glad-hand me. With the founders of The Home Depot, there was zero politics of that sort, and that was one of the qualities I admired most about the company and one I upheld in my businesses.

About a year after Nardelli took over, Alex Calabrese, who had become RSI's CEO and president, was in The Home Depot's lobby waiting to attend a meeting. He was shocked at what Nardelli had done. He phoned me afterwards.

"Holy shit, Ron . . . you won't believe what I just saw!"

His description was appalling. Gone was the corporate history. No more pictures of Bernie, Arthur, Pat, and all early team members working their asses off to create one of the country's best companies. The series of photos extending across the massive lobby was replaced by a single image: a picture of Robert Nardelli.

If I'd had any say in the matter, I would have fired Nardelli on the spot for this change alone. To show that kind of ego was inexcusable.

More very bad decisions were to come, one of the biggest being when Nardelli put the company on an import mission. He told his buyers that they had to purchase a certain percentage of products from Asia. His short-sighted mandate focused just on getting the lowest price, which directly affected our business with his company.

RSI was selling approximately twenty million dollars annually of a vanity and marble top combination to The Home Depot. Thanks to Nardelli's directive, the buyer told us that we had to meet ridiculously low prices to keep the business.

We explained that when they factored in the loss of sales due to out-of-stock conditions from long lead times, the elimination of the in-store service we offered, their additional inventory holding costs, and more, RSI's prices were actually lower than the imports'. But our explanation landed on deaf ears, and because of Nardelli's mandate, The Home Depot switched to the imported products.

You'd never know that the same company that would regularly award RSI vendor of the year could just as quickly throw us out. While you may be one of The Home Depot's top fifteen suppliers, all this can change in an instant. So I never allowed myself to get too comfortable.

Unfortunately, at that time, doing business with The Home Depot was similar to being on a football team and throwing a touchdown pass, only to look up and see the six points not show up on the scoreboard.

Losing twenty million dollars of business was a tough blow. But we were confident we were right, so saying yes would have been a huge mistake.

It didn't take long for The Home Depot to see it had made the wrong decision. In less than half a year, the company realized its so-called cheaper Asian suppliers wound up being more expensive than us for exactly the same reasons we had told them. Six months later, we got the business back. But The Home Depot's earlier decision to drop us never would have happened under the old regime.

This was just one of Nardelli's screw-ups in his short history with The Home Depot. In 2007, he was forced to resign.

After Nardelli was terminated, the board named Frank Blake as The Home Depot's new CEO. He had previously held a position in corporate development in the company and, before that, like Nardelli, had worked at GE.

As The Home Depot's new head, one of the first steps Frank took was to reach out to Bernie Marcus, the company's founding CEO, to seek his advice. He asked Bernie how to bring back the culture that had made The Home Depot so successful. Building on this promising start, Frank went on to become a very capable and productive leader.

An RSI kitchen, 2015.

With Lowe's, which had grown to become the country's second largest home center chain and The Home Depot's fiercest competitor, RSI also had its share of battles; many of these were avoidable had corporate executives taken a hands-on approach, as Bernie, Arthur, and Pat had done. By the early 2000s, we had become Lowe's biggest vanity cabinet supplier. While we had earned respect within the company, we could never have direct conversations with its senior executives.

Meanwhile, at RSI, we were developing our five-year business plan. Part of the process entailed determining where we needed to grow geographically and the manufacturing equipment required to move forward with our expansion. And because of the volume of business we were doing with Lowe's, the company played a big part in our planning.

To get feedback from Lowe's, I wrote a letter to its CEO and told him how I appreciated being his supplier. I then described how RSI was in the process of putting together its business plan. We wanted to make sure we didn't overlook important details, in particular ones that would affect Lowe's. So we asked to set up a meeting at which time we would show where we thought we were headed, receive feedback, and fine-tune if necessary in order to continue being a good supplier. I didn't hear back from him. Instead of responding to me, as Bernie would have done, what did the CEO do?

He simply passed my letter to one his buyers. But rather than interpret what I had written as my commitment to be the best supplier possible, the buyer was insulted by it. She viewed it as a sneaky move where I had gone over her head by reaching out directly to her superior. This couldn't have been further from reality.

Unfortunately, the truth didn't seem to matter in this case. She decided to bad-mouth us to other Lowe's buyers who were in charge of purchasing different RSI products. We did our best to explain to the angry buyer that we were in no way trying to undermine her, but she refused to listen. Her baseless vendetta hit RSI twice.

Several months later, we had acquired Continental Cabinets, a competitor selling kitchen cabinets to Lowe's. After we bought the company, the Lowe's buyer immediately replaced the Continental program with another competitor. Even though our program was far superior to what she was replacing it with, hell hath no fury like a buyer scorned. She threw reason and common sense out the window.

Then, on another occasion, RSI introduced a new kitchen cabinet program. She would not even give us the opportunity to make a presentation to Lowe's. Eventually, she left us with no alternative but to take that same program to The Home Depot, and we agreed we would not sell it to Lowe's. The Home Depot decided to roll it out to all its stores nationwide. That resulted in The Home Depot taking about 30 percent of Lowe's market share of in-stock kitchens.

Negotiations between Lowe's and RSI continued to suffer and eventually broke down to the point where Lowe's threatened to take away RSI's vanity business if we didn't offer a drastic price reduction. But I knew RSI's prices were more than competitive, so we stood our ground.

As a result, Lowe's gave approximately seventy million dollars of our vanity business to one of our rivals. Realizing who the competitor was and its limitations, I knew Lowe's had just shot itself in the foot.

As I had expected, within a year, Lowe's could no longer put up with the new supplier's inability to perform. By that time, Lowe's had assigned a new bath-products buyer, Craig Webber. The good news for RSI was that he was not tainted by the previous buyer's negative rhetoric and decided to work with us to replace the non-performing vanity supplier.

We worked closely with Craig, and the result was a new program we put together for Lowe's. It was a hit; sales volume greatly outperformed our competitor's previous program. In a very short time, the $70 million of business grew to $120 million. In other words, while we initially lost $70 million, in the end, we earned that amount back plus another $50 million. Within the company, Craig became a hero and was eventually promoted to vice president, in part because he had the confidence and foresight to work with a supplier that knew exactly what would benefit his company.

The relationship we had with The Home Depot compared to our experience with Lowe's highlights the difference in the cultures of the two companies. During The Home Depot's early history, we never would have received the kind of treatment from a buyer as we did from the one at Lowe's. She had bad-mouthed and held a grudge against us.

Because of her anger, negotiating with the company became very difficult to the point where we lost a lot of business. And all this happened as a consequence of its incompetent and unengaged CEO not being interested in communicating with one of his big suppliers. As a result, one of Lowe's buyers made an emotionally driven decision not to do business with RSI.

Business can be a battlefield, and I have decades of stories and the mental scar tissue to prove it. Dealing with incompetent businesspeople gave me the toughness to get the job done. And, equally as important, I developed respect and admiration for those that treated others fairly. Their integrity served as examples for me to follow. For instance, negotiating with The Home Depot was not easy. Its founders were tough as nails, but they were always fair and didn't resort to politics, pettiness, or underhanded tactics. In these negotiations, most of the time, both RSI and our customers won, which is what good deals are about.

★ CHAPTER TEN

Sweet Revenge

"I think I can buy your desk for only eight hundred dollars," Ron Shewach, RSI's vice president of operations, told me over the phone. When at Perma-Bilt, I had originally paid more than ten thousand dollars for it, so this was an amazing bargain. Despite this, I told Ron to pass.

In keeping with our lean-and-mean concept, we presented a low-cost image to our customers. If our office looked like the Taj Mahal, customers would believe the price of the products they were purchasing had paid for the elaborate office space, so my operations had to be bare bones inside and out. We also did not have a receptionist. There was a phone in the lobby visitors could use to enter the office. Even our product catalogues were initially printed in black and white. Although the cost of four-color wasn't much more, I knew black and white made RSI look leaner and meaner.

When Ron Shewach called me about the desk, our conversation represented an RSI milestone. It was October 1990. Perma-Bilt Industries had gone bankrupt, and Ron was standing in its headquarters attending an auction. My instincts had proved right about the Leucadia–General Marble deal never closing. Once the company did its due diligence, it dropped out of the purchase, but not without first learning Perma-Bilt's corporate secrets.

After we began shipping to The Home Depot and Pay 'N Pak, we started taking orders from many other home centers. By capturing Perma-Bilt's market share, we expedited its inevitable demise. In fact, we outgrew the nine-thousand-square-foot space we rented from Arkay in less than three months and moved into a twenty-five-thousand-square-foot factory nearby.

Meanwhile, Perma-Bilt's bankruptcy had Ron Shewach on a bargain-hunting mission at the auctioning of its assets. Nearly everything was being sold at around ten cents on the dollar, including my fancy desk. The timing was perfect because RSI needed more equipment and factory space to support its expansion. Revenge reached one of many sweet peaks when RSI took over Perma-Bilt's former 120,000-square-foot headquarters, which is a building I owned in Torrance and was leasing to Perma-Bilt. We rearranged the factory to accommodate RSI's manufacturing process.

While RSI was doing well, I received unwelcomed news. Perma-Bilt's bankruptcy put its parent company in peril. The bank went after Austram, holding it responsible for Perma-Bilt's credit line. And because I was part owner of Perma-Bilt, Austram alleged I was a guarantor, so the company decided to sue me.

Over the next few months, my lawyers were performing their discovery by digging through Austram's internal memos. What surfaced provided a post-mortem account of Austram's deceitful ways. I learned that from the start of my negotiations to sell my 48.5 percent stake, Austram planned to push me out. John Marshall had decided to vote to give Austram absolute control. But it turned out that Austram's deceitful action reinforced my belief that adversity creates opportunity. Austram dropped its lawsuit based on its misleading and groundless case.

I focused all my attention on RSI. Growing at 35 percent per year required additional operating capital. Initially, I thought I could finance the company using my own money. But we were growing so fast I needed outside funding to manage the rapid expansion. For example, I had to order certain hardware components, such as hinges and drawer glides, from China. But before placing orders, I would need to submit letters of credit and obtain a bank line of credit.

I had known Larry Friedman, a vice president of Bank of America, for two decades. Our relationship went back to my Perma-Bilt days. I met with him about getting a credit line with his bank.

"With your good track record at Perma-Bilt and knowing you as well as I do, this isn't going to be an issue. I'll pass it by my credit committee. You'll get approved within the next thirty days," he said.

With customer orders to fill, waiting a month was not an option. I had to increase my parts inventory levels right away. I told Larry about my dilemma.

"You don't need to wait. Go ahead and order now. You'll get approved," he said.

So I placed my parts orders from China. As I was on standby for the bank to approve the credit line, I reached out to Larry periodically for updates. He reassured me that it was in process and approval was imminent.

While I was waiting, I attended an industry trade show in Chicago with one of my closest friends, Harold Kitay, who by this time was also on RSI's board of directors.

We were talking in my hotel room when I received the call from Larry. Bank of America had not approved my line of credit. My stomach sank.

"Larry, so what am I supposed to do now? You assured me it would happen and even told me to go ahead and place orders! I was depending on this. I have payroll to meet and suppliers to pay," I said.

"Don't pay your suppliers' invoices. They can wait," he said.

"That is totally unacceptable," I said.

I hung up the phone.

Harold had been listening to my end of the tense talk.

"What's going on?" he asked.

I recapped the mess.

"How much do you need, and when do you need it?" he asked.

His response was the last thing I expected to hear. I didn't know how to answer.

"Harold, that is not necessary. You do not have to do that," I said.

"You didn't answer my question," he said.

I told him the amount, which was around $900,000. In today's dollars, that would be around $1.8 million. In any case, I had no intention of asking him for it. But I told him I needed it ASAP.

"Done. Where should I send it?" he asked.

He was dead serious, and I could hardly believe it. I had just gotten off the phone wondering how I was going to make payroll and pay my suppliers. Only seconds later, my good friend was solving both problems.

"Harold, you want me to sign something to have it in writing?" I asked.

"No, you don't have to sign anything. You're my friend and my business associate. I trust you. Consider it done," he said.

I was speechless but snapped out of it and thanked him. After our conversation, Harold wired funds to RSI.

Once I returned to Los Angeles, I immediately went to work to secure a line of credit. With Larry and Bank of America out, I met with Security First National Bank. Although Larry's advice to place orders was terrible, I didn't completely blame him for giving it. Based on my solid history with the bank, we were both confident I would receive the credit line.

To my relief, within a week, Security First National Bank approved my credit line. At first, when I had accepted Harold's generous loan, I had planned to pay him back within a month. Now I was able to repay him much sooner.

Harold's friendship was rooted in integrity and trust with a healthy dose of humor and lasted until he passed away a few years ago of a rare heart condition.

Along with needing more cash to fuel our growth, RSI was again running out of room. In 1992, we doubled in size by moving from Torrance into a 240,000-square-foot space in La Mirada, California.

With Ron Shewach as our vice president of operations and Joe Varela as vice president of manufacturing, we never missed a step. Although

Ron with Harold Kitay, 1995.

every move we made was big and complicated, we made sure each was seamless to all our customers. Whether it meant working weekends or evenings or both, we did whatever it took to keep our customers from being negatively affected by the move. In fact, they never even noticed anything had changed. Thanks to Ron and Joe, we avoided many of the typical manufacturing pitfalls startups fall into. Most importantly, we always shipped products on time.

Embedded in RSI's philosophy, and the key to our success, was protecting the integrity of our manufacturing process as our business's most important asset—we would never allow any outside force to cause us to deviate from this model. By offering customers something our competitors couldn't, we had the negotiation leverage necessary to be able to stand our ground, which could be summed up by a steadfast commitment to saying the most basic expression in the English language.

"NO" became one of the key words in RSI's business vocabulary. But salespeople—and sometimes even our own sales executives—often have a passive mentality. This means they are very reluctant to use the word "no" because they think that could result in a lost sale. In other words, on occasion, our sales team inadvertently veered off course. But in RSI's case, a yes mindset could cause us to lose our competitive edge.

So in 1994, when Frank Xavier, who was doing a great job as vice president of sales, came into my office with a yes mindset, I had to set him straight.

"Builders Square wants to buy from us," he said. "But they want sixty-day terms."

The San Antonio–based home improvement retailer had many stores covering a large geographical area and represented a substantial amount of business for RSI.

But our terms were thirty days . . . not thirty-one or thirty-two and definitely not sixty days. Frank knew this. He was afraid, however, that saying no to Builders Square at this stage would lose the sale. So he replied to the company's sixty-day proposal with a "let me check," which led him to speak with me.

"So are you going to give them better terms than what our other good customers get?" I asked rhetorically. "And what happens when these customers find out we gave Builders Square sixty-day terms? How many times have I told you our policy will not be changed?"

Frank's response to them took away our negotiating leverage. The buyer now believed he could receive a concession from us.

"You fucked up," I told Frank. "Had you said no on the spot, they would have known our policy was cast in stone. But now, we are probably going to lose the deal. Never ever again ask me if I will do this."

While I was tough on Frank, my words in no way reflected a lack of respect for him. He was a great team member and a skilled salesman with a strong professional track record. People, including me, liked and trusted him. Unlike me, however, Frank avoided pissing people off. While upsetting others wasn't my goal, if it was an unavoidable consequence in order to move ahead with a decision I had to make, then so be it. Frank, on the other hand, always chose diplomacy over risking rattling nerves. But this time around with Builders Square, I didn't agree with this tactic.

In the end, I was right. Frank went back to Builders Square rejecting its sixty-day-term request. The buyer balked, and the company stayed with its current cabinet supplier. If we had said no from the start, I believe we would have closed the deal. However, almost a year later, Builders Square decided to buy from us, and we ended up selling to it on our credit terms.

Standing our ground with businesses, like Builders Square, protected the integrity of our low-cost position, and it also meant we had to be willing to walk away from a deal.

Celebrating RSI's first five-million-dollar month, 1994.

With RSI continuing to expand, around this time, in 1994, I began putting together a succession plan in order to make sure the organization maintained strong long-term leadership if, for whatever reason, I left or was not able to serve.

I knew the company had the potential for continued growth, but this would be largely contingent on RSI's leadership. In fact, we celebrated a corporate milestone by having our first five-million-dollar month. Thus I thought hard about who would eventually replace me as CEO. Up to this point, I had been completely hands-on, which meant I was involved in nearly every detail of the business. As the company grew, I delegated more and more responsibility to other team members.

In 1995, I appointed a new president. He had done a great job as the company CFO. Considering that I knew him well, the internal promotion seemed like the best move. Unfortunately, while he was an excellent CFO of a smaller RSI, his performance didn't successfully translate to his new role as a head of a rapidly expanding company. In fact, he struggled to the point where I had to fire him.

Now, I no longer had a succession plan. With the leadership position open, workplace politics came into play, which I have *zero* tolerance for.

RSI team at annual party, 1995, left to right: *Ron Shewach, Joe Varela, Alex Calabrese, and Bob Siegel.*

Alex Calabrese continued to impress me. Still under thirty years old, he had worked his way up from materials manager to vice president of operations in only four years. He learned fast and worked hard, and over time, as allies, we fought many battles together where he consistently showed his smarts and mental toughness. With his dedication and accomplishments, Alex would only continue to grow within the company, and all our executives knew this—including our vice president of sales; let's call him John.

While I did not know it at the time but would later learn in an unfortunate way, John wanted to fill RSI's leadership void. Because he and Alex had the same level of responsibility within different parts of the business, he viewed Alex as a rival in his quest to the top. Thus he was determined to take him out of the running.

During a one-on-one conversation John and I had one day, he expressed concern about Alex.

"I think Alex is anti-Semitic," John told me.

"Interesting. What makes you think that?" I asked.

"Because of all the remarks he makes."

"Oh, is that so?" I said.

I didn't express either interest or disinterest during our talk . . . at least outwardly. Inside, however, I had made my decision right away— John had to go.

Alex and I had worked closely together; he had been a loyal employee and colleague, so not for one second did I believe what John told me.

He had made a fatal mistake by lying to me to serve his own interests. RSI was better off without him, and I replaced him with another vice president of sales, Bob Siegel, in less than a year.

Trade shows can be important marketing events. During my Perma-Bilt days, we generated business through them, and with RSI, we continued to do so. As necessary as events such as the Kitchen & Bath Association Show and the National Hardware Show were, I also knew they had their limitations.

We would rent a booth for two or three days. But among the fifty thousand or so attendees walking the exhibit space, only around forty were our targets—and we knew exactly who they were. When they showed up to our booth, this could be our only opportunity to talk to them. But the conditions were not always ideal. A few of them could come at the same time, making it very difficult to have private conversations.

So in 1991, I asked myself, "Do we really need to spend the dollars for trade shows?"

I thought of taking advantage of the trade shows but focusing on only the key individuals I really needed to meet. And I thought I could do this by removing them and RSI from the event itself.

My plan was to rent a hotel room close to the convention center where I would display RSI's products. We would make an appointment with these important individuals to visit our hotel room. In addition to providing us privacy, the setting would add a level of exclusivity and prestige to the meeting.

When I asked the opinions of industry leaders I knew in the building product industry who weren't competitors, they all said the same thing, "Ron, you can't. RSI must have a presence at the show."

Their arguments weren't convincing, so I continued with my plan.

We reached out to the buyers we wanted to meet and were able to set up appointments with most of them. Rather than step into a loud booth crammed with other attendants, they arrived at a one-on-one meeting. We even offered them drinks. They could see our products, and we could answer their questions in a calm and quiet environment without being interrupted. And all of them appreciated the personal attention.

My non-trade-show/trade-show exhibit was a hit for two years . . . until the show sponsors caught wind of it. They made a deal with nearby hotels that prohibited companies like ours from setting up exhibits in their rooms. But knowing I had a successful trade show model in place, I refused to give up my plan. I decided to apply it to fit within the new rules I had to follow.

My plan was to rent a booth at the show, and in order to replicate the hotel-room environment, I would enclose our space within four walls and a door. And getting inside would be through invite only. RSI would offer an island of privacy in an otherwise crowded conventional hall. I pitched my plan to colleagues and industry acquaintances.

Again they told me, "You can't."

I asked why.

"Because you will piss off all the people that cannot get into the booth."

"I do not care about them. I only care about the ones we are going to let in," I said.

Without hearing any convincing objections, I went ahead.

Similar to the hotel room plan, the booth with four walls, each with a photo gallery on the outside of RSI's product line, worked just as well—and maybe even better because my guests didn't have to leave the convention hall to make their appointments.

In 1997, RSI was attending The Home Depot's annual product line review, where competing suppliers would negotiate for The Home Depot's business. This was its way of negotiating for lower prices.

These annual product line reviews are more like business boxing matches. Sometimes the buyers play clean, while other times they enlist dirty tactics. Suppliers are ready to duke it out for as many rounds as necessary, which can last into the early morning hours. For The Home Depot, this was the way to beat up its suppliers to get lower prices.

At the time, RSI was selling The Home Depot medicine and vanity cabinets for its western stores to the tune of around seventeen million dollars annually. General Marble was selling The Home Depot approximately fifty million dollars annually throughout the rest of the country. With our eyes set on winning a national contract, we planned to offer The Home Depot an enticing incentive: Stick to the same prices to maintain our current western footprint, and quote a 10 percent lower price if we could sell to The Home Depot countrywide. The extra volume of a national contract would enable RSI to maintain its margins, even with the reduced price.

My sales team, including Alex Calabrese, was attending the product line review in Tampa, Florida. As always, I was the long-distance cornerman on the West Coast, ready to take a call in the event my team needed my guidance.

Alex made RSI's pitch to John Wickes, The Home Depot's very tough buyer whom we had gone to battle with many times over the years. Then

Alex and his team left the room. Later, after John met with General Marble, he called our team back in and countered our offer.

"Your prices are not low enough for you to gain the national business. In order to keep your business in the West, you'll have to drop your current prices 10 percent," John told Alex.

He'd thrown us a curveball. While completely in line with John's underhanded style, his threat hadn't been what Alex and his team had expected. We thought if The Home Depot rejected our offer, we wouldn't gain a nationwide account but would at least keep the West because we knew our prices were less than General Marble's. This put Alex in a bind; the last thing he wanted to do was to return from Florida having lost *all* of The Home Depot. He left the room and phoned me.

Alex and I talked strategy. With The Home Depot, we knew that we couldn't budge on price because, once we did, the retailer's demands would never stop. He returned to the meeting room.

"I meant what I said," John told Alex, "that to keep our business, you will have to cut your price 10 percent."

"As I told you, John, we would need the extra volume of your national business to be able to lower our price 10 percent," Alex said.

John held his position.

In the meantime, John had also been negotiating with General Marble. He told the company that it would have to cut its prices by 30 percent to be competitive with RSI and keep The Home Depot's business. Unbeknownst to General Marble, this was 15 percent under our 10 percent lower quote. General Marble, desperate to close the deal, agreed.

We understood that refusing to play along with John's sneaky ways could result in losing our business with The Home Depot. At the same time, I knew General Marble would lose money selling at those low prices.

At around 2:00 a.m. Eastern Standard Time, Alex phoned me and broke the bad news. It wasn't what I wanted to hear, but I knew he and his team had lost a hard fight playing by rules that upheld RSI's values. For Alex to say no to John wasn't easy, but he had done the right thing, even if it hurt RSI's bottom line in the short term.

"I am proud of you," I told him.

The next day, I received a call from Bill Hamlin, The Home Depot's vice president of merchandising and John's superior.

"I hate to see you lose this business. But you guys screwed up," he said.

After the deal between RSI and The Home Depot had collapsed, John described to Bill how we had an opportunity to keep The Home Depot's business. But he failed to tell Bill how he was manipulating our price quotations, and I let Bill know this. Bill valued RSI and wanted us to continue being The Home Depot's supplier. He suggested that John and I speak so we could salvage our business.

The next day, John phoned me. He explained how the negotiations went south and it was my team's fault that we lost the business.

"John, I already know what happened. And what you are telling me is not the truth," I said.

"So are you calling me a liar?" John asked.

"Yes and no. Yes, you are a liar. But no, you are not just a liar. You are a fucking liar," I said and abruptly hung up the phone.

A few days later, Bill phoned me. After figuring out what took place during the product line review, he realized RSI had been treated unfairly.

"Look, this is going to work out. You're not going to lose this business," he told me.

RSI maintained the western state business without lowering the price 10 percent. This was the same deal we had during the start of the original product line review.

The Home Depot typically will give suppliers around four months to prepare their factories to fulfill orders for new business, and General Marble was now selling at the low prices it had agreed to. This was the beginning of the end of General Marble. A few months after the company was awarded The Home Depot business and as a result of it selling at crazy-low prices, I found out General Marble was in financial trouble—bad news spreads like a raging fire within the industry gossip mill.

In its effort to not lose business, General Marble chased our prices. Three years before the product line review, its pursuit of market dominance motivated the company to hire manufacturing consultants and open plants in North Carolina.

All the consultants did was complicate General Marble's manufacturing operation by making it far less flexible. And John Wickes, by beating General Marble's prices down, was very instrumental in destroying it—that's the one thing we can thank John for.

Our costs were 30 percent lower than anybody's in the industry, so I knew the only way for General Marble to meet RSI's prices would be for it to lose money. Meanwhile, RSI continued to steamroll over other competitors through our lean-and-mean approach that no one could match.

General Marble's big mistake left it vulnerable. By the fall of 1997, I was ready for my next move. My plan was to buy it, and I made our competitor an offer it couldn't refuse.

I spoke with my team, including RSI's lawyer, Gary Singer, whom we had engaged three years prior and was with the firm O'Melveny and Myers. I ran my plan past him. As any reasonable attorney would conclude, he thought I was nuts for offering to buy with no due diligence. Actually, it didn't require a law degree to think that; anybody with an ounce of business sense would question whether I had thoroughly thought things through.

"Are you sure you want to do that?" he asked, surprised that an experienced businessman like me would even consider such a risky move.

"I am only looking for protection against any liabilities," I said.

Then I explained the simple logic behind what seemed nuts. I just wanted to buy General Marble for The Home Depot business it had. In other words, for what I was estimating to be approximately less than twenty million dollars of General Marble's net book value, RSI would gain nearly fifty million in new business . . . what a no-brainer deal!

I didn't intend to keep operating General Marble's factories; once we took over, RSI already had the capacity to fulfill all our competitor's orders. So I didn't care what General Marble's costs were. Based on RSI's manufacturing expenses, I was certain how much profit we would make once we took on General Marble's sales to The Home Depot. Provided we had the proper legal protection in place, in my eyes I saw absolutely no downside.

Once Gary understood my rationale, the decision made sense to him. That didn't mean he dropped all his concerns. But he went to work putting together the deal according to my terms.

I then reached out to Tom Mara, who was the executive vice president of Leucadia, which owned General Marble. In addition to other companies under the Leucadia umbrella, Tom oversaw General Marble and was thus its decision-maker. I phoned him in his office. We exchanged greetings, and I then went straight to the point.

"Tom, I would like to buy General Marble," I said.

"Well, you're a competitor," he said.

Knowing how much trouble the company was in, I was confident Tom was desperate for solutions. At the same time, he was well aware—as I was when General Marble supposedly wanted to buy Perma-Bilt—of the risks associated with accepting such an offer from a rival.

"Why would I let you come in here and see what we're doing?" He was referring to us performing due diligence at General Marble.

"Tom, I understand and respect that," I said.

And then I made my proposal.

"What I am talking about here is a deal where I do not even have to see your factories. I do not have to see your financial statements either. I will buy your company sight unseen at its net book value so you will not incur any book losses. And we will not perform any due diligence. The only thing I care about is any ongoing liabilities, such as environmental, employee, and financial. I just need the representations and warranties of those liabilities. The bottom line is I am mainly interested in buying your assets. Rather than wait sixty or ninety days, I do not see why we could not close the deal in thirty."

"But what about your financial statements? I'd like to see those," he responded.

I had no intention of disclosing my margins to him . . . or to anyone else for that matter. General Marble had already done this before with

Perma-Bilt. If the deal didn't close, I didn't want General Marble knowing RSI's trade secrets.

"Tell you what. I will get a letter from the bank representing I can write a check. After the deal has closed, I will show you our financials," I said.

Tom told me that General Marble's net book value was approximately seventeen million dollars, which was less than I had estimated. If I was willing to close a transaction in thirty days for that amount, he would agree to meet the following week with our attorneys and structure the deal.

Gary and I flew to Chicago. We met Tom in the law office of General Marble's attorneys. Tom, our lawyers, and I put together a simple deal that afternoon, and then he and I wrapped up the meeting with a handshake. Had Gary had any doubts about what seemed like my crazy plan prior to our meeting in Chicago, all of them were put to rest by the time we boarded the flight back to California.

Over the next few weeks, our lawyers went to work on the purchase agreements. Less than a month later, we were ready to sign the paperwork.

Tom and General Marble's attorneys flew to California, and we closed the purchase in O'Melveny's Newport Beach office, right across the street from RSI's headquarters. This meant RSI began 1998 with fifty million more dollars of The Home Depot's business.

As promised when we initially spoke on the phone, once the deal was signed, I handed Tom RSI's statements.

He compared RSI's performance with General Marble's. A combination of surprise and embarrassment turned his face red.

"Ron, what RSI's done is unbelievable. Here we were losing 20 percent . . . and you're making 25 percent. That goddamn consultant and our CEO, what a bunch of idiots we had working with us!" he said.

After the deal closed, we toured General Marble's facilities. Once we received the company's financials, our speculations were confirmed. Just as I had thought, in General Marble's desperate bid to win The Home Depot's business, it had dug its own grave. In fact, prior to the fourth quarter of 1997, which was when General Marble had begun shipping its products to The Home Depot at the lower price it had agreed upon, General Marble had posted a loss of about two million dollars, an annualized eight-million-dollar loss. The company could not have survived burning through cash at that rate.

With the purchase done, I put behind me a hard-fought war. It began when Austram took over Perma-Bilt. The next battle took place when Austram and John Marshall went against my wishes. They allowed Joe Steinburg, president of Leucadia, parent company of General Marble, to take Perma-Bilt's trade secrets under the pretense of General Marble performing due diligence. And the war ended when General Marble declared defeat and was sold to RSI.

The good news was that it all came to a close amicably. In fact, Tom and I completed the deal with mutual respect, so much so that in the months and years ahead, Tom put a couple of people in contact with me to discuss other business opportunities.

Ten years after my meeting with Joe Steinberg that ended with me threatening to throw him out the window and marked my reentry into the cabinet-manufacturing business, I decided to make amends with Joe, Leucadia's president. I phoned him.

"I am calling to apologize for the way I acted when we met ten years ago," I said.

I explained that during our tense meeting, when he told me about General Marble's plans to buy Perma-Bilt, I had felt like a wounded animal being attacked.

Joe, like Tom, responded like a gentleman.

"Ron, you don't need to apologize. And, by the way, congratulations. You've built a great business," he said.

After I had made peace with my former Leucadia–General Marble adversaries, RSI now needed to ramp up its production to be able to service the approximately fifty million dollars in newly acquired business with The Home Depot.

I phoned Bill Hamlin, The Home Depot's vice-president of merchandising, and told him we had to meet as soon as possible. Fortunately, Bill happened to be in Southern California at the time. We had a friendly relationship, so I invited him to my home in Newport Beach.

We sat in my living room, and I started off by telling him I had good and bad news.

"Which do you want to hear first?" I asked.

"Of course the bad news," he said.

"Bill, as you know, we have just acquired General Marble. And we have to raise the price on General Marble's medicine cabinets by 17 percent, which will be the same price that RSI quoted for your national medicine cabinet business," I said.

At that point, I wondered if I should run for cover behind one of my couches. His face flushed, clearly annoyed with my bad news.

"Okay, what's the good news?" he asked.

"We are going to lower your prices on General Marble's vanity line, which, as you know, represents over 70 percent of your total purchases," I said.

"By how much?" he asked.

"Between 25 and 55 percent, depending on which products we are talking about. So what that means is some of the vanities you are retailing for around four hundred dollars, you will now be able to retail for around two hundred dollars. You will most likely sell many, many more of them as a result," I said.

Bill went from annoyed to gratified since my bad news really wasn't that bad—in fact, it was really good for The Home Depot. He also understood why we had to raise General Marble's medicine cabinet prices.

At the end of our meeting, I let Bill know that chasing RSI's prices is what led to General Marble's demise.

Similarly, by dropping the prices of vanity cabinets and cultured marble tops and manufacturing them on a national scale, RSI made these products more affordable, and the market increased in size as a result—exactly what I had told Bill when we had met at my house. Our relentlessly lean-and-mean business model enabled us to maintain high margins and sell at prices below the competition's. In short order, our products sold like crazy within home centers throughout the United States. This was a triple win: for consumers, retail home centers, and RSI.

★ CHAPTER ELEVEN
RSI's Private Equity History

I n 1993, with my marriage to my second wife, Eleanor, going sideways, I needed to protect my financial interests. Between when we tied the knot in 1980 to our divorce, my career shifted from heading one company, Perma-Bilt, to another, RSI. When I founded RSI in 1989, I was confident that the focused, lean-and-mean business plan would succeed. But success is relative, and back then I never imagined the magnitude of RSI's success.

My divorce attorney recommended I get a professional valuation of RSI. I reached out to Jim Freedman, founder of Barrington Associates, which was an investment banking firm specializing in mergers and acquisitions, capital markets, and strategic advising.

I hired the firm to give a professional opinion of the market value of RSI. Once Barrington Associates completed its work, I used the valuation to negotiate a divorce settlement. Despite being initially upset that Eleanor had gone to such extremes with her choice of divorce lawyers, she and I reached a reasonable and amicable final settlement.

Now that we had overcome that major hurdle, I needed liquidity to pay her off. Jim Freedman introduced me to Marty Jelenko, a managing director of Bankers Trust Private Equity Group. Jim had deep knowledge of RSI's potential and knew Marty would be interested in the company. He and I met in my La Mirada office.

Marty had done his homework and was impressed with RSI. He proposed a valuation of the company based on its earnings over the last twelve months. Bankers Trust offered to pay $15.1 million for a share of RSI, to be determined based on RSI's last twelve months of EBITDA as of June 30. Before shaking hands to seal the deal, I was fully honest with Marty about my present and future intentions:

"I am bringing you in to obtain liquidity to pay off my settlement with my ex-wife and have some cash left over. But I am going to be looking to sell RSI in the near future. If and when that happens, I will be taking you out."

He accepted, and we agreed on the deal on April 1, 1994. As of the signing, Bankers Trust's $15.1 million investment would have represented a 35 percent stake in the company based upon the trailing twelve months ending March 31. Being confident that April, May, and June were going to be strong, I used the company's value on the trailing twelve months ending June 30 rather than March 31, and Bankers Trust agreed.

As I anticipated, RSI showed strong sales and earnings in the three months after the deal closed. The trailing twelve months' earnings as of June 30 were more than the ones of March 31. Because of this, Bankers Trust's $15.1 million investment gave it an 18 percent share in RSI, instead of a 35 percent share. Despite the lower percentage, Bankers Trust would still earn a substantial return on its investment.

After the Bankers Trust deal closed in April 1994, and just as I had told Marty during our meeting, I moved forward with my plan to find an investor that could put in far more than Bankers Trust. Once again, I enlisted the help of Jim Freedman. I asked him to begin an auction process to sell all or most of RSI. His hard work and skill resulted in four serious offers: Kohler Company, Masco Corporation, and two private equity investors, Butler Capital and Saunders Karp & Megrue (SKM), which was the highest bidder.

SKM would purchase a 75 percent stake, which meant RSI senior executives and I would receive $145 million and retain 25 percent of the company. SKM would fund the purchase through two channels: first, borrowing $70 million by leveraging RSI, and second, investing $75 million of its own cash.

Wow! The deal would deliver more cash than I could have ever imagined when I started RSI. Plus, I had the potential to make even more if I continued running the company.

I agreed to move forward with the deal. As a result, SKM's lawyers went to work preparing the buy-sell agreement, which called for the standard reps and warranties and gave SKM the ability to sell RSI after five years.

In addition, I negotiated a two-year non-compete that I would give to RSI's new buyer when SKM sold the company. At the time, the two-year non-compete didn't seem to be an issue for me because I was sixty years old and believed I would retire at sixty-five.

Now that SKM would be buying most of RSI, I had to break the news to Marty. I phoned him and told him about RSI's future; he was completely surprised.

"As we discussed before, I am going to have to take Bankers Trust out now," I said.

"RSI's doing great. Why do you have to take us out now?" he asked.

"I told you I was going to sell the company as soon as possible."

"Yeah, but I never imagined you'd do it so soon. Can't we stay in?"

"No, Marty, because that was the deal we made," I said.

"Ron, you're right," he said.

While I felt terrible for breaking the bad news, I knew RSI had been very good for Bankers Trust. On November 1, 1994, RSI bought back Bankers Trust's shares. By the end of our deal, its initial $15.1 million investment had grown to $17.6 million after only seven months, representing a 28 percent annualized return.

Meanwhile, I began having cold feet about the SKM deal that seemed like the payout of a lifetime. The reason behind my doubts was simple. Back then, debt scared me. So the thought of running a company with seventy million dollars of it turned my stomach into knots. And then there was the part about giving up control. The bottom line was I knew SKM wouldn't take the news well, but I needed to back out.

In November, SKM had completed its due diligence, and the deal would be signed the next day. While the timing couldn't have been worse, I had to come clean about my decision. When I arrived at the office the day before SKM would take control of RSI, I phoned my lawyer, Ron Lazoff. I explained my change of heart.

We then got Jim Freedman on a conference call. I told Jim to inform SKM's John Megrue that I wouldn't go through with the deal as is. Jim remained silent for several seconds.

"Are you fucking crazy?" Jim said. "This is the worst thing to do at the last minute. John will lose his shit. . . . You call him. I won't."

At least Jim agreed to be on the call.

When John answered the phone, I took a deep breath and then told him I couldn't go through with it.

Jim was right. . . . John lost his shit.

"You can't do this!" he said. "We invested over a million in law-yers and accountants who performed our due diligence, let alone three months of our time."

In my most humble and guilt-ridden tone, I explained the reasons behind my decision. While the financial windfall RSI senior executives and I would experience was tempting, in the end, the debt and giving up control were deal breakers for me.

The last thing John wanted was for this whole thing to unravel. He reassured me the debt was nothing to be concerned about and SKM would give me full control of RSI as long as the company continued to perform well. But despite his best efforts, I stood my ground. Naturally, John was not happy. Fortunately for me, however, he accepted it like a gentleman.

A few days later, John had cooled off. Once he got over the shock from my decision, he still wanted to keep the deal alive. He presented revised terms that had major concessions he hoped would address my concerns.

SKM would agree to drop its 75 percent position in RSI to 44 percent. As a result, we would not have to overleverage the company, and RSI would have less debt. The tradeoff was that we would receive $75 million instead of $145 million. Despite the lower payout, the revised SKM arrangement felt right to me. We agreed to move forward with it.

Backing out of the initial deal was really tough to do, but I was glad I made the decision. The revised arrangement allowed RSI to stick to its lean-and-mean values, and the company continued to increase its sales and earnings.

For the first two years, SKM sent its hard-working and talented partner John Clark to attend RSI's quarterly board of directors meetings. But as a result of RSI's success and strong leadership, SKM no longer felt a need to keep an eye on the company, so its representatives stopped attending the meetings. In fact, over the next twenty-six months, we hardly ever heard from SKM.

The previous five years had been profitable with RSI continuing to grow. Alex Calabrese had taken over as president and COO and was doing an incredible job. So at that time, I wasn't ready to sell the company. However, I was bound by the agreement, which gave SKM the right to exit after five years, and in late 1999, John Megrue requested we put RSI up for sale.

I contacted Jim Freedman to spearhead the deal. As before, Kohler Company and Masco Corporation were potential buyers. But this time around, RSI's success meant their offers were much bigger.

The major glitch for me was that both companies required I enter into a five-year non-compete—this was a deal breaker for me. With SKM, I had negotiated a two-year non-compete, and because RSI's future was brighter than ever, I didn't want to sell the company. I also had no desire to retire or stay out of the business. In fact, I figured I could work another couple of decades, so I didn't want to be shut out of competing in that industry. Thus, I refused to agree to a five-year non-compete. But neither Kohler nor Masco would budge from its position.

John Megrue of SKM became furious with me.

"You can't do this! You're a fundamental part of the company, so no one will buy RSI if they think you'd go out and compete against them in two years. Plus you agreed to let us sell it after five years."

"I agreed you could sell RSI, but I did not say you could sell me!" I said.

With that conversation, the battle lines had been drawn. I refused to back down. John tried to convince Masco to buy, but without a five-year non-compete from me, it was not interested.

Desperate to close the deal, John attempted to bribe Alex Calabrese. He wasn't bound to a non-compete and was a key to the company's success, so John tried to convince him to enter into one. He knew Alex and I had developed an inseparable and wonderful relationship and was thereby asking him to betray me. Alex flatly refused.

I gave a lot of thought to where we stood with Saunders Karp & Megrue. I had always had a great relationship with the firm, and especially with John, until this conflict. His attempt to bribe Alex didn't help. In order to keep the peace and resolve this impasse, I decided I would be open to compromising on the non-compete issue.

At that time, RSI was just beginning to get into the kitchen cabinet business. At our relatively small size, we could not even be considered a competitor to Masco or any other kitchen cabinet manufacturer. And so, I called John and told him that Alex and I were going to travel to Detroit to meet with Ray Kennedy, Masco's CEO, and tell him I would give him a five-year non-compete on bath cabinets provided the non-compete would not cover kitchen cabinets. At that meeting, Ray Kennedy agreed.

"That's only fair because you really aren't in the kitchen cabinet business," he told Alex and me.

So, a few days later, we received a letter of intent from Masco to purchase RSI Home Products, which called for a five-year non-compete covering bathroom medicine cabinets and vanities only.

I advised John that it looked like RSI would be sold to Masco and that we were just now waiting to receive the company's draft of a definitive purchase and sale agreement.

While the first draft had other issues I was sure our lawyers could work out, it echoed the non-compete clause we had agreed to in the letter of intent. Our lawyers sent their comments back to Masco's lawyers, and Masco's second draft was consistent with the first with respect to the non-compete.

Our lawyers sent the second draft back with some minor changes, but the third draft came back with a *different* non-compete that precluded us from competing in kitchen cabinets; I completely objected to this.

I immediately called Ray Kennedy and told him what happened, that perhaps his lawyers had changed the non-compete without him knowing about it. Ray said he had never agreed to let us compete in kitchen cabinets.

Incensed, I challenged him. I told him what we had agreed to at the meeting in his office and this was reflected in the letter of intent and the first and second drafts, and at the eleventh hour and fifty-ninth minute, he changed what he had agreed to.

"Are you calling me a liar?" Ray said.

"Yes," I said.

"You can't call me a liar!" he said.

"Well then, I will call you a fucking liar. And this conversation is over!" I said.

I abruptly hung up on him.

Right after, I called John Megrue. I told him about the talk I just had.

"The deal is over, and I am not going to sell to people like that," I said.

Just as I thought he would, John flipped out.

A few days after my tense exchange with Ray Kennedy, I spoke to a private equity executive, as well as to someone who had sold his company to Masco. These people told me it was a typical Masco–Ray Kennedy tactic, changing terms of the deal at the eleventh hour, when the seller is already feeling the dollars he will receive from selling the company. Well, I wasn't that kind of seller. I refused to succumb to its underhanded ways. We never did sell RSI to Masco, and I've never ever regretted that decision. Over the following years, RSI expanded and grew its kitchen cabinet line and actually wound up driving Masco and others out of in-stock kitchens at the home centers. (This was yet another example of sweet revenge.)

What happened points to what I've learned about the importance of maintaining integrity, no matter what. Throughout my career, a few people have tried to screw me. Very few succeeded. And even among those that initially did, they eventually got theirs, which is why I'm a firm believer in the saying, "What goes around, comes around." Integrity will always prevail in the end, and that's one of the main reasons it's the value I stand by most.

In fact, I like to think the *I* in RSI also stands for *integrity* because that's how the company operates. The same could not have been said for Masco; at the time, "integrity" could never have been part of its name because the company didn't have much and this showed in its culture.

Meanwhile, the investment fund SKM used to buy its position at RSI was in its sixth year, which meant the fund needed to pay off its investors. But because the relationship between John Megrue and me had soured, SKM flew its senior partner, Jim Saunders, to California to negotiate with me. We didn't reach an agreement.

In order to resolve the deadlock between SKM and RSI, I reached out to the man whose negotiation skill I had counted on before. I asked Jim Freedman to broker a deal. As I had hoped, he came through.

We agreed that RSI would pay $132.5 million for SKM's 44 percent share of RSI. That meant SKM would receive almost four times its investment of $35 million. Apparently, however, that wasn't good enough for John Megrue, and he attempted to re-trade our agreement. He sent John Clark to let me know this.

Under orders from his boss, John Clark flew to meet us at RSI's Newport Beach headquarters where he asked us to pay more. Based on what I knew of him, I'm sure he was making the request only because his boss had put him up to it. And based on what he knew of me, I'm sure he wasn't thrilled with doing John's bidding. But because he was the messenger, John Clark bore the brunt of my response. I listened to the increased amount John Megrue was proposing and could not believe that SKM was trying to change the agreement we had made.

"Absolutely not! No way!" I told John Clark.

Knowing that my anger was flaring, I forced the meeting to come to a quick close before I completely lost it. I reached for his briefcase, gathered his paperwork, and shoved both at him. And then I escorted him out of our office.

The final amount remained at the $132.5 million we had originally agreed upon. On June 1, 2000, the deal closed, and SKM and RSI parted ways. SKM may have been bitter about not getting what it wanted in the end, but the bottom line was that SKM made a very profitable decision investing in RSI.

I believe John Megrue, despite creating so much unnecessary conflict, may still hold a grudge against me. Meanwhile, John Clark has moved on to another private equity firm. He held himself to high ethical standards, which I respect him for, and I'm certain the feeling is mutual.

Less than two years after we bought out SKM, we negotiated a private equity deal with Lehman Brothers Holdings. On February 22, 2002, the global financial services firm took a minority position in RSI. We then bought it out five years later in 2007. Lehman's investment yielded the firm a 22 percent annual return.

A little over a year later, we did another private equity deal with Onex Corporation. On September 30, 2008, Onex's investment gave it a 50 percent share of RSI. Considering the time frame, Onex made a great investment in RSI.

The financial crisis began in 2007 and blew apart September 15, 2008, with the collapse of the aforementioned Lehman Brothers. Fifteen days later, Onex was half-owner of RSI.

Over the next almost four and a half years, people across the world were struggling to regain financial security after tremendous losses in the stock market. In particular, the US kitchen cabinet industry took a major hit during the deep, deep recession. Yet RSI gave a 48 percent return, annualized at 10 percent, to Onex. While the industry as a whole had shrunk by over 60 percent, RSI sales were off less than 25 percent. And even better for RSI, as a result of our substantial purchasing leverage, as well as low fixed overhead, our costs came down significantly, which allowed us to actually grow margins during the Great Recession.

Going back to 1993, with my divorce from Ellie that initially triggered RSI's search for private equity, I now had the marriage behind me. I was an eligible bachelor surrounded by friends who wanted to set me up on dates. One of these matchmakers was Sandi. She was the wife of Allan Liebert, who was my very close friend. Allan and I had a lot in common, so when we first met, we developed an instant friendship that deepened over the years.

Left to right: *Ron and Ellie, Sandi and Allan Liebert, Avalon, 1988.*

Throughout my marriage to Ellie, we spent lots of time with Allan and Sandi. We had dinner at each other's homes, our children became friends, and we spent holidays together, even traveling as couples.

Sadly, in 1990, Allan died of colon cancer. Ellie and I were still married at the time, and we provided Sandi as much support as we could. A couple of years after Allan's death, Sandi began dating. She would often ask Ellie and me to meet the men in her life so we could vet them and provide her our opinions.

After Ellie and I divorced in 1993, Sandi and I maintained our friendship. Now that I was single, she would try to set me up with some of her girlfriends. At the time, I was not interested because I already had a girlfriend in Newport Beach.

Meanwhile, I continued to look for potential partners for Sandi. My girlfriend thought she had the perfect match for her. I made the introduction, but in the end, Sandi didn't feel any spark with the guy. During this time, the romance with the woman I was dating had fizzled, and Sandi and I continued our platonic friendship.

We continued seeing each other, including on the tennis court, and eventually our friendship evolved into a romance. On the one hand, this made sense: We had been close friends for decades, shared the same values, and were both single and interested in marriage. I was also drawn to her loving, energetic, and fun-loving personality. On the other hand, if you had asked either of us prior to becoming a couple if we would fall in love with each other, we would have laughed and said you were nuts.

Ron and Sandi on a glider ride in Hawaii, 1995.

While our common interests and attraction connected us emotionally, the 1994 Northridge earthquake really brought us together. Sandi was living in Encino, which is a neighborhood close to the earthquake's epicenter. As a result, her house sustained damage, and she couldn't stay in it. Meanwhile, I was living in a rented house in Newport Beach. At the time, we had already been spending weekends together, so I told her, "Since you cannot stay in your house, why not just move in with me?" From that point, we were living together.

Ron and Sandi in the Caribbean, 1996.

Gigi Thomas, a real estate agent who was looking for a house for me to buy in Newport Beach became a friend of mine. She knew Sandi and was very fond of her. Gigi wasn't Jewish but appreciated our culture. She would ask me to teach her Yiddish words. One of them was "bashert," which means "destiny" or "it's meant to be."

"Ron, it was bashert. This earthquake brought you and Sandi together," she said.

I laughed and said jokingly, "So God created this earthquake that killed all these people and caused all this terrible destruction just so Sandi and I could get together? He must *really* think we're something special!"

Maybe we were—and still are—something special because Sandi and I married on April 28, 1996, at our house in a small ceremony where we were surrounded by immediate family members and my close friends Harold and Pearl Kitay.

Because Sandi and I had built most of our lives in Los Angeles's San

Fernando Valley, where we both had raised our respective families, our move to Newport Beach signaled a fresh start. With the exception of my lawyer, Ron Lazoff, who lived in Newport Beach, all our friends were in the Los Angeles area. Thanks to Sandi's outgoing personality, we involved ourselves in the Orange County community where, over time, we made many really great friends.

Sandi and I have a history that spans decades, starting as friends and evolving into husband and wife. I love her very much and feel very fortunate to have such a wonderful wife for, as of this writing, twenty-five years.

Ron and Sandi, 2018.

★ CHAPTER TWELVE

RSI's Secret Sauce

In 2005, we decided to apply RSI's winning culture and operating efficiencies to other building material products.

With Alex's phenomenal track record at RSI, we moved him out of his role of running the company's day-to-day operations so he could be in a position to lead our expansion plans. This meant we had to find another president and CEO to replace Alex. For this major task, we decided to look outside the company.

Given how much RSI's rise was a result of our culture that was unique within the building-products industry, we knew we needed someone who both respected and would uphold it.

We worked with an executive recruiter in a four-month-long search and selected a candidate. Let's call him Jim Jones. He had an impressive background, including a twenty-year career running one of General Electric's appliance divisions.

Before we brought him on board, we hammered in the importance of our culture, the integrity of our low-cost manufacturing process that we upheld no matter what, and the importance we placed on saying no—even at the cost of losing business—if doing so was necessary to stick to our values.

"I love your business philosophy. I'll enhance it and live by it," Jim said.

That reassurance, combined with how we believed RSI would benefit from Jim's career at GE, convinced us to bring him on. With a new leader at RSI, Alex and I took a hands-off approach and allowed him to do his job.

While entrusting highly qualified people to fulfill their duties without micromanaging has served me well throughout my career as a business leader, my strategy hasn't always worked. And this was a perfect example.

Without us knowing it at the time, Jim was saying one thing yet doing another: He promised he would enhance and protect RSI's culture, but we later learned that just thirty days into his new job he began making changes that we would have never allowed in a million years.

One major misstep he made was to begin to implement GE's operating philosophy into our operating procedures . . . big mistake! Our success didn't come from running like GE. In fact, its values were totally different from ours. His reasoning was there was no way RSI could continue to maintain our high margins while at the same time growing the company. And he thought doing things the GE way was best.

While we were not initially aware of Jim's unacceptable conduct, within months, the series of changes he made snowballed into a size that made Alex and me take notice. That and what we began to hear from our executive team. For instance, Alex and I learned about a leadership conference Jim had sent them to.

We then reviewed the invoices for the event. Upon further investigation, we found out the weekend conference took place in Salt Lake City. Alex and I were appalled to see what the conference was teaching our executives; it was the complete opposite of RSI's philosophy!

It was as radical as a philosophy conference working to convert Christians into atheists. This event, combined with all the other big changes we found out about, made me furious with Jim. But I was probably even angrier at my executive team. Shouldn't they have known better? I was shocked they didn't tell us right away, the moment they realized the new CEO was compromising RSI's culture.

On the one hand, I understood why they kept quiet. Jim was in charge, so it was their job to follow orders. This put them in a difficult position: Do they stick with what the head of the company tells them, even if they disagree, or essentially undermine his leadership by coming to Alex or me?

On the other hand, the executive team had been part of RSI's rise from the beginning. We had worked as a tight-knit operation, a business family really, and they knew that RSI's culture was the formula to its success. Compromising on *any* of our values would cause us to lose our unrivaled competitive edge.

Eventually, they did the right thing (but not nearly as fast or as thoroughly as I expected them to) by giving us enough small bits of information for us to realize we needed to step in. And step in we did . . . or more like storm in!

I met with Jim, and under no uncertain terms, I made my point clear: "You are fired," I said.

Jim didn't see it coming, and I was fine with that. In my mind, he was already a low point in RSI's past, and I was ready to move on without him. We had *a lot* of work ahead of us, after all, to undo the mess he had created. So six months after he was hired, he was gone, and Alex had to step back in and run the company.

Our next move was to let the executive team know our disappointment: "The minute you knew things were going sideways, you should have told us. But you did not out of fear. Well . . . shame on you! Hell, you should have been willing to break down Alex's door if that was what you needed to do to tell us what was going on. Our company has always been about doing what is best for the business, no matter the consequences!" I said.

Part of Jim's termination included confiscating his corporate computer. When we reviewed it, all our concerns were confirmed. He was emailing Alex and me messages telling us what we wanted to hear: that he would uphold RSI's tradition of saying no to our customers, such as The Home Depot, if saying yes meant compromising on our values. For example, he vowed he would not let The Home Depot knock our prices down.

Meanwhile, he was going behind our backs telling our sales team to give our customers all kinds of concessions Alex and I would have never allowed. In other words, he was saying yes, under circumstances Alex and I would have flatly said no.

Once Alex was in charge again, he dug deeply into what Jim had done, and we couldn't believe how much RSI's culture had eroded under Jim's brief watch. Far from laziness, his single-minded effort to implement his vision of how the company should be run and the culture it should have was actually undoing what made RSI great. Fortunately, the damage could be fixed. But we needed to change course right away.

Prior to Jim's brief tenure, RSI's executive team had worked tirelessly to make RSI into the country's largest bathroom vanity, cultured marble countertop, and medicine cabinet manufacturers. We refused to budge even an inch if it threated our relentless pursuit of being the leanest and meanest company in our industry. In our hard work to blow away the competition, even the smallest change for the worse was absolutely unacceptable.

With Alex back in his leadership position, he went about making sure we'd never repeat the same mistake again—what a wake-up call! Continual improvement meant always learning from our missteps.

Jim's effort to make us less like RSI and more like GE could have been far worse had we not cut him off when we did. So as much as I viewed his tenure as a big mistake, in the end, our team gave Alex and me the information we needed to get to the bottom of what was going on and take corrective measures within only months. In the case of other companies, years can go by before a bad leader is given the boot. Imagine how much damage is done, often irreversible, under those circumstances.

Alex and I realized RSI's culture was embedded in every aspect of our business. But it wasn't explicitly defined in writing. This complacency is what allowed Jim to implement what would have otherwise been obvious to everyone as a move against our way of doing business. Never again! We would take this negative blip in RSI's history and turn it to our advantage.

Business culture is like religion. One of the most important roles of regular attendance in houses of worship is to keep reminding attendees of the beliefs they commit to uphold.

What RSI was missing was a clear-as-day credo, a set of values that would remind our employees, on a regular basis, of the tenets that guide us. So in 2005, we went about creating them. They are as follows:

Recognize and Respect Our Roots.
Always remember that RSI is—first and foremost—a manufacturing company. Every management decision should protect, enhance, or strengthen efficiency and productivity.

Stand Up for What You Believe.
Disagreement—even when it's heated—ensures that alternative solutions are always heard and considered. When offered respectfully and professionally, differing points of view help, not hurt, our business.

Educate and Advocate.
Remind customers that everything RSI does for them has value. Without RSI's prudent policies, operating costs could skyrocket and result in higher prices and longer manufacturing lead times.

Be Vigilant about Cost Control.
Focus on cutting costs every day. Recognize the long-term value of continuously reducing costs, even if only by a few basis points at a time.

It's OK to Be Tough.
Be uncompromising about standing up for and enforcing our policies. They reward us with superior margins that fuel innovation and growth.

Speak Up.
There is no such thing as a crazy idea or a ridiculous question at RSI. Share your ideas. Ask your questions. That's how we learn, innovate, and improve.

Live and Learn.
We all make mistakes. When your turn comes, admit it and accept responsibility. But most importantly, learn from the error—and try not to repeat it.

Adversity Creates Opportunity. Really.
Embrace challenges and realize that they create opportunity. RSI's existence and success resulted from adverse circumstances.

Lead Decisively.
Leaders make difficult choices. Measure all options against what you know is best for the company and then act. It's impossible to lead effectively from atop a fence.

Honor Your Commitments.
Make commitments carefully and thoughtfully. Being true to your word demonstrates integrity and strength of character, both for you and our company.

Cost Awareness.
Knowing the cost of every SKU we manufacture is critical, as is the accuracy of those costs. Beat the costing of new products to death. There is no such thing as overkill here.

Create an Atmosphere of Professionalism and Respect.
Treat everyone with whom you come into contact—employees, customers, and vendors—with dignity and respect. Even when you are tough or play hardball, do so with integrity.

There's Strength in Simplicity.
Implement only those policies and processes that keep manufacturing as easy and uncomplicated as possible.

Know the Competition.
As good as we are, we must always be one step ahead of our competitors. We have to constantly challenge ourselves and our processes. In today's competitive landscape, it's all about playing hardball—and playing to win.

Succession.
A key indicator of your effectiveness as a manager is how well you develop your direct reports. Have you identified your successor? Are you doing everything possible to educate, train, and encourage these individuals? Moreover, are your people developing their people? If not, now's the time to start.

Give Customers 100% All Day, Every Day.
Do whatever it takes to make quality a top priority and to provide perfect service every day. Our goal: 100% fill rates with 100% on-time shipments. Eliminate the concept of "backorders" from your thinking.

And then we distilled these to the acronym VICO: value in, cost out. We made big VICO banners and hung them all over our factories. Now everyone knew what RSI was about. Whether it was the executive team or the factory workers, following the tenets empowered everyone to speak up if there was a better way to run and continuously improve RSI. From the assembly lines, men and women came up with ideas. For example, a factory worker would tell his supervisor, "Gee, if we moved this piece of machinery here, instead of where it is now, we could save us time in the assembly operation." And if it made sense, you bet that the suggestion would be implemented.

We introduced regular meetings with our executives and supervisors, driving home what defined us. They weren't long and tedious ones. Rather, they lasted five, maybe ten minutes: brief and no-nonsense reminders of who we were and how we ran RSI.

The impact of the tenets that guided RSI was made loud and clear during my travels to Asia. In 2005, I was in Shanghai on vacation. As an endlessly curious company owner, which speaks to the tenets "live and learn" and "know the competition," I was interested in touring some cabinet factories.

While I had traveled to China before, it was my first visit to Shanghai. I was amazed at the metropolis's massive size (boasting then a population of more than twenty million), its breathtaking skyline, and how rapidly it adapted cutting-edge technology on a grand scale not seen anywhere else in the world.

With a gigantic manufacturing sector, I wanted to see some of the area's bathroom and kitchen cabinet factories. Our guide arranged for us to meet with local business owners and take factory tours of companies selling products in the United States.

I recall one particular factory making vanity cabinets we toured that had 363 employees. Based on RSI's lean-and-mean system, I calculated that we were able to turn out the same number of cabinets with fewer than eighty people. After visiting a few factories in China and seeing how inefficient they were, we even considered exporting higher price-point products to China.

So when people ask, "How do you compete with China with its low wages?" my reply doesn't require a brain surgeon to figure it out. In fact, throughout my history at RSI, I've been asked, "How do you do it?" countless times.

For example, over the years, RSI has interviewed twenty or so potential private equity firms and two strategic buyers, Masco and Kohler, which were competitors that would have merged RSI into their companies. Every time their teams reviewed our management presentation and dug deep within our company, they would always want to know the magic or secret sauce behind our accomplishments.

But the answer was there was no secret sauce; nothing of the sort could be discovered by walking through our factories. You needed to look no further than the tenets to see how we worked. That's not to say the tenets are easy to live by.

At RSI, they manifested in the combination of a thousand efforts—big and small. Major examples of these were the attention to detail we put into our products and services, inspiring everyone at RSI to perform at his or her best, and our amazing leadership.

From RSI's start, I constantly looked for what could be improved and acted upon it right away to make it better. And then I pushed myself to see if I could find even more room for improvement. This obsession with continual improvement flowed from me and into the company's management, fully becoming part of our business's DNA. And as RSI grew, it grew stronger.

So if someone were to come in and tell us, "Wow! You're perfect," our reply would be, "No way. We are not perfect. While we can never be perfect, we can always strive toward it and become better as a result."

RSI's eye toward self-criticism was both encouraged and rewarded. I recall one of our plant managers, John Shivley, brought us a proposal to rearrange our assembly production lines to make them more efficient.

Although the upgrade would cost around three hundred thousand dollars, his suggestion made sense, so we implemented his plan.

When it was done, I went on a plant tour. The factory was humming as efficiently as I could have imagined; I was really happy to see the obvious improvements John had envisioned that resulted in the increased material flow. I was so thankful for his commitment to doing his job so well. In fact, within less than a year, the investment paid for itself. This was a prime example of upholding VICO.

"Really amazing, John! I am so proud," I told him.

"Ron, thank you . . . really. But we can do so much better than this," he said.

I was baffled. It all looked so great.

"How?" I asked.

And then he told me.

Many, many bosses would have taken his words as bad news. "Christ, you just got me to spend three hundred thousand dollars changing this plant, and now you're saying we need to spend even more money? Why didn't you make those changes in the first place?"

But I would have never said that because I know better. The reason John hadn't suggested implementing the improvements he now saw as necessary was they occur on a progression. When you're on a course of constant improvement, once you reach a milestone, you're now ready to catapult to the next one. Your goal is to always do better. The higher you move up, however, the more refined your process becomes, which makes it tougher to find areas in which to get better. But because we believed our process was never-ending, we were relentless in our quest for perfection. That's why, rather than get upset with John, I appreciated his insistence to keep improving and making sure we were running as lean and efficiently as possible.

John's actions were examples of the tenets "speak up," "cost awareness," and "stand up for what you believe." For RSI's long-term success, I needed to listen and reward team members, like John, for their dedication to excellence, which reflected the tenet, "create an atmosphere of professionalism and respect."

"Get with Alex and put your plan together. Present it to me, and if it makes sense, we will do it," I said.

Another instance of our commitment to continual improvement was our monthly product meetings where we used value engineering. This means to bring production costs down, sell a product for less as a result, and thereby bring greater value to the consumer, which represented the tenets "be vigilant about cost control," "give customers 100 percent all day, every day," and "cost awareness."

Realizing its benefits, we value-engineered the shit out of our products. We assembled a team comprising the production and engineering departments. We looked at the products that had the highest sales volume. Then we dissected them and analyzed all the parts.

The overarching challenge we placed before ourselves was to reduce cost while not compromising quality. To accomplish this goal, we answered questions such as: "What can we do different?" "Will changing a dimension on a certain part improve the performance while cutting cost?" "Can we standardize it with other products?" Going to great lengths to find solutions to these questions is an example of "be vigilant about cost control."

In all the years we had product meetings, we always found a way to cut costs, however small, while maintaining quality.

Value engineering and John's example are two of many that show the strength of RSI's culture, which appears in the tenet "recognize and respect our roots." And we upheld the tenet "live and learn" by pushing ourselves to find a better way to do something and then saw how we could improve upon what we initially thought was best.

Although outsiders appreciated what we had accomplished, some had doubts that we could maintain our perfectionist culture over the long term.

This was demonstrated in an exchange I had in 1994 when Masco was considering acquiring RSI. The global home improvement and building-products giant had underneath it companies that were household names in cabinets (which meant its companies were RSI competitors), paint (such as Behr), plumbing (Delta, Hansgrohe, Peerless, and others), windows, and more.

At the time, Alan Krauss was Masco's group president. He toured our plant and reviewed our management presentation.

"Ron, your operating expenses are 9.5 percent of sales. You should be commended for that low number. And I think you can achieve the growth you've projected for RSI, but based on my experience, I can tell you that as you get larger, it's going to take more people to run your company. So that 9.5 percent will increase to around 14 to 15 percent," he said.

Our business plan was to grow RSI from around seventy-five million dollars to two hundred million dollars in sales over the next two to three years.

"So in other words," I said, "in two to three years, as our company grows, our operating expenses could be about the same percentage of sales as Masco's."

"That's right."

In his eyes, 14 to 15 percent would make us as good as Masco. I let him know right away why I took issue with his point: Yes, growing from seventy-five to two-hundred fifty million dollars would require more people, but our operating costs (covering administration, sales, and marketing) as a percentage of sales would go down because we would increase only our variable costs such as materials and labor.

In other words, despite our growth, we wouldn't need to hire one more CEO, one more president, and one more CFO. We wouldn't need to hire one more vice president of sales, finance, and marketing. While we would need to add more lower-level positions for sure, the number of big-ticket salary-earners would remain the same.

"In fact, my bet is that when we reach that level of sales, our operating expenses will be *lower than* 9.5 percent," I said.

"I absolutely don't agree with you," he said.

"Okay, that is your opinion," I said.

I'm sure as the group president of the kitchen and bath cabinet division of a company many, many times bigger than ours, Alan thought he was smarter than we were. And I'm sure he thought I was being short-sighted, naïve, and maybe even arrogant by outright disagreeing with him. Instead, in my mind, his division was complacent and we never were.

While we were in disagreement, it didn't require resolution because, in the end, we did the private equity deal with SKM and not Masco.

All my predictions proved right. By 2000, RSI was doing over $250 million in sales *and* our operating expenses went down, to the tune of around 8.5 percent—a significant feat according to Alan, who was convinced that the exact opposite was inevitable. That year, when SKM tried to sell RSI, Masco once again took interest in our company. Like the first time around, the executives, including Alan, toured our plant and reviewed our management presentation. And just like the first time around, Alan was impressed.

"Ron, you should be commended on your 8.5 percent operating expenses. But, as you know, as your company grows, your operating expenses will grow right along with it," he said.

With those words, I realized he didn't remember our previous conversation.

"Also, you're turning your inventory seven times a year—that's a great number. But you can't expect to keep that pace up as you grow," he added.

RSI had leveraged economies of scale (as companies grow in size, they are able to produce at a lower per unit price) to an extent that even the group president of a huge company with a worldwide footprint and many, many times larger than ours couldn't believe was sustainable.

In fact, Masco's kitchen and bath cabinet business alone brought in around 1.5 billion dollars in sales a year. While Alan was convinced that operating expenses would go up and inventory turnover would go down, RSI had done the exact opposite for both since we had last debated the topic. I thought it was time to remind Alan of this.

"Remember when you were here in 1994? You told me that RSI's operating expenses of 9.5 percent would increase to around 14 to 15 percent, which would make us as good as Masco. Well, thank God we never got in Masco's league because now our operating expenses are just a little over 8 percent. I told you then that they would go down, which is exactly what happened.

"And I'm telling you now as RSI continues growing, our operating expenses will go down, not up, even more—as hard as that may be for you to believe. And as far as our inventory turns are concerned, you think seven times is great, and you expect it only to go down from there. But to be honest, I think it sucks. And you can count on the fact that I'm all over our operations team to bring that up to closer to eight turns!"

Alan's face turned red as he suddenly recalled our conversation a few years back. In the end, we didn't do a deal with Masco this time either. This would mark my second time rebuffing its attempts to acquire RSI.

A David-versus-Goliath comparison seems inevitable, given Masco's twelve-billion-dollar size that made it the industry's largest player in home products manufacturing. The conglomerate was a roll-up of many companies that, in and of themselves, were big. Meanwhile, RSI was far smaller but continually taking market share from our gigantic rival through our zero tolerance of mediocrity, poor performance, and politics.

While RSI was battling with its customers, The Home Depot and Lowe's, there's no question that we were fighting multiple campaigns. Masco was not about to concede defeat to its much smaller competitor. And at RSI, we never looked at anything we did as sacred, which pushed us to constantly and relentlessly improve.

Here was RSI, fully aware of our size and realizing how much room we had to improve and grow. And then there was Masco, a giant company whose mindset seemed like, "No one is better than us," which resulted in its complacent leaders. Alan was doubting RSI's ability to keep improving because Masco's culture was the polar opposite of ours. If Masco's attitude was, "We're good enough," RSI's was, "While we are proud of where we are, we can always get better."

You bet that if I was RSI's competitor and saw how it was run, I'd be losing sleep thinking, "If they can make these kinds of margins, why can't we?" And I'd be putting constant pressure on everyone within the company to do whatever was necessary to improve as fast as possible. This speaks to RSI's culture.

While our rivals big and small became comfortable with a "business as usual" attitude that justified their actions, we were relentlessly increasing efficiency, lowering costs, and staying above the competition. Outdoing our competitors had pushed us to pursue excellence. But I would say that beating our own performance had always been an equal motivator. And RSI had my relentless self-criticism to thank for that.

★ CHAPTER THIRTEEN
Losing Mom and Dad

Without question, my own inner critic far surpasses that of any outside voices. I've always been tough on myself. You'll see this in all aspects of my life. From running RSI to playing on the baseball field when I was a kid, I was never ever satisfied with any past accomplishment. After all, one major screw-up in the present would erase any prior feats in an instant. In this regard, I guess that means I owe my parents for a lot of RSI's success.

I learned well from my mom and dad and their constant critiques. They could definitely be hard on me, but I also realize they were products of their environments. They grew up during difficult times and within families that suffered under ruthless Russian and Western European anti-Semitism.

In my dad's case, I hand it to him for starting his career as a janitor in a sheet metal factory and eventually climbing his way up to launch Perma-Bilt—that required immense courage and hard work.

While he wanted me to take over his business, I know he struggled listening to his adult son questioning everything, telling him where the company he built needed to be improved, and challenging how he ran it. My dad was a smart man, and hearing criticism from me was not easy. And looking back, I realize I could have been more diplomatic during our tense conversations.

Had I not been so ambitious and outspoken and been more passive, I am sure we would have avoided some of the conflicts we had. While I could not imagine putting my ambition aside for the sake of improving our relationship—that just would not be me—I could have handled the day-and-night differences between our personalities better.

But beyond the natural tendency for parents to not want to take orders from their children, my dad, in general did not like confrontation. And here I was, someone who never shied away from it if necessary. He continued with this tendency till his last days.

When he was diagnosed with multiple myeloma in the mid-1980s, his doctor asked me, "Do you want me to tell him or do you want to?"

"I will take care of it," I said.

The moment after I broke the terrible news, we never talked about his cancer again. He just could not bring himself to acknowledge his disease, so the C-word was never mentioned.

Despite his fears of death, my dad actually lived four years beyond the initial diagnosis. Almost every Sunday, I would go over to his house and make him breakfast.

Decades before he was diagnosed with cancer, he had become some-what of a health nut giving up all the foods he loved so much. Previously, he ate corned beef, pastrami, and hot dogs . . . but no more. Every morning, he drank hot water with lemon. He replaced the cured meats with cooked vegetables and bland chicken.

One day toward the end of his life, I made my usual round at the deli to get him breakfast, which would be smoked salmon and bagels. To that I would add scrambled eggs and onions I would cook for him.

I stood in front of the long deli case and looked at all the things my dad used to love to eat. With his life nearly at its end, I wanted to provide him some comfort in the form of food, and I would refuse to take no for an answer.

When I arrived at his house, I said to him, "Dad, I brought you some corned beef."

"You know I don't eat that shit," he said.

"You know what, Dad? What do you think? Is it going to kill you? You are dying, okay? So eat the fucking corned beef. You used to love it," I said.

I had not planned on saying what I did, but afterwards, I was glad I finally brought up the topic none of us talked about. As much as most of him wanted to resist, he gave in and ate his sandwich. Or more like he devoured it.

"Oh my God, so good, so good!" he said.

He was terrified of the disease taking over his body. But the joy on his face as he chomped through the sandwich made me feel good—for a moment the comfort food gave him relief from his biggest fears.

Contrast the feeling of satisfaction I had that day with how I felt at his funeral. After he passed, my mom and I met with the rabbi who would perform his memorial service.

"So tell me things about Sidney," he said.

I have to admit that focusing only on the positive, which I knew we needed to do, was a tall order coming from a son who had had such a tough relationship with his dad. But my mother and I did stay positive. One aspect we agreed on was his sense of humor and charm. The way he could make people laugh was memorable and truly a wonderful quality.

The day of the service, I was filled with sadness. My dad was gone, and I had to face it. I was prepared to cry at the funeral.

Once the rabbi gave his eulogy, however, I realized I had predicted my response wrong. The rabbi covered Perma-Bilt's history:

"And then Ron joined Sidney's company. At Perma-Bilt, they were a great father-and-son team. They got along well. As a result, they ran a successful business together."

I could not believe the words coming out of the man's mouth.

"What you are saying could not be farther from the truth!" I thought. "We locked horns constantly, to the point where I often did not respect his business judgment and where I threatened to leave."

I did not expect the eulogy to be a tell-all about our difficult relationship, but I also did not think the rabbi would describe it so inaccurately.

By doing so, he cut my mourning at the service short. Although his description was completely outside reality, hearing it reminded me of the truth, which was how different my dad and I were.

After my dad's passing, my mom stayed in their home as a widow for the next several years.

By October 2005, my mother's health had deteriorated to the point where she was placed under hospice care in her Encino home.

I would call her three to four times a week to check up on her. She would usually pick up the phone with a jovial "Hello!". . . eager to speak to the person on the other end.

But ever one to say the glass was half-empty, after I said, "Hi, Mom. How are you?" she would realize it was me, and her voice would suddenly take a gloomy tone.

"Oh. Oh. I'm okay," she would say with a slight groan in her voice.

This was her way of letting me know I should ask how she was doing so she could complain. After several years of her initial bright and cheery greeting turning to negative and gloomy in order to get my sympathy, I had had enough of it. I thought about what do and decided to let her know about my plan during one of our calls. As always, she was ready to complain.

"Mom, I want to call you, and I want to talk to you often. But I just want to hear more positive stuff. I do not want to hear constant negativity because it does not make me feel good. So I am telling you right now, the next time I call and you do that, then I am going to wait another week to call you. And if you do it again, I will wait two weeks. And if you do it again, it will be three weeks."

After that conversation, our phone calls became much more pleasant. I did not even have to wait a week to call her.

Despite her overall negativity, I realized how much she loved and cared for me. Her constant criticism was definitely part of her personality but also her way of trying to help improve me.

She had been in hospice for three months when I took a weeklong trip to Europe. I returned home and phoned her. We had a brief conversation where I told her I had arrived back safely.

Fifteen minutes later, I received a call from my mom's caregiver. She told me my mom had just passed. Filled with sadness, I also felt grateful I had had a chance to speak with her right before she died. I also realized that she had waited for me. She wanted to know her son had made it home safely before passing on.

CHAPTER FOURTEEN

Tell Me Why I Can't: Taking What I Learned to a Different Industry

Eight Feet

For years and years, that was the standard ceiling height for a house. In fact, I grew up with eight-foot ceilings, and so did nearly everyone else I knew. But over time, in California and eventually in most other states, ceiling heights grew to nine feet.

So, using my contacts with homebuilders, including many prominent ones, I asked them a simple question:

"Why can't we make homes with eight-foot ceilings?"

The reply I heard was a variation of a phrase I detest:

"Because you can't."

Ever since I can remember, I have asked why. And throughout my life, *because you can't* has often been a red flag—fighting words—to stir me into finding out why I can't or even if I really can.

Back when I was a kid, I frustrated my zayde as I peppered him with questions as he *tried* to tell me the story of Noah's ark. My poor grandpa eventually gave up because his pain-in-the-ass grandson couldn't stop doubting the whole hard-to-believe Bible story.

My challenging the credibility of Noah's ark as a child turned into "why can't we split the company stock?" during my early days at Perma-Bilt and then "why can't we compete with Asia?" when I launched RSI.

And whenever my why was answered with "because you can't" and followed up by nothing or some explanation that didn't convince me . . . well, that was basically my call to action. Now, my job was to prove the naysayer wrong.

I am fully in favor of seeking contrarian opinion. If the answer to my question or the point someone makes proves my idea wrong, I am the first to welcome that information. I will change course without thinking twice about it. But "because you can't" without backup evidence is a lazy and completely insufficient answer. And when it came to the basic questions I had about the homebuilding industry, so many of my *whys* were met with the phrase that only fueled my search for real answers.

In 2007, I embarked on a new business venture. At the time, as president and CEO of RSI, Alex Calabrese was doing an incredible job, which meant that as chairman, I did not have to be involved in the company's day-to-day operations.

Overall, if I'm confident I hired the right person, my management style is hands-off. But if someone on my team asks me for advice or help, I will provide it. When Alex was first appointed president in 1996, we would meet several times a day where he would lean on me for advice. But as the years passed, Alex took on more responsibility and grew into his role. As a result, we would speak less often. I was only involved in policy, long-range planning, hiring, and high-level decisions. Eventually, Alex was running the company's day-to-day operations and required very little input from me.

While my responsibilities at RSI grew less, at seventy-three years young, I was far from ready to retire. So I began looking for other business opportunities, ones that would allow me to tap into the same creative side that inspired me to start RSI after Austram's CEO told Perma-Bilt employees that "the days of Ron Simon are over." RSI went on to be an American success story, which resulted in sweet revenge.

During my years at RSI, homebuilders subcontracted us to supply them with our products, as well as their installation. Working closely with the homebuilders, I gained an in-depth look at the industry. I saw its strengths and weaknesses.

When compared to manufacturing and distributing products, as RSI did for The Home Depot and Lowe's, being a subcontractor to home-builders is far more complicated. This is mostly because builders have to deal with multiple external variables they have little control over.

For example, because they are not manufacturers, they depend on the trades to build their houses. Having to rely on subcontractors who sometimes do not perform to adequate standards can result in higher costs, poorer quality, and multiple bottlenecks that create delays in com-pleting projects.

Next, builders were making money on land values, not on the houses themselves, and the more the homes sold for, the greater profit the build-ers could realize. This revenue model is fundamentally flawed. In my mind, houses should be treated as any other consumer product. In other words, just as RSI successfully did in the cabinet industry, manufacturers and suppliers should constantly be motivated to find ways to lower costs, enhance value, and make their products more affordable overall.

Contrast that with other US manufacturers, such as the auto indus-try. For decades, domestic car manufacturers had little motivation to improve quality and sell at more affordable prices. They had a firm grip on the market and were making tons of money. But then with fierce foreign competition (at first from Japan), domestic automakers had to shape up or risk losing market share. US companies increased efficiency and reliability and provided greater value to consumers.

If it weren't for foreign competition, US-made cars would probably cost twice as much as they do today and be of lower quality. In other words, consumers would have suffered at the hands of complacent car makers.

Sadly, in the case of homes, Americans are crying out for more affordable housing, and builders just are not responding. A degree of complacency plagues the industry. If you backed into an airplane propeller and survived, would you back into it again? That's what I see many homebuilders doing. The US government bailed the industry out during the Great Crash of 2008 by refunding income taxes homebuilders paid over the prior five years.

So what do homebuilders do? Instead of focusing on lowering costs, they raise prices to take advantage of market demand. Then when an economic downturn comes along, such as a recession—whammo!—market demand decreases and land values plummet. Now developers are stuck with a huge leveraged investment—in other words, land they overpaid for. This cycle has happened repeatedly.

Realizing the weaknesses of the industry, my entrepreneurial side kicked into high gear.

Based on my understanding of the manufacturing and homebuilding industries, I came to an exciting conclusion: Done right, two-thirds of the current on-site labor to build entry-level houses could be reduced, and the time to build homes could be shortened to less than thirty days, compared to 120-plus days, which was the industry standard.

At the same time, experience had taught me to stick with what I knew. Otherwise, the pitfalls of delving into areas outside my knowledge base could spell trouble.

I realized that homebuilding had two phases: One I understood, and the other was outside my expertise.

Building the house, called vertical construction in the business, was the area I thought could be greatly improved. I believed building a house was no different from manufacturing any other product. In other words, all components should be engineered to exact dimensions so they can all come together in an assembly operation.

Land entitlement and development, on the other hand, which includes the grading of the land and adding the infrastructure necessary to produce a finished lot ready for the house construction, were outside my experience. I would defer those aspects to experts.

I set out to prove that the homebuilding industry could offer quality, affordable housing. In short, just as RSI had made positive disruptions in kitchen and vanity cabinets, we would do something similar in the homebuilding industry. If successful, the change could be revolutionary.

To receive expert feedback, I shared my ideas with other builders. I went straight to the top. Thanks to RSI being a supplier to the largest public homebuilding companies, I knew many of the executives. The input I received was far from promising and instead was very frustrating. Most of them told me my concept was impossible to achieve.

But when I asked for reasons they thought I was crazy, none of them provided me with logical explanations that took apart my idea. I heard a series of "because you can't." To me this was a sign of how much they were entrenched in the status quo, hadn't thought of new solutions to old problems, and didn't like to be challenged.

One conversation even wound up damaging a friendship. When I questioned my friend about the practices of the homebuilding industry, he said, "Ron, are you trying to tell me that, as a successful homebuilder, I don't know what I'm doing?"

"No, that is not what I am saying. I am just asking questions. I do not have the answers, and that is why I am seeking your input. So . . . tell me why it can't be done."

Some of his responses just didn't make sense to me. Meanwhile, he became visibly upset with my questioning.

"Ron, you don't know what the fuck you're doing. You *think* you can do these things. Well, you can't!" he said.

That was the end of that conversation. And, unfortunately, our friendship began to drift apart.

The naysaying (and especially the "you can't!" part), combined with the lack of any clear evidence that demonstrated my plan was crazy or stupid, only further fueled my ambitions. In my mind, being told you can't do something basically because it has never been done before is a great reason to move forward.

In order to execute my plan, I knew I needed to bring on experienced homebuilders because I was new to the industry. I engaged Kevin Crook, who had a fine reputation as an architect to several homebuilders. I also brought on a construction manager, Todd Richardson, whom a home-building subcontractor recommended to me.

Todd had an impressive resume. He had been responsible for build-ing approximately one thousand homes a year in Southern California as a construction manager for Centex, a major homebuilder later bought out by Pulte.

When we met, I told him bluntly, "If you do not believe you can build a two-thousand-square-foot, one- or two-story house in less than twenty days, you should not accept this position."

He shot right back.

"With the right controls and processes, I know I can," he said.

"Then why is it taking you 120 days now?" I asked.

He gave me all the reasons. And they were legitimate, a major one being that homebuilders were not providing consumers standardized products. For instance, they would offer upgrades and give buyers multiple options—even ones that would alter room sizes and complicate design and construction. Such customization created homebuilding bottlenecks. And the opposite is true as well: Standardization creates manufacturing efficiency.

Having brought on the first key players of my team, RSI Con-struction was born. We immediately went to work and developed two home designs: One was 1,624 square feet, and the other was 1,964. Both matched and in some cases exceeded the quality of comparable entry-level homes being built.

Around this time, in 2007, I was introduced to and became friendly with Miguel Pulido, mayor of Santa Ana in Orange County. I told Miguel about my plans to launch an affordable housing program. The details I provided caught his attention.

The price point and home specs I proposed were what Miguel knew most of the city's hard-working residents could afford and desperately needed. RSI Construction would finally make single-family residences affordable to his constituents. Our prices were within the budget of residents earning approximately 60 percent of the average income for the area.

By the end of our conversation, he was begging me to launch my venture in his city. He wanted Santa Ana to be an example of something that could spark other communities to encourage affordable home construction.

Miguel offered two empty lots on South Orange Avenue. The city would contribute the lots at no cost to RSI Construction if we would sell the homes for $125,000 and $140,000, respectively—a remarkably low price for Orange County where the cheapest houses hovered around $300,000 at the time.

While Miguel had his constituents' best interests at heart, running a business, especially homebuilding, has taught me that you're always going to encounter obstacles—no matter how promising your plan. Some neighbors near the proposed development came down with a case of NIMBY (not in my back yard). The main argument against the construction went along the lines of "it will attract the wrong kind of people to live in the neighborhood." That thought infuriates me.

Nurses, police officers, firefighters, and other upstanding citizens could not afford to buy houses in many areas where they work. Are they the wrong kind of people? Why should someone object to having any of these fine men and women living next door? I would welcome hard-working, responsible people in my own neighborhood any day.

But the NIMBY complaints that plague all California were beyond my control. Unfortunately, between neighbor grumbling and other red tape we had to cut through, it took over six months for the contract between the city and RSI Construction to be negotiated and signed. And eventually the deal would have probably died had it not been for Miguel championing this project and ramrodding it through.

After nine months of difficult negotiation, the plans, following the construction methods we had developed, were finally approved. RSI Construction committed to complete the work within fifteen days after the foundations were finished.

So the race began. From the start, our every move was scrutinized and documented—the city had a photographer visiting and capturing images three to four times a day during the vertical construction.

Despite RSI Construction being examined under a microscope, I didn't lose any sleep over it because my hiring decision proved right. Todd Richardson did a great job developing an effective construction plan, and he continued his impeccable work managing the entire project.

By the fourteenth day, both houses were completed, and sod was being laid on the front lawns. And by this time, the construction drew public attention. LA's ABC Channel 7 featured the project in a TV report.

Because of the high demand for these two homes, the city held a lottery to ensure fairness in selecting the homeowners. The lottery had eligibility requirements, including salaries that could not exceed 60 percent of the annual wage and proof of residency in Santa Ana. The lucky winners were two wonderful, hard-working families that otherwise could not afford a home in Santa Ana.

As of 2021, the original owners still live in their homes and have maintained them at a very high level—even more so than their neighbors, whose NIMBYism nearly killed the project. So much for their worries that the houses would attract "the wrong kind of people."

With the success of RSI Construction's affordable housing model, we were contacted by the mayor of Buena Park, also in Orange County, who explained his city had nine vacant lots. He wanted us to repeat what we had done in Santa Ana. Similar to that project, Buena Park offered to discount the cost of the vacant lots, which enabled us to sell the houses in a lottery at affordable prices. The city would not incur any out-of-pocket expenses. Typically, municipalities would discount the price of the lot, as well as provide cash subsidies, so the builders would not lose money.

Having a very low land cost allowed us to sell the homes at affordable prices. Because RSI Construction was able to build houses for far less than any other homebuilder, Buena Park now had affordable houses without offering subsidies at the city's expense.

Similar to the positive outcome in Santa Ana, the Buena Park homes had a happy ending. Residents that could otherwise not afford to buy in their community became owners of these quality homes.

RSI Construction had proven that quality housing could be built in less than thirty days. With our model proven, we set our sights on a commercial project. In order to create the lots for the houses, we would need to first purchase and develop the land beneath them. But because we had no experience in land development and the related construction, we needed to recruit a president who had an extensive homebuilding background.

We found a former regional president of a large homebuilder to potentially fill the role. As I had done with Todd Richardson, I asked the prospective president if he thought our vertical process was achievable. He was excited and expressed belief in our construction model.

We then purchased enough land in Menifee, California, to build 103 homes. While Menifee was growing, the land values were still relatively low. With the project moving forward, we created a brand name, "The New House by RSI."

For our process to succeed, we needed to drastically depart from the traditional way homebuilders market and build their products. Typically, model homes are built on-site, so buyers can see both the house and where it will be located. In order to cut costs, we took a different approach.

We constructed our model homes in a yard adjacent to our factory, which was approximately thirty miles away. So rather than see the model homes on-site, buyers would make an appointment and travel to our factory. This would cost less by centralizing the sales process; these models could serve many communities we could develop in the future.

Next, our homes were engineered with eight-foot-high ceilings, instead of the nine feet that had become the standard throughout California. This enabled our prefabricated wall panels to fit flat on a truck bed, resulting in lower freight and material costs.

The result of the home's overall design was superior construction quality at a price around twenty thousand dollars less than the competition's.

We even included features as standard items that were typically upgrades, such as granite countertops, choice of cabinet finishes, and stainless-steel kitchen appliances.

But the new president disagreed with our perspective.

"No one will drive thirty miles to see off-site models. And no one will buy a house with eight-foot ceilings," he said, effectively rejecting The New House's strategy.

"Why not?" I asked.

"Because everyone else is offering nine-foot ceilings and their model homes are on-site," he said.

"Yeah, but we are the only ones to offer them at prices that most people can afford. Think about it. . . . Would you rather live in a house with eight-foot ceilings or no house at all?" I asked.

My logic made sense and his didn't. Why were nine-foot ceilings so important? I wasn't over seven feet tall like LA Laker's legend Kareem Abdul Jabbar, and neither were our homebuyers.

Unfortunately, this was just the beginning of our disagreements. Despite the president's protests, we built them the way we had proposed.

In the final analysis, our president was an extremely capable home-builder with a long series of career successes. But he was stuck in the same status quo mindset in regard to home marketing and building that I was determined to break away from. I knew the status quo was failing to answer one of the country's most pressing questions: How do we provide homes to a population desperately in need of affordable housing?

Just as our smaller Santa Ana and Buena Park projects had done, when we scaled up our plan, it met my expectations as well. In fact, the Menifee project proved to be so successful that a development by KB Homes, one of the nation's largest homebuilders, couldn't compete. It shuttered its project located about two miles away from ours.

In addition, a sales manager from Richmond American, which was also constructing homes near us, ended up buying one of ours. Today our homes, with their eight-foot ceilings, have comparable resale values to others in the Menifee area with nine-foot ceilings.

Two affordable houses built by RSI Construction in Santa Ana, 2009.

Next, we built seventy-seven houses in Beaumont and twenty-six in San Jacinto, California. We achieved an unrivaled twenty-eight-day vertical construction cycle. When it came time to sell, market conditions could not have been worse. These houses, as well as the ones in Menifee, were being built in the midst of an economic slump. They came on the market in 2008 and 2009 during the Great Recession, which was brought on in large part by the collapse of the residential real estate bubble.

While residential construction projects throughout the country were put on hold or had gone belly-up, because of our homes' tremendous value, they were all sold before even finished. To more than prove our point, even though the country was facing tough economic times, the demand for affordable houses was still great, and we were providing people homes to move into.

As I gained more and more experience in the home-construction industry, I continued to maintain my stance of not participating in the land development business and owning thousands of lots. In fact, my position became stronger as a result of what I viewed were the downsides of large-scale land development. Typically, you need to have a huge land inventory, and its value rises and falls with the economy. Homebuilders who accumulate land to build on can be hit hard during economic recessions because its value can decrease significantly. Furthermore, we needed to focus on refining our home-construction process, which required razor-sharp dedication.

An alternative would have been to build in planned communities constructed on land that very large developers had purchased, entitled, and finished, which they, in turn, sold to homebuilders. The benefit of this plan was that we wouldn't need land development expertise.

The downside was the many design restrictions and pricing requirements the homebuilders had to follow to participate in these projects. Furthermore, because our products would be out of line with most of these planned communities due to their lower prices and the simplicity of their design, that road wasn't available to us.

As a result, we came up with the idea of building replacement houses for homeowners living in very old properties. We initially focused our efforts in Orange County because it was in our corporate backyard. That way, we could be closely involved with each phase of the construction. We determined we could promise homeowners a fixed price and an unrivaled ninety-day construction period, which included the demo of the old house, preparing the lot for new construction, and completion of the new house.

Over the next year, we bought around forty teardown houses in Costa Mesa, California. We replaced them with new homes, sticking to our ninety-day commitment.

We then started building houses for people who owned older homes in Orange and LA Counties. Combined, we built over one hundred of these houses and again proved that we could stick to our tight timeline.

While our construction process worked, we could not scale it up due to factors out of our control. Dealing with city planners and neighbors infected with NIMBYism, obtaining construction permits, and resolving other bureaucratic hurdles created significant delays. If we could cut through government red tape, we could without a doubt realize our vision of quality, affordable housing completed in industry-leading times. But experience has taught me that red tape can strangle the life out of any positive innovation. Getting permits from the city to build one infill house would require the same time it would take to get permits for one hundred tract homes in a new project. Because of the need to have so many project managers, our program was not scalable.

To reach the volume necessary for our home-construction business to be effective and viable, in 2014 we founded a new entity, RSI Communities. We recruited Todd Palmer, a very experienced and capable executive who had been a regional president at Standard Pacific, a major homebuilding company.

Once at RSI Communities, Todd built a team in two states: California and Texas. Over the next three years, Todd did a great job, and RSI Communities became very successful. But over time, it became clear that although we respected one another, we were not always on the same page regarding how to achieve our goals. For example, we did not agree on certain marketing and construction methods. Also, in 2017, the value of home-construction companies was peaking.

Our ideological differences combined with favorable market conditions motivated us to come to a mutual agreement to sell. It was an amicable split where we maintained our friendship, and Todd's team and my team benefitted. After a little over three years of operation, we sold RSI Communities to William Lyon Homes for just under five hundred million dollars.

The ups and downs I experienced on the road to realizing my home-building vision are common to nearly every successful startup. What kept me on track are the tenets RSI put into words in 2005 but have been part of who I have been for most of my life.

The New House showed that bringing affordable housing and great value to the American consumer was possible. But dealing with all the bureaucratic and political obstacles has made it very challenging. Shouldn't providing such a common-sense need for hard-working American families be our government's top priority?

★ CHAPTER FIFTEEN

The Importance of Comic Relief in Business

There's no other way around it. Business can be war. If you're not strong-minded and an out-of-the-box thinker, and if you don't have innate business sense, your competitors will outperform you. In fact, every successful company owner has a long list of battle stories from the front lines.

You've already read about some of mine, and there'll inevitably be more in my future. In my case, the worst battles usually came as a result of the lack of business intelligence of the people we were doing deals with.

The pressure is always building, so finding ways to blow off steam on a regular basis is important because it serves as a release valve. Otherwise, you risk blowing up or burning out, which isn't good for anyone. Over my career, I've found many outlets to relax and clear my head in order to arm myself for the next fight.

Golf is high on my list, although those that have played with me will probably debate whether I'm really relaxing—I've been known to occasionally let my temper take over when my competitive and self-critical side has kicked in.

I recall my friend Allen Segal, a successful commercial real estate broker, inviting me to play a round of golf at the Newport Beach Country

Club. At the time, I was still pretty new at the game. We were at the first hole, and I approached the tee with a 3-wood because it was a short hole and pulled the ball out of the fairway.

Angry, I grabbed the club and hurled it in the air. My golf swing may have been off that day, but I still had my trusty baseball arm. The club went up and then didn't come down; it got stuck in a tree right next to the tee.

Al said, "Let me have one of the kids here climb up and get it."

"Al, I don't even deserve to have the club for missing something so easy," I said feeling utterly stupid.

I went on to play the round without the 3-wood that was lodged in the tree. The next morning, I opened the front door to pick up the newspaper, and my golf club was waiting for me on the porch.

Another personal pastime is playing practical jokes and making people laugh—clearly a carryover from my mischievous past that started as far back as I can remember.

Fortunately, as an adult, I don't wreak havoc on those around me like when I was a kid. Back then, I couldn't help but drive my parents nuts with my Dennis-the-Menace pranks. To their relief, I outgrew that stage, but I do still enjoy keeping those around me on edge. To me, levity in business is important.

From an early age watching Mr. Steinman maintain his unforgettable sense of humor, despite losing everyone he loved in what he joked were the Nazi "consideration camps," I learned the power of comedy and its ability to help businesspeople—as well as doctors—lighten the pressure they carry with them in their work.

My cardiologist, Dr. David Abrahamson, is a vegetarian. In other words, he's the opposite of me. I took a photo with him in front of spareribs and brisket I had just barbecued and then taped it to his office wall for all his patients to see. The image was accompanied by the caption, "Do not believe a word Dr. Abrahamson tells you about his diet." He, like me, has a sense of humor and appreciated my joke; it got a lot of laughs from his patients.

I also have a remote-controlled fart machine. It has mysteriously appeared on more than one occasion underneath an unsuspecting person's chair.

Ron with his vegetarian cardiologist, Dr. David Abrahamson.

Imagine a small dinner party. I choose the shiest person as my victim. We all sit down for our meal. I then take my remote and press the button without anyone seeing me.

We all hear a fart, and everyone knows where it came from, but politely no one says anything. A few minutes later, I go for round two. Now I let the fart rip for longer. Even if the victim and others at the table wanted to act as if nothing had happened, the gas noise has spread around so fast and loud that there's no denying it.

Meanwhile, I sit back and watch the entire disaster unfold: the victim who can't control the fart sound creeping out underneath and the guests who wonder what's going on with the person who can't stop passing gas.

"I . . . I didn't do that!" the person tells everyone at the table.

Then I make things worse.

"Oh really? Then who did it?" I ask.

I'm trying my hardest to maintain a disapproving look when all I really want to do is burst out laughing and relieve the poor victim of this prank. Finally, I let the person off the hook by taking responsibility for my gag.

I would file the fart prank under the rookie folder because, while hilarious, it doesn't take a whole lot of sophisticated planning. Another stunt I pulled took three months to organize.

By the end of 1991, the Soviet Union ceased to exist, and Russia emerged as an independent nation. Before its collapse, Mikhail Gorbachev was its last leader. Through his famous policies of *glasnost,* which means openness and granted more civil liberties to Soviet citizens, and *perestroika*, which means restructuring and signaled sweeping economic reforms, he gave freedoms to individual Soviet states that fueled their quest for independence.

With Gorbachev out and the Soviet Union no longer, Boris Yeltsin became the first president of the newly minted Russian Federation. He quickly privatized the country's biggest state-owned entities, and as a result, a small group of Russian elites became really rich, really fast. Many of them used their sudden wealth to make investments outside of Russia.

My friend Bob Wynn was a successful Hollywood producer and director. He had a long list of credits to his name, including nationally televised award shows and hit TV series, such as *Real People*. As a result of his decades in the entertainment industry, Bob had important connections with famous performers such as Mikhail Baryshnikov and high-ranking Russian politicians. He offered to introduce me to the head economic advisor to Boris Yeltsin.

I was having lunch with my top executives and told them about my pending meeting with the Russian official.

"Bob wants me to meet him because those oligarchs are buying US companies for huge amounts of money," I said.

My colleagues couldn't believe that even for a second I'd consider something like that. Keep in mind that just a year before Boris Yeltsin became head of the Russian Federation, the United States and the Soviet

Union were fighting the Cold War.

For decades, our nukes had been pointed at each other, and a provocation from either side could have triggered an attack destructive enough to blow up planet Earth. While the Cold War was over, mistrust and tensions between the two countries lingered.

"Wait a minute," one of my executives said. "You would even think of selling RSI to the Russians? Are you crazy?"

"Hell, if someone wants to pay us four or five times more than any other strategic buyer would, I have to at least listen to what he has to offer," I said.

I knew how opposed my executives were to my making a deal with Russian businessmen. And this is what inspired my practical joke.

After that conversation, we all dropped the topic. Until one of them brought it up a few weeks later.

"Hey, Ron, did you ever talk to that Russian guy?" he asked.

"You know, as a matter of fact, I have a meeting with him next week," I said.

I lied . . . sort of.

Yes, I did have a meeting—but not with the Russian oligarch. Instead, it was with someone I hired to play him. Between my prior lunch with my executive team and that conversation, I had been planning my prank.

Previously, I attended a petrochemical symposium in Silverado Resort in Napa, California, sponsored by a multi-national engineering firm. My friend and I were invited to the event because we had purchased a patent that converted methane to ethaline and were researching how to further develop the technology.

A Saudi prince was invited as a guest speaker. Addressing the room full of executives, he launched into an over-the-top anti-American tirade. His rant offended many of the attendees, that is, until they realized it was a joke and the prince was really a professional impersonator.

The man went by the stage name Mr. Put Ons, and he was a master actor who could play a posh Englishman, a Saudi Prince, and best of all, a Russian government official.

I hired him for the role of Dr. Alexi Alexandroff, a made-up person, who would be Russia's highest-ranking economic advisor.

Dr. Alexandroff was at the center of my stunt, so we had to make sure the actor's delivery was spot on. Together, Mr. Put Ons and I invented his character and the role he would play. I gave him information on members of my team, and he would use this to get them really bad.

Meanwhile, at RSI, we planned a big party to celebrate hitting a major corporate sales milestone. During the event, at the Four Seasons Hotel in Newport Beach, we would also honor our customer of the year.

I let my executive team know that I had invited Dr. Alexandroff to the celebration because part of making a serious offer to buy RSI required him to meet the senior executives. This description fit perfectly with the American stereotype at the time of Russian government officials being obsessed with spying on foreigners through their KGB, the Soviet version of the CIA.

According to the story I invented, Dr. Alexandroff's busy schedule of international travel meant he could see us only on the day of our party. And even better, all RSI's executives would be in the same place, so it made the perfect excuse for Dr. Alexandroff to attend. While in today's world of instant internet fact-checking, anyone with a smartphone would have figured out this was a hoax right away, this was pre-Google, so there was no easy way to check the man's identity.

I then did my best to convince them it was a fantastic idea.

"I invited Dr. Alexandroff to come here and speak to us. It would be a great opportunity for him to meet all of us. He even offered to answer your questions. It'll be a fun evening," I said.

My words didn't change their minds. They still couldn't believe I'd cut a deal with the Soviets. And everyone probably questioned why I would use our company's biggest event to introduce him to us.

For the evening of the party, I hired a Russian violinist. The young woman provided elegant background music during the cocktail hour. Then Dr. Alexandroff entered the room.

"Is that him?" one of my executives whispered to me.

"Oh, God, how did you know?" I asked.

"I could tell by the way he was dressed," he said.

"Oh, really? You are very perceptive," I said.

His reply made me proud of all the planning I had done to make the prank seem legit.

After the cocktail hour, all of us took a seat at our tables. I then introduced the room to our honored guest:

"It is going to be a great evening. We will hear the esteemed Dr. Alexandroff talk about Russia's current economic situation.

"After he speaks, he has kindly offered to answer any questions you have. But rather than ask them directly, he requests that you write your questions down on the notepads at your table and then someone will come by to pick them up. As you can imagine, there is a language barrier, so Dr. Alexandroff would like to read your questions ahead of time. That way, he can answer them properly."

When it was time for Dr. Alexandroff to deliver his presentation, he approached the podium at the front of the banquet hall and started his talk.

"It's really a pleasure to be here," he said. "And I'm so happy to officially announce we're buying your company. So now, you'll be working for the Russians."

Mr. Put Ons nailed the accent. None of the guests would question whether he was really Russian and buying RSI. I looked around the room. If there were a word that could describe the expression on people's faces after his shocking announcement, it would be "fuck." If there were a sentence, it would be, "Damn, we're fucked!"

Dr. Alexandroff paused to allow everyone to digest his bombshell news. He then continued.

"Part of our buying decision required us to investigate all your company's top executives. Now that the Soviet Union is no more, there has been an unprecedented openness and collaboration between the KGB and your CIA, so we know everything about you. This is part of our due diligence before we buy companies."

I glanced at my executives. Some were shifting in their seats while others had tensed foreheads. They were all nervous as hell.

"Mr. Norton Krinsky," Dr. Alexandroff said. "Can you stand up please?"

He rose to his feet and all eyes were on him.

"You're the chief financial officer of this company. Is that correct?"

"Yes," Norton said.

"And I understand you're cohabitating with your significant other," he said.

Norton stood silently in disbelief.

Dr. Alexandroff didn't wait for a response.

"I believe in your country what you're doing is called shacking up. Well, in our country, we call it unacceptable. So either you have to get married, or we'll have no other choice than to throw you out."

Dr. Alexandroff performed a couple of more stunts like that, messing with company executives, and the crowd eventually figured out that they had fallen for an epic gag.

While this was definitely one of my more elaborate stunts, it is one example of many, many I've plotted and successfully pulled off throughout my career. I have used jokes and comedy to lighten my mood, as well as that of those around me, and always enjoyed being around people that have a sense of humor.

But I don't think pranks go just in one direction. I'm fully aware that I have to be equally willing to take what I dish out. Actually, as a career prankster, I have to be *even more* vigilant because my victims are always seeking sweet revenge.

Fortunately, the plus of being street-smart is that I have a solid sixth sense. I've proudly caught many practical jokes directed at me before falling for them since I always have my guard up. Recently, however, after twenty-five years of diligent effort, my team finally got me. And I have to hand it to them—they duped me 100 percent.

As much as running a company is thrilling and a job I'd pick above any other, the work is nonstop, often stressful, a huge responsibility, and the battles are relentless. Part of easing the pressure of the tough business world is to take things less seriously once in a while. Laughter is medicine, but not everyone shares the same sense of humor. Plus, in the workplace, you must walk a fine line between kidding and not offending anyone. Unfortunately, some people figure it's safest just to avoid any joking altogether. But that would make for a workplace that wouldn't be fun for me.

In fact, being a risk taker and jokester, I take my chances in adding humor when it feels appropriate and maybe even necessary to lighten things up. And being constantly aware of what's going on around me, I'm always on the lookout for new practical jokes to add to my playbook. But because I've earned a reputation as a prankster, to pull a gag off successfully requires more and more creativity on my part.

In 2005 during my visit to Shanghai, I found the perfect opportunity to play a great joke, and it would be one to liven up my usually very serious board of directors and our meetings.

Several months prior to my trip, I was introduced to Alex To. Having spent many years in China, Alex now lived in Newport Beach. He had worked in Shanghai for the financial arm of General Electric, and he and I had become friendly. During one of our conversations, I described my plans to visit China and how I wanted to tour kitchen cabinet factories and retail showrooms.

"Ron, that's great. Let me show you around China. I've got lots of business connections in Shanghai. I could introduce you to people and be your guide," he said.

His offer was too good to refuse, so I took him up on it. I knew he was a good guy prior to our trip, but afterwards, I thought even more highly of him.

When we arrived in the massive and modern Chinese city, I toured several factories and showrooms that made and sold products similar to RSI's. Seeing the major inefficiencies of Chinese cabinet manufacturers inspired me to consider competing head-to-head with them *on their own turf.*

During my trip, Alex To arranged for me to meet the general manager of Kohler China, a subsidiary of the US company founded in 1873 and best known for its kitchen and bath plumbing products. The GM was of Chinese descent; we'll call him Peter Chang. My plan was to interview Peter as a prospective manager to run RSI's sales and marketing in China.

When Peter and I met in Shanghai, I described RSI's low-cost manu-facturing operations, how they were better than what I saw in China, and how we could be very competitive selling our products here. But after talking to him, I knew he would be a lousy fit for RSI.

I just flat out didn't like the guy. The GM's personality, and in particular his arrogance, was 100 percent at odds with RSI's practical and down-to-earth culture. So right away, I abandoned the thought of hiring him.

But the meeting was not a total loss. I realized it was perfect fod-der for a memorable gag I could play on my board of directors—Byron Allumbaugh, Gilbert LeVasseur, Harold Kitay, and Tom Tucker, as well as three Lehman Brothers executives because the company was an RSI investor. In all, with Alex Calabrese and me, there were nine of us.

Throughout my trip in China, Alex To was a real jokester. We pulled off some hilarious pranks because he could keep a straight face through practically anything. Seeing his acting and comedy chops convinced me my plan would work. After returning home, I told Alex To about the joke I planned to play and his role in it to be Peter Chang.

"God, I'd *love* to do it! That would be hilarious," he said.

So with Alex's green light, I charged ahead. To successfully pull this off to a group of street-smart men who knew me well would require a water-tight plan.

Back in Newport Beach, I circulated an email to the board of direc-tors describing how I had an amazing business opportunity for RSI to expand in China. I let them know I wanted to get their opinion during our next meeting.

On the day we met, as always we sat in our boardroom. Alex To, play-ing Peter Chang, was waiting outside for me to call him in. I reminded everyone of how excited I was about this huge opportunity.

Next, I told them that our guest, Kohler China's GM, had planned a trip to the United States to attend a meeting at the company's Wisconsin headquarters. I had arranged for him to see us in Newport Beach during his stateside visit. In other words, he was here today, ready to talk to us, and very interested in joining the RSI team. Then I went in for the really hard sell.

"Can you imagine what this could mean for RSI? And when I met Peter Chang, I got even more excited. He was totally on-board with our low-cost model. As a matter of fact, we are on the same page with just about everything, which, as you all know, is very rare."

I then circulated his resume; it was the one the real Peter Chang had handed me when we had met in Shanghai.

"Listen, gentlemen," I said. "Peter is very qualified, and I cannot wait for you to meet him. I am going to invite him in now. I want your candid opinion afterwards about whether you think we should go ahead with the program and hire this guy."

I then called Terri Stephens, my assistant, to send in Peter. He entered the boardroom, and I introduced him to the group and told them that Peter was happy to answer their questions.

"Do you think RSI could be the low-cost producer in China?" one board member asked.

"No way!" Peter said. "There's no such thing. You could *never ever* have the hope of doing that. So you might as well give up that dream!"

"I'm sorry, but I'm confused," another board member said. "Ron told us you'd met with him in Shanghai and you were very excited about being a low-cost producer, representing RSI in China, working for RSI and all kinds of other things . . ."

"What?! I *never* said any of that!" Peter replied. "I have no idea why, but Ron made all that up!"

Then he went on a short rant criticizing RSI. The board members all looked totally baffled. Meanwhile, I sat there listening, not saying a word, and doing my best to look like I was fuming. They all knew me, and if they saw my expression, they had no doubt that I was ready to explode, which I then did.

"What the fuck are you talking about?!" I said. "You sit here in our boardroom, and you have the nerve to humiliate me and insult this company in front of the entire board? I want you out of here . . . *right now!*"

I walked over and grabbed him by the arm. As I dragged him to the door, I told him, "Get the hell out of here and wait in the lobby. I will have my assistant write you an expense check."

He left and I closed the door.

I took a seat, still visibly mad. The board sat in silence, probably in shock over how this meeting that had started so positive and exciting turned ugly so fast and how pissed off I got.

"I have never been so humiliated in my entire life! Unbelievable," I said.

The whole group was feeling bad for me now, so they tried to help me out.

"Well, Ron, you know it's better we found out about this guy now, rather than after hiring him," Byron said.

"My God, Ron," another one said. "We've never seen you this angry before. I didn't know you had a temper like that. I mean, you must have been really embarrassed. I'm having trouble even believing what just happened."

I gave myself a few moments to calm down. I was now ready to continue with the meeting.

"Okay, guys, you know I just came back from a great trip to China. We were introduced to a lot of people and saw a lot of factories. Alex To was kind enough to act as our guide there. He used to manage the General Electric fund in China. I invited him here today, and he is waiting outside. I wanted you to meet Alex, so we could all thank him for managing a very fruitful trip," I said.

I got on the phone and called Terri.

"Please send in Alex To," I said.

When he entered the room, the board members at first all had confused looks on their faces. Peter was now Alex To. They then quickly figured out they had just been majorly duped.

The serious weight of the board meeting suddenly lifted, and now everyone was all smiles.

"Ron! We're going to really get you if it's the last thing we do!" a board member said.

We all broke out in laughter.

While they never did get me back for this one, they'll probably never forget how good I'd gotten them.

Teasing close friends and business associates about their idiosyncrasies and joking about racial stereotypes are part of my DNA. I find it always lightens tense situations.

While racial discrimination is a terrible part of our society, I believe political correctness has gone too far and has fueled conflicts that otherwise might not exist.

When I was growing up, jokes about race and ethnicity told by so many comedians—mostly Jewish and Italian but a few Irish and some Blacks—were widespread and hysterically funny. Most made fun of their own backgrounds and were in no way racist.

To laugh at yourself can be the funniest humor. My very close friends, whether Italian, Black, or Asian, would tease each other all the time with jokes that today could be considered racist. But because of the love and respect that we had for one another, they were not taken that way.

For example, when I was pitching for my high school baseball team, a fast ball got away from me and hit a Black batter in the head. I was scared to death that I had killed him. I ran to the batter's box to help him, yelling, "Are you okay?" As I reached down, he was already getting up and jokingly said to me, "Of course I am, Jew Boy. Your fastball couldn't hurt a fly."

Laughing, we then hugged each other, and I returned to the pitcher's mound. This is an example of two kids without a racist bone in their bodies that liked and respected each other. Imagine that conversation today. Despite today's pressures to be politically correct, I feel fortunate to have my sense of humor still intact.

★ CHAPTER SIXTEEN

Giving Back:
My Most Rewarding Investment

For years, I had cringed when I saw my dad stammer in front of others. And when I started junior high, I was frightened the same would happen to me.

From the outside, my life looked fine. My mom and dad loved me and provided my basic needs. I was an average student who sailed through my classes without much effort. I had plenty of friends and loved sports.

Every kid wants to fit in, and the ones that say they don't are often the ones that care the most. I certainly didn't want to be the victim of people teasing and laughing at me, and I was terrified my stammering would make me stand out. I managed to develop ways to get by without anyone noticing. But part of me always worried that I'd be caught, which explains why just the thought of speaking in front of my class would scare me to death.

I've long since overcome my fear. Although still not a fan of public speaking, I'm fine doing it. One benefit of my struggle is that I can relate to any kid who has ever felt stupid, suffers from low self-esteem, or struggles with something that seems too big to handle. In fact, one of the greatest gifts my professional success has provided me has been the ability to give back. I'm grateful that I can help young people overcome the obstacles keeping them from reaching their potential.

In 2002, I started the Simon Scholars program, whose mission is to give scholarships to disadvantaged high school students. Unlike most scholarships that provide only college support, our program begins during the students' junior year in high school. Many of our students had no hope of attending college, so by reaching them in high school, we broaden the horizons of these first-generation university students, guide them through this unfamiliar and often scary territory, and support them in transitioning to college and beyond, as well as provide financial aid.

In 2002, David Dukes became CEO of my foundation, which at the time operated the Simon Scholars program. We began our program with ten students in Orange County. The next year, we started chapters in Santa Fe, New Mexico, where my son, Steve Simon, lives and in Atlanta, Georgia, where my daughter, Dr. Kathy Simon Abels, was residing at the

Ron and his daughter, Dr. Kathy Simon Abels,
at a Horatio Alger event, 2016.

Ron and his son, Steve Simon, 1995.

time. My grandson, Ben Drutman, has also contributed immeasurably as executive director of the Simon Scholars program in Southern California.

In 2020, we accepted more than 130 new students, adding to the over 650 Simon Scholars who were already in the program. The following year 190 new students will become Simon Scholars. In three years, over one thousand young men and women will be participating.

While all Simon Scholars have overcome tremendous adversity in their lives, my children were blessed to come from secure and stable backgrounds, protected from violence and poverty. But, as I've learned, children of privilege also have roadblocks. For example, when they become adults and enter the professional world, they frequently struggle earning respect on their own merit. They are often perceived as spoiled or entitled or both, which means their accomplishments were handed to them, rather than brought about through their own hard work. I've certainly seen my share of kids who grew up in wealthy families that fit the stereotype of children that turned into undisciplined and irresponsible adults.

I didn't come from a rich family. My parents made it clear they would meet my basic needs and the rest was up to me. As an adult, I appreciated the lessons I learned from earning money and hard work when I was a kid. I wanted to instill the same values in my own children. When they would compare themselves to their peers and want the same things their friends got from their parents, I would tell them, "I don't want you to be like these rich spoiled kids."

During their college years, I thought it was important for them to experience the real-world challenges of adulthood, despite being in the protective university bubble. As a fulltime student at the University of Denver, my son worked as a restaurant sous chef, which is physically demanding with long hours. To this day, he navigates his way through a kitchen like a pro and cooks amazing dishes. Kathy, while at Occidental College with a full class load, was flipping burgers in a fast-food joint. She asked me one day, "Dad, don't you feel bad your daughter works in a hamburger stand?" To her surprise my answer was, "Just the opposite. I'm more proud of my daughter than ever." And I meant it. She could have taken the easy path, but she chose the more disciplined one of juggling work and school. And the result spoke for itself—she graduated summa cum laude, went on to earn her PhD in clinical psychology, and had a private therapy practice before assuming the role of president of the Simon Scholars program.

My two children have succeeded on their own without riding on the coattails of their dad's legacy. And they've done so through being humble, working hard, demonstrating a deep compassion for others, and a commitment to giving back by improving the world in which they live.

The initial objective of the foundation was straightforward: provide financial aid to underserved students. But as the program evolved, Steve and Kathy saw how deep the needs of at-risk youth were and how the foundation could make a huge difference in their lives. My children used their professional training to create a program that moved far beyond granting scholarships to bright and ambitious students.

Today, Simon Scholars provides students resources to succeed in the long term. Ninety-six percent of our high schoolers have been accepted to nearly two hundred colleges and universities, including ones throughout California's flagship UC system, as well as in the Ivy League.

The instant a young person earns a spot, he or she is a Simon Scholar. This title means the student will participate in a six-year program that begins during his or her junior year in high school and continues through four years of undergraduate studies. It is designed to prepare him or her to succeed in high school, earn a four-year college degree and in some cases a graduate degree, successfully enter the workforce, and give back to the community. While Simon Scholars have worked hard to earn the scholarship by meeting high standards, most don't fully understand what an honor and privilege it is until they actually start in the program.

From immediate support, such as our monthly curriculum program, SAT prep courses, and college application assistance, to intense and exciting leadership conferences and retreats, as well as college tours, we take a whole-person approach to meeting the needs of our scholars. This means our programs address the multiple aspects of a young person's emotional and academic development.

Simon Scholars come from some of the toughest backgrounds you can imagine: drug addiction within their families, absentee parents, poverty, lack of emotional support at home, violent neighborhoods and schools, and all the other traits of a rough childhood environment. In other words, Simon Scholars are fighters and survivors.

Many of the events Simon Scholars participate in give them access to experiences they would have otherwise never had. For instance, during the college tour, students visit the nation's most elite public and private universities. For some, this is the first time they've ever gone outside their immediate communities, let alone boarded a plane and toured a spectacular university campus.

The visit exposes them to an academic setting that inspires them to think beyond their high school years and imagine life in a sprawling and intellectually stimulating college environment. Once they enroll in a four-year university, they are eligible for our needs-based scholarship and to be part of our alumni program.

Each year, we hold a three-day leadership symposium and invite several college admission recruiters, who interface with the scholars. Because the colleges know that Simon Scholars have a graduation rate above 90 percent, many offer them full rides.

To be a Simon Scholar means the student has demonstrated excellence from an early age, despite multiple setbacks. Sometimes it's a little spark we see that tells us the kid has the potential—possibly unknown to him or her—to do amazing things. With the impressive track record of our students who demonstrate high achievement in college, as well as the workforce, we know what to look for when selecting future Simon Scholars.

Rather than reject or deny the struggles they've overcome on the road to become Simon Scholars, our program provides them the resources to use their adversity to motivate them to become successful.

Students who are selected to be Simon Scholars also exhibit innate leadership qualities, and we provide them tools to further use their voice to improve the lives of those around them. Many scholars have expressed that through their participation in the program and their subsequent accomplishments, they've had a positive impact on their siblings, families, and communities. They've developed leadership skills far beyond what they thought was possible.

Each Simon Scholar has an internal desire to succeed. Thus peer support is an ideal way to collectively harness the individual drive of our scholars. By bringing them together, we give them a broader life perspective and support from fellow highly motivated students representing diverse backgrounds.

Seeing firsthand the life-altering results of engaging, supporting, and nurturing students has been deeply gratifying. Simon Scholars have overcome innumerable obstacles, and they have done so through immense determination, intelligence, and self-reliance. Our foundation's role in supporting these students is the greatest investment I've ever made.

Like any solid organization, the Simon Scholars program continues to grow and evolve. For example, its success inspired us to introduce the Simon Scholars Leadership Association (SSLA). We know that to become effective leaders, our scholars require discipline, decision-making skills, and strong character. The goal of the SSLA is to model and foster these qualities within our scholars. We have recruited prominent professionals who are leaders within their industries. While their career paths vary, they all share high achievement and a belief in our country's capitalist system, as well as a passion to positively support and influence the development of underserved youth. Their experiences and life lessons inspire, guide, and connect with our scholars.

From the rise of competing superpowers to the domestic challenges we see on the news every day, our country faces a near endless list of obstacles that call into question the reality of the American Dream.

But taking a long view of US history, we see that our nation has held true to its promise of rewarding those that work hard while staying on a course of continual improvement—the greatest winning streak in human history! I'm proud to have played a small but personally very meaningful role in our country's success story. Our optimism, pragmatism, spirit of innovation, and tough work ethic are what have always fueled our economic engine, one that has solved the world's greatest problems and will keep doing so because of the momentum we've built over generations.

Thus I steadfastly reject any disruptive force that runs counter to our country's capitalist values. The Simon Scholars program exists today only as a result of what America has to offer. And I'm proud that this organization will help instill in others for generations to come the love and respect for my country that has been my guiding light.

Without a doubt, our nation has many self-inflicted wounds from mistakes and bad decisions we've made. But without question, we've been an unstoppable force for healing and goodness around the globe. Just looking back on my own family's short history on these great shores, I am astonished at how far we've come as a nation.

As immigrant Jews in LA, my parents dealt with in-your-face discrimination absolutely unthinkable today. But no matter what bigotry they were dealt, they never ever allowed others' hatred and ignorance to turn them bitter. They never ceded their pursuit of the American Dream to someone else's stupid and narrow-minded belief that it wasn't for them to go after.

The easy way out for my parents would have been to connect anti-Semitism here with the same cancer they had escaped that infected all of Europe. "Here we go again!" Belle and Sidney Simon could have told themselves and felt shame or like victims and then resented their adopted country. But rather than succumb to that, they refused to complain. In fact, they reacted just the opposite. Throughout her life, my mom was known to tear up when she heard the national anthem. And when Kate Smith, the First Lady of Radio sang "God Bless America," you could bet my mom would have to go grab a handkerchief. Far from corny or melodramatic, my mom's response reflected her deep love of her country. She never took for granted what America gave her and her family.

I thank my parents for passing on to me not the poison of resentment but, rather, the passion of what is possible here. They were true patriots because they experienced America's ugly side yet focused on the greatness that far outshone the darkness. My mom and dad instilled in me a gratitude for what this country has to offer. And this appreciation inspired me throughout my life and motivates me to inspire others today.

While I reaped the rewards of being raised in the Land of Opportunity by building businesses, many argue that prosperous landscape no longer exists. They are wrong! Even though times have changed, opportunities abound. I know because I see really big and amazing ones everywhere and am still looking to seize new ones.

From the examples provided by the Simon Scholars—who hopefully will someday become our nation's leaders—I have no doubt the American Dream is alive and well. We are a country that offers unrivaled possibilities to those who are willing to work hard and pursue excellence.

Simon Scholars that go on to become first-generation college graduates demonstrate that you can come from incredibly tough circumstances but your hardships can be a bridge, rather than a barrier, to realizing your wildest dreams. And I'm proud that my foundation has given young people the resources they need to tap into their greatest potential.

In 2005, almost three years after launching my foundation, I was honored to receive the Horatio Alger Award, which the Horatio Alger Association of Distinguished Americans presents every year to about twelve men and women.

The organization's namesake was a successful author whose books were tremendously popular in the late 1800s. His best sellers were rags-to-riches tales of boys who overcame their impoverished circumstances and went on to become wealthy and famous men.

While Alger passed away in 1899, today the association, founded in 1947, is dedicated to spreading the belief that "hard work, honesty and determination can conquer all obstacles." Award recipients have triumphed over adversity and, as a result, achieved remarkable success. Through its Horatio Alger Endowment Fund, the organization provides needs-based scholarships to undergraduate and graduate students.

Ron with Byron Allumbaugh at the Horatio Alger Awards Ceremony, 2005.

Past award recipients represent a wide swath of society, including baseball legend Hank Aaron, President Ronald Reagan, businessman and entrepreneur Wayne Huizenga, former secretaries of state Condoleezza Rice and Colin Powell, entertainment industry mogul Oprah Winfrey, and many other famous men and women.

To be named among the country's most outstanding citizens was an honor, and because my foundation's purpose was to help young people realize and reach their fullest potential, I hoped the award would further inspire Simon Scholars to overcome the challenges they faced.

While I was thrilled to receive this very prestigious honor, it also presented a huge challenge for me. I would be receiving the Horatio Alger Award at a celebration that took place in our nation's capital and was a three-day event, which included breakfasts where we would meet scholarship recipients, member luncheons, an inaugural reception hosted at the Supreme Court, and the awards ceremony.

The last event gave me pause because I would have to present acceptance remarks. Despite being a business leader for decades, I had always been a reluctant public speaker. Now, I was expected to deliver a short speech for a huge award whose purpose was to inspire those who had received scholarships. In other words, I felt the pressure.

I had about six months to prepare, which meant the butterflies fluttered in my stomach for half a year. My nerves grew worse as the event drew nearer. On the day of the ceremony, they reached their peak. As I sat waiting for my turn to speak, I did my best to relax. When my time to accept the award came up, I approached the podium and, despite the jitters, forged ahead.

In my speech, I described how this was the greatest day of my life because "it just doesn't get better than this." I addressed the scholarship recipients by congratulating them on overcoming seemingly insurmountable obstacles. Despite all the difficulties they faced, I told them not to forget to give back. I encouraged them to trust their instincts and believe in themselves and reminded them that they will play an important role in making our great country even greater.

Last, I expressed my gratitude for what this nation has provided me and thanked my wife Sandi, my family, and the 3,400 RSI associates for their hard work and dedication.

Ron and Sandi with Supreme Court Justice Clarence Thomas at the Horatio Alger event, 2005.

I worked through the nerves, and thankfully, my presentation went smoothly that evening. After that speech, every subsequent event where I had to publicly speak has been a breeze in comparison. With the delivery behind me, I imagined myself like the many kids who paged through Horatio Alger's famous books. After reading his words, they realized their own weaknesses didn't need to hold them back and, in fact, could become a source of strength once they overcame them.

Facing the challenge of speaking in front of over a thousand of this country's very prominent and prestigious leaders gave me the confidence to continue giving speeches to other large groups afterwards—public speaking became a lot easier.

In 2015, I was given another large platform to deliver remarks when I was awarded the Orange County Innovator of the Year Award. I received the honor for the Simon Scholars program's work and RSI's efficient and low-cost bathroom and kitchen cabinet manufacturing that competed with China, as well as RSI Construction's affordable housing.

Ron receiving the Orange County Innovator of the Year Award, 2015.

Establishing the Simon Scholars program fulfills, in part, my desire to leave a meaningful legacy. As much as I have enjoyed the work in creating successful businesses, my work does not stop there. My foundation supporting the Simon Scholars carries my values forward and assures me that it will help others achieve.

But my legacy shows in other ways, ones that rarely get the spotlight but make me very proud nonetheless. Those that especially fill me with satisfaction concern people I've influenced, knowing my interactions spread far wider than I imagined at the time.

To manage RSI's fast growth well, I had to hire amazing people who were up to the major tasks ahead. One of the first guys I brought on was Joe Varela. I needed someone to run the factory, and he was the perfect fit. I already knew Joe well because he worked for Perma-Bilt where he showed his smarts and was an incredibly hard worker with real integrity. Once Austram took over, he was fired along with many others I would eventually bring on to join me at RSI.

I made Joe vice president of operations. Joe is a prime example of the hiring decisions I'm most proud of. For the following decades during which he served as VP, he helped RSI meet the challenges of its rapid expansion. Joe retired at seventy years old and left as a permanent member of the RSI family. He continued to attend company parties and stayed in touch with me and the management team.

Joe always had a big heart that he put into his work and family. Unfortunately, during retirement, that same heart started to struggle keeping up with his body. He suffered from a condition that grew progressively worse to the point that, after seventeen years in retirement, his doctors told him they had done everything possible and they had run out of treatment options. . . . In other words, death was near.

At eighty-seven years old, Joe was three years my senior. He gave me a call to let me know this would most likely be our last conversation. During our talk, he wanted to thank me for what RSI had provided for him and his family.

"Ron, back when you did the private equity deals, you told me that I would be set for life afterwards and that I would be able to take care of my family. And you were right. You did exactly what you said you would, and I wanted to thank you for that," he told me.

"I am the one that should be thanking you, Joe, for the wonderful contribution to the success of the company," I said.

Then there was Gonzalo Verduzco. He was born in Mexico and immigrated to the United States. At the time I hired him, he was working for a furniture company in LA as the lead man on its assembly line. A salesman had told me about this guy who was a disciplined, intelligent, and extremely hard worker that would be the perfect fit for RSI.

I poached him from the furniture business and hired him as RSI's first factory employee. He worked as the lead man on our first assembly line. Joe Varela ended up being Gonzalo's boss. Gonzalo was around forty years old at the time he worked for RSI and stayed with us for about twenty-five years.

My wife Sandi will never forget the conversation she had with Gonzalo at our company picnic one year. He reflected on his time at RSI.

"I'm so grateful to Ron for giving me such a great position and won-derful future," he said. "It helped me build a house for my parents in Mexico, for me to buy a house in this country, and for my wife and me to send our kids to college."

His gratitude brought tears to my wife's eyes. And his words are an example of the countless unforgettable rewards I have experienced for my commitment to take care of my team by making sure they shared in our profits. We all prospered together through RSI's remarkable rise.

★ CHAPTER SEVENTEEN
Selling My Company

I have always thought it far better to promote from within an organization than to recruit a CEO from the outside. At RSI, I was very fortunate that I made Alex Calabrese, who grew up in the company, my successor. But who would be his successor?

While we had a very talented and loyal executive team at RSI, we did not think we had anyone that could fill Alex's shoes. So when the time came to get him out of the trenches to spearhead our plans to diversify by acquiring companies manufacturing other building material products, we had to recruit from the outside. We made attempts at it, and each one did not work out. The last effort was disastrous and eventually led to the sale of RSI.

Once a very successful investor told me it would be extremely difficult to find a CEO to run RSI. That person was none other than Warren Buffett. This is how I met him.

Back in 2008, my friend Mike Yanney was asking me what future plans I had for RSI. He and I had met when we both received the Horatio Alger Award in 2005. Mike had spent his career in finance. In 1984, he established America First Companies, which later became Burlington Capital Group LLC. It was one of the Midwest's largest private-investment banking firms.

Our shared business experiences and our similar personalities resulted in us becoming good friends. We both respected one another's career accomplishments and our commitment to excellence.

Mike's Midwest roots and his work in banking brought him in contact with the best and brightest financial minds, including Warren Buffett.

"I know him really well," Mike told me. "Let me check with Warren and see if he would be interested in investing in your company."

When a friend offers to make an introduction to the Oracle of Omaha, you do not think twice about it. I thanked Mike for reaching out to Warren on my behalf. Mike phoned me the next day.

"Ron, I gave Warren a brief summary about RSI. He's very interested. He wants you to give him a call," he said.

Mike provided me Warren's direct number, and I dialed it right away. You would think someone as famous as him would have an endless number of gatekeepers. But to my surprise, I did not have to go through any layers of administrative red tape. In an instant, I was speaking to the world's most renowned investor.

"Hi, this is Warren," he said.

"Hello, Warren. This is Ron Simon. I am a friend of Mike Yanney's," I said.

"Of course, Ron. Tell me what you've got," he said.

Cordial, to the point, and absolutely devoid of politics, the CEO of Berkshire Hathaway was exactly as I had imagined him to be, and I respected him for it. I gave him a five-minute, high-level history of RSI.

"I'd be very interested. Can you send me something?" he asked.

"Or course. I will overnight it so you will have it first thing tomorrow. Warren, I tell you what. I normally would require a confidentiality agreement before sending, but something tells me I can trust you," I joked.

"You can," he said.

As promised, the executive summary arrived at his office the next day. In the world of private equity, after sending information, I would have typically expected to hear back a week later. Although that was not RSI's speed of doing business, I learned I had to be patient in working with other investors . . . with the following exception:

Warren called me back the same day after receiving my executive summary.

"Ron, you've got a great company. I am so impressed. How in the hell do you make these kinds of margins, despite the tough business environment you're in?"

When one of the greatest investors in history gives you a sincere compliment, you take a second to let the message settle in. Especially because you know he's a zero-percent bullshitter.

"Well, that would take a long time to explain. But, yes, we have these margins, and that trend will continue; the company has a bright future," I said.

"I believe you. I would love to see how you take on your competitors. It would be fun to watch you go out and destroy other companies. . . . But to be very honest, you're not the type of business I buy," he said.

After hearing the bright analysis of RSI, I was surprised with his conclusion.

"Why not?" I asked.

"Because in order for you to achieve what you have, there has to be a great leader and a great management team. And when I buy a company, I have to make the assumption that the leader won't be there," he said.

I understood his point. Once companies are purchased, CEOs have less skin in the game. They may take their payout, run off, and go play.

"For example," Warren added, "I have See's Candies. There's a great guy running it, and I hope he stays for a while. But if he ever leaves, I could probably find five highly qualified guys to step in and keep it running just as well. But in RSI's case, it takes an exceptional person at the helm to achieve RSI's level of success. Few of those people are available, and they are extremely difficult to recruit. So I gotta pass," he said.

"Warren, I do understand, and you have no idea how much you have impressed me. Number one, how responsive you were is a tremendous indication of why you are so successful. Number two, your insight is incredible. I cannot disagree with anything you said, except I will tell you that I have a guy running the company day-to-day that I have no question could step into my shoes tomorrow morning," I said.

"I know, Ron. I've heard that before. But I'm not going to bet the store on it. Good luck. Keep me updated. I'd love to know how you do," he said.

I knew Warren had made up his mind. So, as much as I would have enjoyed partnering with Berkshire Hathaway, I was not going to try anymore to convince him. I gave him my sincerest thanks, and we ended our call.

A process that would have taken weeks with most private equity and strategic buyers took only two days with Warren Buffett. And, specifically, the back-and-forth required only two short but high-impact phone calls.

My firsthand experience with him convinced me of how he has accomplished so much in his career. While he has many aspects of a regular guy—humility, directness, and sincerity—behind the down-to-earth exterior is a business genius running one of the world's most successful companies.

Our brief interaction was also an unforgettable endorsement of RSI. When one of history's greatest businessmen says how impressed he is with the company you built from scratch, that's a conversation you'll always remember.

In hindsight, it warned me of the difficult road ahead. When the time came to diversify RSI into other product categories, Alex would be the best qualified to take on this huge responsibility. But recruiting someone to fill his shoes was going to be very tough.

What Warren told me also pointed to everything I had achieved at RSI *and* what I could accomplish elsewhere. At this time in my career, I sought to use what I had learned to push myself to seek new and interesting entrepreneurial opportunities.

Six years after my conversation with Warren Buffett, in 2014, the company was soaring and was an excellent IPO candidate. Thanks to all that Alex had accomplished, our plan that year was to take RSI public, continue to operate and grow it with a new leader in the trenches, and use some of the capital from the IPO to gain liquidity for myself and other RSI team members.

As a first major step, we found a new CEO for RSI. Alex then became executive chairman. We even began the process of selecting a banker to lead the IPO. We believed the CEO would be very capable of running RSI as a public company because in his most recent post, he successfully took a company public. And prior to that, he had turned around a cabinet manufacturer that was selling in the mid-price range that RSI was planning to enter with a new program it had developed.

Unfortunately, under our new CEO's watch, RSI's performance began to suffer: Profit margins shrank, and our two biggest customers, The Home Depot and Lowe's, were unhappy with our new leader. Because of all this, we had no choice but to terminate the new company head and abandon our IPO plans. Instead, we made the decision to sell RSI.

But first we needed to turn RSI around—and fast—to position it for a sale that could deliver a value comparable to what it was before the new leader came on board.

So Alex was put back into his CEO post, and this time, he was responsible for a turnaround that made the last one he was in charge of seem easy. That was the one where we terminated our appointed CEO who had headed one of GE's appliance divisions. As we had come to expect from Alex, he worked nonstop until he restored RSI to greatness.

So it was yet again, mission accomplished for Alex. But this time around, it took its toll on him. Reflecting on what Alex went through in order to return RSI to how he had left it before becoming executive chairman, I remembered what Warren Buffett had told me.

He was so right—it takes a very special talent to continue to grow a company like RSI and maintain margins that are two and a half times that of its best performing competitor. And when most of your business comes from two giant home centers, like The Home Depot and Lowe's, you're guaranteed that the battles will be relentless and the victories always hard fought. With all their buying power, they fire at you almost nonstop in order to get lower prices. You can take only so many bullets before the wounds really become too painful.

This meant I knew exactly how Alex felt. The endless clashes I had so many years ago, before I sold Perma-Bilt to Austram, left me wanting out as fast as possible. The big difference in my case was that I was in charge of a company much smaller than RSI.

As far as Alex was concerned, he had been fighting in the trenches with The Home Depot and Lowe's for two decades. Add to that the burden of being left to clean up the messes less capable CEOs had made for the company he loved so much.

In the end, he was burned out and needed a break from all the havoc. That's when we made the difficult decision to sell. In December of 2017, American Woodmark purchased RSI for $1.2 billion.

As we had done many times in the past, we could have engaged Jim Freedman to sell RSI through an auction process. We did discuss RSI's sale with other strategic buyers, but in the end, we decided that American Woodmark would be the best home for RSI because of the promises its CEO, Cary Dunston, had made to us.

"We have such a strong interest because we admire RSI," said Cary, "especially how you treat your employees. We'll preserve RSI's values and culture and take what we learn in order to improve American Woodmark."

Cary went on to say that he planned to make RSI a subsidiary. Doing so would enable it to stay true to its winning formula, which included profit margins that were much higher than American Woodmark's. In other words, RSI would carry on as the industry's lowest cost producer, and its employees would continue to be in a comfortable environment.

The CEO's promise to take care of RSI's employees was important to us because they had played such a big role in the company's success. Based on what he said, he understood why I valued them so much, and he would absolutely continue on just as our executive team had done. So we decided to forego the auction-type transaction and sell to American Woodmark.

On December 29, 2017, the purchase closed. The following appeared in a news release American Woodmark published that day:

> *RSI and its subsidiaries will operate as subsidiaries of American Woodmark*
> *going forward with their existing brands, channel strategy and operational*

philosophy remaining. American Woodmark will continue to be managed by its existing management team, led by Cary Dunston as Chairman and CEO.

We were relieved that the company put in print the pledge it made to preserve RSI's successful philosophy. We had received some stock as part of the sale. Shortly after the transaction was announced, its value jumped from $96 to $140. But despite this good news, the sale felt bittersweet. We had given up our baby, and we could only hope we had left it in the hands of a loving new family.

On several occasions prior to the deal closing, Alex had told Cary that he and David Lowrie, RSI's senior vice president and CFO, were willing to stay on and help as long as they were needed. Alex wanted the transition to go smoothly and American Woodmark to maintain the momentum our executive team had built. Specifically, Alex sought to make sure the new parent company would take advantage of the many synergistic savings that would greatly enhance its margins. And he knew that he and David could help ensure that would happen.

If I had been in Cary's shoes, I would have jumped at Alex's offer. And any CEO in his or her right mind certainly should have done so as well. The two were the leaders of a company that had margins unheard of in the industry and ones that American Woodmark most likely couldn't have maintained without their guidance. Well, not Cary. The day the deal closed, he asked Alex and David to leave. That remarkably incompetent decision signaled what was to come.

In an almost 180-degree turnaround from what Cary had assured us, he and American Woodmark began to unravel RSI's culture. Rather than learn from RSI and pass those industry-leading lessons on to his company, RSI was folded into an inferior company. And because of that, American Woodmark began to lose what gave RSI its competitive advantage. But do not just take my word for it. The company's investors and Wall Street analysts realized what was happening, which you can see by how the company's stock has plummeted.

Today the old RSI no longer exists. Almost all the very talented leaders are gone and, with them, RSI's culture that revolutionized the kitchen and bath cabinet industry. I am heartbroken by all of this.

So, in March 2019 when I heard that American Woodmark and the rest of the American Kitchen Cabinet Alliance (AKCA) had run to Uncle Sam to help them compete with Chinese imports, my blood boiled.

If American Woodmark had done what it had promised to do, which was to learn from RSI's culture and operational efficiencies, it could have taken to market the mid-priced stock program that RSI had developed prior to the sale. By doing so, it would have successfully competed directly with China and other Asian manufacturers.

So just by sticking to its promise, American Woodmark would have never had to go begging for the US government to step in, which to me is both outrageous and embarrassing.

Instead, the AKCA filed one of the largest ever trade cases against China with the US Commerce Department and the International Trade Commission. The official complaint charges China with manipulation and unfair trade practices. According to the AKCA, the US kitchen cabinet and bath vanity industry and the 250,000 workers it represents have lost between two and four billion dollars of business.

On the AKCA website, the group states, "The American Kitchen Cabinet Alliance aims to stand up to China's cheating and level the playing field for American workers and protect an iconic industry." And on its Twitter page are images of vacant factories representing manufacturers that have been put out of business due to Chinese cheating.

The subsequent news and headlines describing AKCA's petition were both provocative and persuasive: "Putting American Kitchen Cabinet Workers First," "Fighting Back against Illegal Chinese Trade Practices," and "One of the Largest Trade Cases Filed against China to Protect a More Than $9.5 Billion American Industry."

In response to AKCA's complaint, the US Commerce Department launched an investigation to determine whether China is guilty as charged. To my deep disappointment and frustration, steep tariffs were eventually levied on imports of Chinese cabinets.

As my experience founding RSI showed, China's prices are much less for one reason only—stock and semi-custom US cabinet prices are much too high. While the term "trade war" is attention grabbing, the reality is that in the case of the US cabinet industry, the war is not actually about unfair trade. Instead, it's about whether the incompetence of the leaders within these domestic industries should be rewarded.

As a proud patriot who has an unwavering commitment to US businesses and the American Dream, I am steadfastly opposed to the US kitchen cabinet manufacturing companies calling on the US government to protect them from their own ineptitude. Business survival should be determined via marketplace competition, not by federal subsidies that prop up manufacturers that can't compete in terms of execution, costs, and product quality. American manufacturers should stop looking for handouts from Uncle Sam and his taxpayers in order to offset their own failure at staying competitive. Rather, they need to take a hard look in the mirror and see their flaws and shortcomings—no excuses.

Where are their fight and creativity? Where is their drive to never give up and instead roll up their sleeves and jump in the ring with their opponent? With billions of dollars on the line, this appalls me. Way before RSI revolutionized the US cabinet industry, foreign manufacturers of everything from VCRs to cars pushed US companies to innovate and lower their costs to be competitive.

With tariffs in place, incentives to produce more efficiently disappear. Plus, the tariffs fail to accomplish the intended results and instead encourage the same old same old, as we're seeing with the current situation.

Once tariffs were levied on the Chinese-manufactured kitchen cabinets, the American companies previously buying from China shifted their purchases to other countries like Vietnam, whose prices were similar to China's.

According to the *Wall Street Journal*, the result has been same price and likely lower quality for consumers and, as of October 2020, a trade deficit with China higher than ever. Plus, US factory production didn't rebound with this tariff tactic.

What were they thinking? If Vietnam's prices were close to China's and it was not cheating or dumping, should we place tariffs on that country's products too? And if buying shifts to still another country, do we levy tariffs on that one as well?

The bottom line is Chinese companies were making a legitimate profit, and the fact that the buyers of the Chinese products could switch to other countries like Vietnam points out how wrong the AKCA was and how much time and resources it wasted in submitting baseless claims.

In addition—and worse—tariffs slapped on Chinese goods drive prices up, *and this hurts American consumers.*

Rather than survive by running for help, businesses and their leaders should get off their asses and figure out how to compete head-to-head with their Chinese and other Asian rivals.

RSI had successfully driven Chinese competition out of the opening price point of the kitchen and bath cabinets. As a result, Chinese manufacturers moved up to the mid-price point and semi-custom products. They knew they could offer far lower prices because US companies like RSI do not exist in those segments.

After declaring victory at the opening price point, and prior to our sale to American Woodmark, RSI was ready to compete with China in the mid-price point range. And I am confident, had American Woodmark kept RSI's values, Chinese manufacturers would have gone running in the opposite direction just as they did when we went head-to-head with them.

While RSI was ready to duke it out with Chinese manufacturers, most American cabinet manufacturers have thrown in the towel. Rather than dig deep within themselves and tap into their competitive drive, they ran to Uncle Sam for help. Shame on them!

This amazing country has taught me from an early age that nothing is impossible. At the same time, I had to learn from many mistakes, which were great teachers showing me what *not to do*, as well as what *to do*, and how to work with integrity and humility.

Thus when I see the AKCA reports complaining how impossible competing with China is, I know how wrong they are. Asia was RSI's first competitor. So don't tell me you can't compete because RSI did and won.

I am opposed to US government intervention, except in those countries playing games that result in practices counter to free trade. Deferring to Uncle Sam to apply tariffs rewards incompetent US manufacturers, reduces competition and the game-changing creativity it inspires, and hurts US consumers. But most importantly, protectionism runs counter to the capitalist vision of our country that, for generations, has roused people around the globe to reach their highest potential.

Rather than play the role of the victim to an unfair oppressor and look for government-sponsored lifesavers, America's greatest companies have succeeded by out-innovating and outcompeting rivals within our borders and throughout the world.

So if Asian countries can make a profit, why can't we?

Answering that big question was what pushed me to come up with creative solutions that resulted in starting RSI, which grew from the fire in my gut, lit by Austram's betrayal after buying Perma-Bilt. My company's ascent, eventually driving Perma-Bilt and the Aussies out of business, was a clear case of sweet revenge. But that was decades ago.

With RSI's purchase, American Woodmark could have had a no-brainer giant success on its hands. The demise of RSI has been very upsetting for me, the RSI executives, and many of RSI's loyal employees to watch. And recent events indicate we may be witnessing American Woodmark in its final throes.

On July 14, 2020, American Woodmark issued a press release, as well as a Form 8-K, which is a report companies publish informing investors about important changes within the organization. Both announced that effective July 9, 2020, S. Cary Dunston had retired as president, CEO, and member of the board of directors at the young age of fifty-five.

My initial reaction was, "Wow! The board finally got some sense in their heads." But the report continued on that the board had elected Scott Culbreth, the CFO, as the new president and CEO. I'm glad these directors do not sit on a hospital board. They would probably make one of the accountants chief of surgery.

During the due diligence process when we sold RSI to American Woodmark, Alex and Dave Lowrie, RSI's CFO, spent many hours with Scott and came away with a great understanding of his capabilities. They concluded that he seemed like a nice guy but was not up to our standards as a CFO—let alone CEO material.

The report further stated that also effective on July 9, 2020, R. Perry Campbell, the company's senior VP of sales and commercial operations, was terminated as a result of an internal investigation that found he exhibited a behavior that violated the company's policy and values. Because they were dismissed on the same day, one can assume that he and Cary were both involved in whatever caused Perry to be fired.

Those events of 2020 were not a total shock to us. Back in 2017, about a week after the deal closed, we began to realize we had grossly misjudged the character of American Woodmark's leadership team. Alex and I both feel this was one of the biggest mistakes of our careers.

But rather than mope and do nothing, I, along with Alex Calabrese, David Lowrie, Gary Singer, and Jerry Liu, created a private equity company that we named RSI Equity Partners. This is the same team responsible for RSI's success.

We asked ourselves, could this be a repeat of when I sold Perma-Bilt? Should we put together a team of mostly ex-RSI employees to create a new RSI that can and will compete with Asia and kick the shit out of the companies that hide behind Uncle Sam? If this sounds like sour grapes, I guess you can say that on an emotional level it is. But on an objective level, the facts clearly speak for themselves.

Alex and I were bound by a three-year non-compete agreement that expired at the end of 2020. So in the meantime, we were focused on building affordable housing. My passion for it had continued since 2009, which is the year I proved that working with cities to obtain city and county land at affordable prices could enable us to produce quality houses at affordable prices. But reaching this goal didn't come without struggle.

Over time, we became so frustrated in attempting to work with cities like Los Angeles that we threw in the towel. Mayors would tell us,

"Having affordable housing is one of our most critical issues," and "The state is mandating us to do it."

Meanwhile, none of these politicians attempted to remove the many obstacles that would free us to go forward. I became convinced that all government officials cared about was getting reelected, and because most of their constituents were opposed to affordable housing, these politicians wound up saying one thing to us, but their actions were the polar opposite.

We pretty much gave up counting on unreliable political leaders. Instead, we began building houses on land that we purchased at market prices. After selling our homebuilding company in 2018, the need for affordable housing was far greater than in 2009. It became a top priority, and the state began imposing very strong mandates, as well as providing financing.

So in late 2019, we again set out to explore the possibilities of working with the cities. We designed and engineered very comfortable and appealing two-story apartments that could rent for as little as six hundred dollars per month if the city would provide the land at no cost and waive the impact fees. They also would not have to provide subsidies. In other words, it would not cost them a penny, and in some cases, they would be able to charge for the land if the rents could still be affordable.

We presented our concept to many city officials. They were blown away by the new strategy. But it ended there, déjà vu of what we went through in 2009. So again, we threw in the towel. We succumbed to the warning of "you can't fight city hall."

Meanwhile, the thought of getting back into the cabinet business still lingers in all our minds. So stay tuned.

HAPPY 80TH BIRTHDAY DAD

For my eightieth birthday, my daughter, Kathy, gave me this piece of artwork that reflected my life from the time she was about four years old until I was eighty.

I LOVE YOU, KATHY

*It shows the places she and I went,
as well as the highlights in my personal and professional life.*

★ ACKNOWLEDGMENTS

While the role of a book's acknowledgments is typically to thank those who helped write it, I find that far too limiting. I have been blessed by having had a wonderful life with a wonderful family, friends, and colleagues. As a result, I am using this section to thank those who influenced my personal and professional journey. Without their contributions, this would be a far less meaningful book.

First and foremost, my thanks and love go to my wife, Sandi, for making the last twenty-five years the very best of my life.

My two children, Steve Simon and Dr. Kathy Simon Abels, have dedicated the past seventeen years to create and grow the Simon Scholars program into the most effective scholarship program serving underprivileged high school students in the country. I am so grateful to my children for establishing such an amazing and wonderful program, one that will be endowed for generations to come. I am also very proud of the solid and responsible people they are, the wonderful lives they have led with honesty and integrity, and the respect they have earned within their communities. My daughter, Kathy, gave me three grandchildren. Allison Drutman is a practicing attorney. Jamie Drutman graduated with honors from Carnegie Mellon University with a degree in theater directing. And Ben Drutman, who at the young age of thirty has taken over as executive director of the Simon Scholars program in Southern California, is carrying on the family legacy by fulfilling his responsibilities with passion. Concurrently working full-time at the program and earning his bachelor's degree in organizational management in 2019 demonstrate his discipline and work ethic. I am confident he will continue to grow the Simon Scholars program to serve many more deserving kids.

Ron with grandchildren, Jamie (left), *Allison* (back), *and Ben* (front right), *1995.*

Ron with grandson, Ben, and great-grandson, Leo, 2019.

Ron's grandchildren, left to right: *Allison, Ben, and Jamie, 2007.*

Although my parents and I did not always see eye to eye, I was very fortunate to have them as my mom and dad. They both were caring and loving people who wanted only the very best for me. How they tolerated the challenges in raising me, I'll never know. What I do know is how blessed I was to have them as my parents.

And the love I received from my grandparents, Meyer and Anna Langer and Sarah Simon, will forever be in my heart.

I would be remiss if I didn't acknowledge the positive influence Mr. Steinman had on my life. A salesman in my grandfather's luggage store, he was a Holocaust survivor with a great sense of humor and a positive outlook.

Many great people have played an important role in my life as close friends, business associates, or both. So many of them have, in their own ways, contributed to my success.

Let's begin with Terri Stephens, my very able and sweet executive assistant for the past twenty-four years. She is my right arm, and in running a very efficient and organized office, she makes my work life very, very comfortable, dealing with my moods and idiosyncrasies like no one else. I'd be lost without her.

Going back to my Perma-Bilt days, I had a great relationship with the very capable executive team of Paul Vert, CFO; Frank Xavier, VP of sales; Norton Krinsky, comptroller; and Ron Shewach, materials manager. Frank, Norton, and Ron joined me to start RSI. Rhonda Hosford and Gloria Alvillar, both long-time Perma-Bilt employees, also were part of the RSI team as the first members of the administrative staff and contributed greatly to RSI's success.

One of the best professional decisions I ever made was to hire Alex Calabrese in 1990. He is a key part of my succession plan. Not only was Alex responsible for most of RSI's success, but also, our thirty years of working together has developed into a great personal friendship. Alex is like a son to me.

I have been blessed to have had the following business associates and friends who have all played an important role in enriching my life:

Allan Liebert and I met in 1978, and it was love at first sight. We became instant friends and partners in a business venture. My ex-wife Ellie and I became very close with Allan and Sandi, whom I would marry six years after Allan's passing in 1990. As married couples, the four of us spent a great deal of time together. Also, Allan acted as my attorney on a few occasions.

In 1959, I met Harold Kitay when he was a Perma-Bilt customer. Harold, Tom Tucker, and Gil LeVasseur became three of my closest and most trusted friends and great advisors. All became directors on the RSI Board, and Gil is on the board of my foundation. Sadly, Harold passed away in 2013. In 1994, I met Byron Allumbaugh who was the CEO of Ralphs Grocery Co., a large supermarket chain. Byron joined the RSI Board in 1995. I learned a lot from him on running a large business. Byron, along with George Argyros, sponsored me in becoming a Horatio Alger member, which is a major highlight in my life

Jim Freedman, a leading mergers and acquisitions advisor, managed every private equity deal that RSI did. He is one of my most trusted advisors, as well as a good friend. Jim also serves on my foundation's board.

Gary Singer became RSI's corporate counsel in 1995 when he was a partner with O'Melveny and Meyers, a national law firm. Over the years, Gary headed up our legal team on five private equity deals, two major acquisitions, and the sale of RSI Home Products and RSI Communities. He became a very close member of our team, as well as a very trusted friend and personal confidant. In 2017, I persuaded Gary to retire from O'Melveny and Meyers and become senior VP and general counsel for RSI, as well as chairman of my foundation's board. Gary contributed greatly to RSI's successes.

In 1993 when I had the idea of giving scholarships to underserved kids while they are in high school rather than wait until they get to college, I asked Doug Freeman to act as my attorney in establishing my foundation. I appointed David Dukes as CEO, and David did a great job in getting the Simon Scholars program organized and operating. Also, as a surprise for my seventy-second birthday in 2006, David created a book on my life, which I will always cherish.

To all the many associates of the RSI companies, which are too numerous to name, thank you for your hard work and creativity, which contributed so greatly to our success. You all should be very proud of what was accomplished. And to everyone running the Simon Scholars program, thank you for your drive, determination, and passion in creating opportunities for our scholars that they otherwise might not have had. As a result, many of them will be in a position to give back to their communities.

We were very fortunate to have a great group of suppliers that supported RSI's startup and growth. Without their contributions, RSI could not have achieved the success that it did.

To Pat Farrah, Bill Hamlin, Dave Heerensperger, Jim Ingliss, Ken Langone, and Bernie Marcus, leaders of the companies that were RSI customers that I personally did business with, thank you for your help in making RSI a great supplier. You made us a better company, and we will always respect and be grateful to have had you for business partners.

And to the many other associates of RSI's customers, thank you for your support and for having the confidence in our ability to support you.

Todd Palmer joined our team as CEO of RSI Communities and, with the great team of associates he put together, took our homebuilding to great heights. My thanks to Todd and all of his team.

I have had so many good friends that have enriched my life that are not mentioned in this book, and I am grateful to them all.

Finally, I thank Lawrence Ineno for the guidance he provided throughout the process of writing my book.

★ NOTES

Chapter One

10   *SS* **Polonia**   "Lloyd's Register, Steamers & Motorships" (PDF), London, 1938-1939, accessed August 31, 2020, https://plimsoll. southampton.gov.uk/shipdata/pdfs/38/38b0708.pdf.

Chapter Two

29   **seventy-five thousand Yiddish-speaking Eastern European immigrants**   website for Breed Street Shul Project, "Historical Information" page, accessed April 21, 2020, https://breedstreetshul. org/historical-information/.

38   **had failed to appear for his court hearing.**   Cecilia Rasmussen, "Girl's Molestation, Murder in 1949 Prompted Tougher Laws," *Los Angeles Times*, August 29, 2004, https://www.latimes.com/archives/ la-xpm-2004-aug-29-me-then29-story.html.

38   **Stroble had been arrested for exposing**   Ibid.

39   **But in a case of clear negligence**   Ibid.

39   **Linda's body was found**   Ibid.

39   **drew coast-to-coast attention**   Ibid.

39   **Two days after**   Ibid.

39   **"I had to kill her**   Ibid.

39   **He confessed**   Ibid.

39   **"Every home in this neighborhood**   Ibid.

39   **It would take decades**   Ibid.

40   **"I've been drinking**   Ibid.

40   **Despite his insanity plea**   Ibid.

40   **trial lasted twelve days.**   Ibid.

40   **The defendant's attorneys appealed**   Ibid.

41   **He was executed**   Ibid.

41   **child molestation was only a misdemeanor**   Ibid.

41   **short film, initially funded by John Wayne**   Ibid.

Chapter Three

54   **SS, or Schutzstaffel**   "The SS," History.com, updated June 7, 2019, https://www.history.com/topics/world-war-ii/ss.

Chapter Six

99   **On the evening of August 11, 1965**   "Watts Rebellion," History.com, updated June 24, 2020, https://www.history.com/topics/1960s/watts-riots.

100   **The stepbrothers' mother**   Douglas Martin, "Rena Price Is Dead at 97; Catalyst for the Watts Riots," the *New York Times* online, June 29, 2013, https://www.nytimes.com/2013/06/30/us/rena-price-is-dead-at-97-catalyst-for-the-watts-riots.html.

100   **As the crowd swelled**   "Watts Rebellion," History.com, updated June 24, 2020, https://www.history.com/topics/1960s/watts-riots.

Chapter Seven

118   **Beverly Hills restaurant, founded by Jimmy Murphy**
Pat Saperstein, "Jimmy Murphy, Founder of Jimmy's Restaurant in Beverly Hills, Dies at 75, *Variety* online, February 3, 2014, https://variety.com/2014/scene/news/jimmy-murphy-founder-of-jimmys-restaurant-in-beverly-hills-dies-at-75-1201084747/.

Chapter Nine

147   **Robert Nardelli, one of three top General Electric executives**   "Home Unimprovement: Was Nardelli's Tenure at Home Depot a Blueprint for Failure?" transcript of podcast, Knowledge@Wharton, the Wharton School, June 10, 2007, https://knowledge.wharton.upenn.edu/article/home-unimprovement-was-nardellis-tenure-at-home-depot-a-blueprint-for-failure/.

Chapter Eleven

173   **Jim Freedman, founder of Barrington Associates**   "LA 500: Jim Freedman," August 14, 2017, *Los Angeles Business Journal* online, https://labusinessjournal.com/news/2017/aug/14/la-500-jim-freedman/.

Chapter Twelve

193   **population of more than twenty million**   "Population of the urban area of Shanghai, China from 1980 to 2035," Statista, accessed July 26, 2020, https://www.statista.com/statistics/466938/china-population-of-shanghai/.

Chapter Sixteen

243   **The organization's namesake was a successful author**   *Encyclopedia Britannica Online*, s.v. "Horatio Alger," updated July 14, 2020, https://www.britannica.com/biography/Horatio-Alger.

Chapter Seventeen

256   **have lost between two and four billion dollars of business.**   Joe Deaux, "U.S. Cabinet Makers Seek Giant Trade Case Against China Imports," Bloomberg, March 6, 2019, https://www.bloomberg.com/news/articles/2019-03-06/u-s-cabinet-makers-seek-giant-trade-case-against-china-imports.

256   **On the AKCA website**   website for American KitchenCabinet Alliance, accessed July 26, 2020, https://kitchencabinetfairtrade.com.

256 **And on its Twitter page** AKCA Twitter page, March 27, 2019, https://twitter.com/AKCAUSA/status/1110944783860670464/photo/1.

256 **"Putting American Kitchen Cabinet Workers First,"** Mark A. Trexler, "Putting American Kitchen Cabinet Workers First," *Washington Examiner* online, March 7, 2019, https://www.washingtonexaminer.com/opinion/op-eds/putting-american-kitchen-cabinet-workers-first.

256 **"Fighting Back against Illegal Chinese Trade Practices,"** website for Showplace Cabinetry, "Fighting Back against Illegal Chinese Trade Practices" by Paul Sova, accessed July 26, 2020, https://showplacecabinetry.com/showplace-academy/news-views/fighting-back-against-illegal-chinese-trade-practices.

256 **"One of the Largest Trade Cases** PR Newswire, from news release by American Kitchen Cabinet Alliance, March 6, 2019, https://www.prnewswire.com/news-releases/american-kitchen-cabinet-alliance-initiates-one-of-the-largest-trade-cases-filed-against-china-to-protect-a-more-than-9-5-billion-american-industry-300807831.html.

257 **According to the *Wall Street Journal*** Josh Zumbrun and Bob Davis, "China Trade War Didn't Boost U.S. Manufacturing Might," *Wall Street Journal* online, October 25, 2020, https://www.wsj.com/articles/china-trade-war-didnt-boost-u-s-manufacturing-might-11603618203.

259 **On July 14, 2020, American Woodmark issued a press release** website for American Woodmark. Press Release: "American Woodmark announces Leadership Transition," July 14, 2020, https://investors.americanwoodmark.com/news-market-information/press-releases/news-details/2020/American-Woodmark-Announces-Leadership-Transition/default.aspx.

259 **as well as a Form 8-K** United States Securities and Exchange Commission, Form 8-K for American Woodmark Corporation, July 14, 2020, https://d18rn0p25nwr6d.cloudfront.net/CIK-0000794619/c1217093-7f25-4a03-a81e-d984b79e60f4.pdf.

★ INDEX

References to photos and illustrations are given in *italic* type.